GW01605034

Motor Sports
A Pictorial History

The early races: depicted on the sides of the Michelin building in the Fulham Road, London, England.

Motor Sports

A Pictorial History by RAYMOND FLOWER | Foreword by Graham Hill

Collins Glasgow and London

(Preceding Page)
John Cobb, a great performer on the Brooklands Outer Circuit, with his 23 litre Napier-Railton, seen here winning the 1937 Broadcast Trophy race. His lap record at 143.44mph (230.84kph) stands in perpetuity.

Published in 1975 by
William Collins Sons
& Co. Ltd.,
Glasgow and London

ISBN 0 00 434550 9

Printed in Spain
D.L.: S.S. 480/75

Contents

For

PETER FLOWER

Now graduating
from two wheels to four

Foreword by Graham Hill

THE STRANGE THING IS that it hasn't been done before. Because, despite those 6,000 books in the Royal Automobile Club's library which Raymond Flower talks about, the fact is that up until now there just hasn't been a straightforward history of the sport that tells us how it happened without putting us to sleep. Neither have we seen such an authoritative text, complemented by such evocative pictures, before this publication.

What started as the sport of kings and old-fashioned aristos is now mass entertainment. But this does not alter the fact that it's still the king of sports. I started as a mechanic, dismantling engines for Colin Chapman for a pound a day, visiting the Steering Wheel Club, where the racing fraternity forgather, once a week. Here, soaking up the racing chat faster than my beer, I picked up some of the folklore of motoring along with my early drives – and perhaps some of the nostalgia for the days when cars had a more individual look and you could see the expression on a driver's face as his rival shut the door on him on the last corner.

I certainly do think that the background story of motor racing is tremendously important for anyone who wants to understand what it's all about today; which is why I welcome Raymond's spirited account of all the various aspects of motorsport since its beginning, set out in such a lively way and coupled with pictures that tell a story in themselves.

I wish this book every success.

CIRCUIT
des ARDENNES 1906
DURAY
sur LORRAINE DIETRICH

GRAND-PRIX
A·C·F 1906 Sarthe
SZISZ
sur RENAULT

Author's Preface

IN THE LIBRARY of the Royal Automobile Club in London there are some 6,000 volumes covering every aspect of motoring over the last eighty years. Among them are to be found complete sets of the *Autocar*, the *Motor* and so forth since before the turn of the century. With so much source material available, in fact, the problem is obviously one of selection and more exactly what to leave out. A blow by blow account of each classic event, after all, would be as bulky as the New York telephone directory (and just about as indigestible!). I have tried, therefore, to trace the main lines of motorsport's development and to capture, as far as possible, the feel of each period. At moments, admittedly, this may be more subjective than others. My father was a pioneer motorist who took the first car to many parts of the Middle East, and I myself (though far from being mechanically minded) have spent a good deal of my life in the world of motoring. From 1949 to 1956 I was actively involved in sports car racing and rallying, and during that time I had the good luck to know, and often compete against, many of the great figures of the sport. It was, if you like, a golden era for us amateurs who raced for fun and were prepared – if necessary – to pay for our pleasure. Best of all, perhaps, was the free and easy atmosphere as we met again and again through the summer in various parts of Europe for the next rally or race; and although horizons have now expanded and the stakes become so much greater, I suspect that some of the bounce and fizzle has been lost in the process. So, exhilarating though I find the present scene, it is with a touch of nostalgia that I record my appreciation to those stalwart spirits – notably Ernest McMillen, Mike Llewellyn, Fitzroy Raglan and George Phillips – who so often shared the wheel with me.

I owe a debt of gratitude, likewise, to Edward Montagu for hospitably giving me the run of the Montagu Motor Library and to Eric Bellamy, the librarian, for steering me around it; to Gordon Pearce for doing the same through our well-guarded archives at the RAC in Pall Mall; and to Stanley Gillam's ever-welcoming staff at the London Library (who might easily have been foxed by a subject like this, but needless to say weren't). So many other friendly enthusiasts in France, Italy, Germany, Scandinavia and the United States have helped me in one way or another that it is difficult to express my appreciation properly. But apart from these I undoubtedly owe the best dinner in town to Hugh Begg of London Editions, who together with Tony Salmond of the BRDC spurred this book on, to Ronald Barker who so sportingly read the manuscript to its great advantage and to Cyril Posthumus who checked the captions. And, of course, to Jeanne Griffiths, who got together the pictures; Sally Windle, who somehow turned my illegible scrawl into a tidy typescript, and Diana Mansour who knocked it all into shape for the printers.

To all of these kind and helpful friends, my thanks.

Beginnings

IN THE SUMMER of 1769 – the year that James Watt patented his steam engine – a number of Parisian big-wigs were invited by the Foreign Minister of France to inspect a three-wheeled wooden vehicle, designed by a Frenchman named Cugnot, and propelled by a curious, kettle-like contraption which was mounted at the front. They watched it run successfully under its own steam for twelve minutes at a speed of some six miles per hour (over nine kilometres per hour) before finally crashing into a wall. Their host, the Duc de Choiseul (so often credited with having precipitated the French Revolution) was apparently interested in the military potential of the device. Yet inadvertently he sowed the seeds of an even wider social upheaval. For with those twelve minutes the story of motoring can be said to have begun.

Admittedly, it was a slow process of gestation. But so, after all, had been the steam engine, when it is remembered that Hero of Alexandria had described a primitive steam reaction turbine as far back as the second century BC. In 1788 an American steam car, designed by Oliver Evans and built by Robert Furness, appeared on the scene, and for most of the nineteenth century efforts were concentrated on non-condensing, high-pressure 'puffers', which in England at least were regarded with such disfavour that savage legislation, such as the notorious 'Red Flag' Act of 1865, was introduced to curb their development. It was in 1885, however, that the real breakthrough occurred when Gottlieb Daimler (a pupil of Nikolaus Otto) finally developed the internal combustion engine, using petroleum spirit. Two years later, during the Paris Exhibition, he demonstrated his invention in a boat running on the Seine. Here it caught the eye of Emile Levassor of Panhard & Levassor, a wood-working machine factory, who saw that such an engine could be used to propel a road vehicle. Securing the rights from Daimler, he proceeded to design a layout which in many ways is unchanged even today (the drive of his first car was taken through a clutch to a set

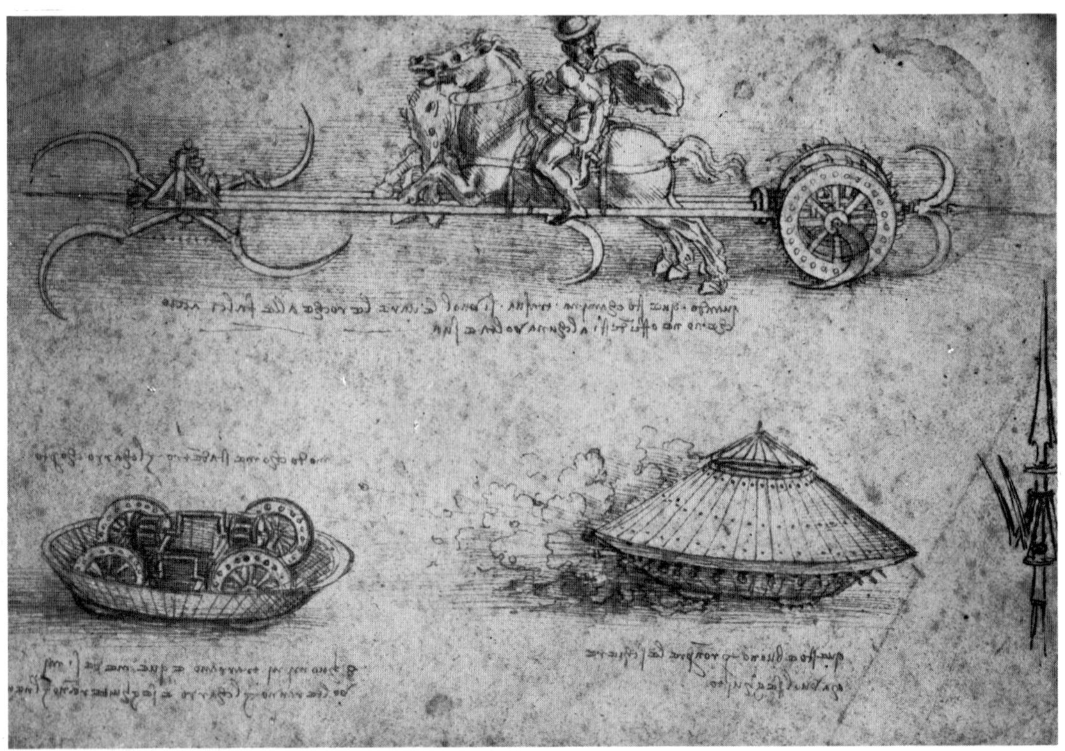

Motor sport in the fifteenth century. A 'Trojan Horse' complete with scythes, and a futuristic armoured car, as envisaged and drawn by Leonardo da Vinci.

Transport of delight, or the heady aroma of speed in the late nineteenth century. Achille Philion (below) of Akron, Ohio, on his steamer built in 1892. Cugnot's steam carriage (right), intended to tow guns, now in the Musée des Arts et Métiers in Paris.

of reduction gears and thence to a differential gear on a countershaft from which the road wheels were driven.)

Although Léon Serpollet produced his famous 'steamer' around the same time, and early American taste still favoured steam cars, firms like De Dion Bouton soon switched to internal combustion, and over the next few years the supremacy of the petrol (or gasoline) engine was overwhelmingly established. While in Germany both Gottlieb Daimler and Karl Benz were busy improving their products, the real pioneering centre of the motor car was in France. And hardly were the first bone-shakers on the road than competitive sport began.

Serpollet's streamlined steam car (below), one of several he built, was advanced for its day in 1902.
Early Teutonic high-wheeler (left) 1891 Benz. Its engine was under the seat, above the rear axle.

Birth of a Sport: the Paris Races

A Benz (left) entered by Emil Roger in the Paris-Bordeaux race of 1895. Twenty-three cars took part in the event and nine of these finished. The committee which organized the race developed into the Automobile Club de France. A Peugeot phaeton four-seater (above) in the Paris Rouen Trial of 1894. Peugeot came second and third in this race in which the first to arrive (but not the winner) was a De Dion steam car.

HISTORICALLY SPEAKING, the first motoring event took place in Paris on 20 April 1887. Organized by a journalist named Fossier, this consisted of a run of some twenty miles from Neuilly to Versailles and back. But since Georges Bouton, who completed the course with his De Dion Bouton in an hour and fourteen minutes, was the sole participant, it was hardly a rousing success – any more than the next recorded competition at Longchamps, which attracted only two entrants, both on steam tricycles. (The Serpollet broke down, and the De Dion again romped home, this time completing the twelve-and-a-half-mile lap in forty-one minutes.) A third race, staged at Vincennes, once again attracted just a solitary starter, and police stopped the event after Lacaux's De Dion nearly ran over a spectator in the middle of the track.

But obviously these fledgling affairs can hardly be considered seriously, and the Paris–Rouen Motor Trial held on Sunday 22 July 1894 is usually reckoned to have been the world's first motor competition. Sponsored

The five Opel brothers (left) showing their paces. Left to right: Carl, Wilhelm, Heinrich, Fritz and Ludwig.
Three of the brothers, Wilhelm, Heinrich and Fritz, took part in the sport as drivers, Wilhelm being the overall winner of the 1909 Prince Henry Trial.

Prototype Renaults (left) on the Quai d'Orleans, Paris, in 1899, with (left to right) Marcel Renault seated in the 1897 quadricycle, Louis Renault driving the first voiturette of 1898, and Paul Hugé in the first 1899 model.

by *Le Petit Journal* it was open to 'horseless carriages' of all descriptions, and among the 102 prospective entrants were an astonishing assortment of four-, three-, and two-wheel vehicles powered by steam, petrol, and electricity, as well as a confection apparently propelled by the weight of its passengers. In the end only twenty-one machines actually turned up at the starting line, but of these no less than seventeen reached Rouen successfully. They were headed by Count de Dion in a steamer of his own make, who covered the 79 miles (127km) in 6hr 48min at an average speed of 11.66mph (18.77kph) although through a technicality the first prize of 5,000 francs was awarded jointly to the petrol-engined Panhard and Peugeot.

If nothing else, this trial was a remarkable demonstration of reliability, since eighty per cent of the starters were in at the finish, and it aroused almost as much excitement in Paris as the notorious Dreyfus case did three months later. That autumn three of the most prominent enthusiasts – the Baron de Zuylen, the Marquis de Dion, and the Chevalier René de Knyff – formed a committee which set about organizing a full-scale race from Paris to Bordeaux and back, a distance of 732 miles (1,178km). Of the twenty-three cars which started from Versailles at dawn on 11 June 1895 nine completed the course; and although the honours (and a prize of 12,000 francs) went to Emile Levassor who, driving his 600cc two-seater Panhard single-handed, romped home 48hr 48min later at an average speed of 15mph (24.14kph), the regulations specified four-seaters and he had to concede the titular first place to Koechlin's Peugeot (which came in six hours behind him!).

From the technical point of view, the race demonstrated the superiority of the petrol engine over steam, since eight of the finishers had petrol-driven cars against a single steamer; and it also marked the first appearance – though admittedly a disastrous one – of pneumatic tires on André Michelin's Peugeot. What is more, it gave a tremendous boost to motoring as a whole.

Motor racing now became a national sport – in France, at any rate. The original group of friends that had met in the Marquis de Dion's house grew into the Automobile Club de France, formed on 5 November 1895, which organized no less than thirty-four further city-to-city races over the next eight years, culminating in the tragic Paris to Madrid of 1903.

As curtain-raisers to the developing saga of motor sport these nation-to-nation marathons could hardly have been bettered, and even today the memory of the early 'classics' tingles one's spine with a dream of power, danger and high endeavour. Perched hazardously somewhere above the rear axle in a rudimentary bucket seat (with often just a toolbox for the mechanic) behind a roaring, unsilenced engine, with no windshield (windscreen) or mudguards and virtually no suspension or brakes, the drivers had to wrestle to keep control of their monsters down primitive dirt roads and through clouds of dust or blinding rain at speeds that would still take some beating, even in a modern international rally. They were beset with every kind of difficulty: early morning mist, dust or rain and mud, blowouts and mechanical breakdowns. But they loved it. To men like de Knyff, Charron, Girardot, de Caters, Fournier, the Renault brothers, Jenatzy, Zborowski and Edge, this was the greatest sport ever devised. Many of them were rich men driving their own cars that had been specially built for any given event, and over and above the intoxication of speed and the splendid uncertainty of it all, they were intent on proving to the world that their machines were capable of covering great distances fast and reliably.

> The long winding road stretches out before you, reaching from the capital of one great country to the centre of another . . . Hundreds of miles of straight road, narrow road, right-angled corners, treacherous turns, maybe mountain passes, rough surfaces, and dangerous obstacles, all enveloped in a dense pall of dust caused by

the cars which are preceding you and which you are endeavouring to overtake . . . the unknown presents itself at every yard . . . and as you wrestle mentally and physically with all the difficulties of the trial the excitement of it enters your soul, and you realize this is a sport of the gods.

Or so rhapsodized one of the early sportsmen.

The most famous of the city-to-city races (of which a full list is given in the Appendix) were the Paris to Marseilles and back in 1896, the Paris–Amsterdam–Paris in 1898, the Paris–Berlin of 1901 and the Paris–Vienna of 1902. And finally, of course, the unlucky Paris–Madrid in 1903 which caused such a holocaust that it was stopped by the French government at Bordeaux. This 'race to death', as it became known, was a tragic end not only to an epochal series, but to unrestricted racing on the open roads of Europe.

All the same, these 'dust and glory' classics with their heady spectrum of high living and acute discomfort, of danger and achievement, and above all of adventure and good fellowship, can be said to have laid down the ground rules and created the traditions which were to govern motor sport for the next fifty years. Their nearest parallels in later years were the South American cross-country races (which Juan Manuel Fangio describes so vividly in his autobiography), the Mille Miglia, and certain of the great Alpine Rallies of the thirties and early fifties.

At some phenomenally small hour of the morning, the cars were started off at two-minute intervals, amid a deafening roar of engines and a blue haze of lubricating oil. An official handed over the route card, the timekeeper shouted 'Partez!', and the monsters sped off through packed crowds of spectators carrying paper lanterns who had camped out all night. Soon the troubles would begin: an engine governor sticking, a broken spring, or the inevitable punctured tire which had to be replaced with the wheel still on the hub. Cars passed and repassed each other continuously, driving blind through choking dust to overtake or being pelted with stones and gravel from a faster machine as it went by. At villages and towns that were 'neutralized' (that is to say, where the cars were allowed a given time to pass through, usually preceded by a cyclist) the competitors were smothered by flowers thrown by the excited throngs in the streets, who pressed champagne, food, cigars and cigarettes on them – which, mixed up with grease, lubricating oil and tools, made a disgusting mess of the cockpit. To finish at all costs was the aim, but it often required both luck and ingenuity. Charles Jarrott's exploits in the Paris–Vienna, for instance, read like the script for a thriller. On the second day of racing the wooden chassis of his 13.72 litre Panhard '70' collapsed with a crack just short of the overnight stop at Bregenz. To all intents and purposes, his chances of continuing were nil. Nevertheless, he and his mechanic (in this case George Du Cross of Dunlop's) felt that if only they could strengthen the frame by some means or other, it might hold out for the next stage to Salzburg at least.

A drill and some bolts were secured, but all attempts to find four long pieces of wood were in vain. 'I was just getting into bed and had turned to put out the light, when my eye fell upon a stand used for carrying a tray, and in a second I perceived that the four legs of that stand were exactly what I wanted,' Jarrott recalls. It was too late to ask the hotel management if they would sell the table – which they would probably have refused to do anyway – so he and Du Cros decided to act at once and argue later.

The trouble, of course, was to demolish the stand without waking the whole place up. Next they had to drill four holes in each length of wood so that in the morning they could bolt the pieces on each side of the broken chassis frame. 'Never have I known any wood that was so hard,' Jarrott went on to relate. To get greater power with the drill, Du Cros had the idea of drilling against the wall. 'He was delightfully successful, but the trouble was that he drove it through too far, and brought down half the plaster. And then,

Arriving just behind Gabriel's Mors at Bordeaux in 1903, was Louis Renault in a 30hp car of his own make. Here he learnt from his brother Fernand of Marcel Renault's

fatal accident in the tragic
Paris -to-Madrid race.

Advertisement for motoring headgear (left) at the turn of the century. With open cars and dusty roads, some form of cap was as essential for men as veils were for women.

Camille Jenatzy (right), the Belgian driver known as the 'Red Devil', was a colorful character, famed for his duels with Count de Chasseloup-Laubat for the first land speed records, and winner of the 1903 Gordon Bennett cup on a Mercedes. He was killed during a shoot on his estate, being shot by a friend, following an unfortunate practical joke. He is seen here standing beside the 16hp Mercedes that he drove in the 1899 Tour de France.

in endeavouring to show how easy it was on another portion of the wall, he succeeded in bringing that down also.' At this point Jarrott bored a hole through his arm instead of through the wood, and for the next half hour they were tearing up the bed-linen to make bandages. 'There was nothing in the room we did not utilize for something or other,' he confesses ruefully, 'I hate to think what must have been the expression on the proprietor's face when he discovered what had taken place.'

But the trick worked and by seven o'clock the following morning they were roaring up the Arlberg past the wrecks of numerous other machines that had come to grief. They reached Salzburg just in time to scotch a rumour (which *The Times* correspondent was in the act of cabling to London) that they had been killed in a smash. Even so, their troubles were far from over, and at one point in the final stage Du Cros had to lie full length along the hood (bonnet) with a towel wrapped round the pipe to hold the water in the radiator. And then, just five kilometres before Vienna, another catastrophe occurred. Through distortion of the chassis frame, the gearbox broke, and huge pieces of aluminium fell out into the road. Jarrott seized a bicycle and pedalled off over the pavé to get help. He returned to find Du Cros being towed to the finish behind a horse-drawn cab. This was more than he could stomach. Slashing the rope, he jumped behind the wheel, somehow

jammed first gear in, and was off just as the exhaust box fell off. Belching smoke and flame straight on to the road and sounding like a maxim gun, the gearless monster stormed virtually out of control across the finishing line, and expired. Not another yard would it move. But it had completed the course.

What all too tragically turned out to be the last of these marathons, the Paris–Madrid race of 1903, was the most ambitious event yet to have been held, covering 816 miles (1,313km), passing through Bordeaux and over the Guadarra mountains to Madrid. It attracted a record entry of 216 cars, ranging from the enormous Mercedes, Panhards and Mors to a 6hp De Boisse (as well as 59 motorcycles) of which 179 were actually flagged off at two-minute intervals. (So long was the queue that the leading car had already passed through the control at Tours before the last motorcycle started.)

To pin-point the blame for what happened would be difficult. It may have been the vast, uncontrolled crowds of spectators who packed the verges of the road all the way to Bordeaux – three million people were estimated to have watched the race – or the ruthless efforts of some designers to keep the larger machines down to the weight limit of 1,000kg regardless of security which was at the root of the holocaust that followed. To be sure, far too many cars that reached speeds in excess of 80mph yet had next to no braking power were involved in collisions with dogs and livestock and even other competitors. The figures were never officially published, but at least five drivers and their mechanics were killed, including Marcel Renault, the constructor, and Lorraine Barrow, a popular British sportsman, as well as a number of spectators.

When the news of the tragedy reached Paris, the authorities ordered the race to be stopped and for the cars to be 'arrested' on their arrival at Bordeaux. Unhappily, too, the recriminations that followed somewhat overshadowed the extraordinary performance that Fernand Gabriel put up in his 70hp

PISART

Camille Jenatzy (above) cornering with his 120hp Mercedes in the 1906 Circuit des Ardennes in Belgium. He finished tenth, the winner being Duray in a 120hp De Dietrich. Plenty of dust as Salzer's 14 litre Mercedes (left) rushes through Bastogne in the same race. In this year seven cars averaged 60mph (96kph).

The first woman to compete in the *Grandes Epreuves.* Mme Camille du Gast (right) took part in the 1901 Paris-Berlin on a Panhard with Prince du Sagan as 'mechanic'. She is seen here with the 30hp 5.7 litre De Dietrich at the start of the 1903 Paris-Madrid. When lying sixth in the race she stopped to help her team mate Stead, who was seriously injured.

Mors: having started some five and a half hours after the first car had left, he overtook no less than 163 other competitors along the route to be first in at Bordeaux, and with this epic drive rang down the curtain on motor racing in its earliest and most stirring form.

The Gordon Bennett Cup

THE ENGLISH, meanwhile, were still dedicated to the horse. Motor cars were virtually forbidden fruit in Victoria's England, and if a motorist ventured out on to the public highway he did so at his peril. Until 1896 his speed was restricted to 4mph (6.4kph) in the country and 2mph in the town; he had to be preceded by a footman not less than sixty paces ahead; and if the rider of a horse so much as put up his hand, the car was obliged to stop. Sir David Salomon and the Hon. Evelyn Ellis both brought machines over from France and put them through their paces in private grounds, but once they drove out on to the open road they were, as it was gloomily put, 'subjected to annoyance at the hands of the authorities'. Nonetheless the motor lobby persevered, and its efforts were rewarded with the Light Locomotives Act in November 1896 which finally made it legal for motor cars to circulate on English roads at a speed not exceeding 14mph (22.5kph).

To celebrate this lifting of the shackles,

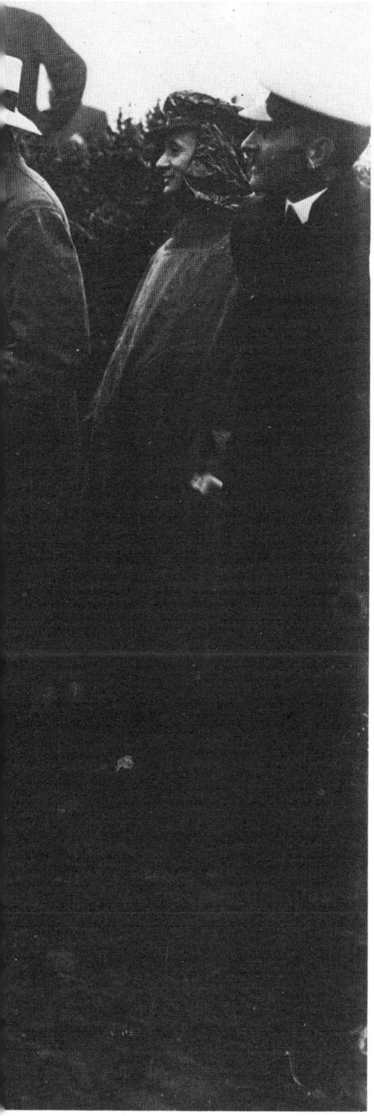

All eyes on Camille Jenatzy (above), seen chatting with officials at Kilrush while awaiting the start of the 1903 Gordon Bennett race which he won on his Mercedes.
How *Illustrated London News* readers got their first sight of the cars and drivers for the same race (right). The British cars were painted green as a compliment to Ireland, where the race was held.

THE INTERNATIONAL MOTOR-RACE FOR THE GORDON-BENNETT CUP, JULY 2.

Drawn by A. Hugh Fisher.

80 H.P. Peerless Car
Mr L. Mooers

Napier Car
45 HP Mr. S.F. Edge.

ENGLAND

UNITED STATES

Mr Alex Winton

Mr J.W. Stocks

Mr Ch. Jarrott

80 HP Winton Car
Mr Percy Owen.

The Gordon Bennett Trophy

Chv. R. de Knyff

FRANCE

Jenatzy

GERMANY

Baron de Caters

70 H.P. Mors Car
M. Gabriel.

60 H.P. Mercedes Car
Mr. Foxhall Keene.

70 H.P. Panhard Car
Henri Farman.

A. HUGH FISHER

an 'Emancipation Run' was staged from London to Brighton. On a foggy, wet November morning, after a hearty breakfast during the course of which the Earl of Winchilsea ceremoniously tore up a red flag, some thirty cars set off from the Metropole Hotel. Headed by the Panhard-Levassor on which Levassor had won the Paris–Bordeaux race the previous year, along with another Panhard which had even more recently won the Paris–Marseilles and a Daimler landaulette containing no less a personage than Herr Gottlieb Daimler himself, the procession included four Léon Bollée tricycles, an Arnold dog-cart, a steam bicycle, five electric vehicles and a breakdown van full of spares (which, as it turned out, used up most of the replacement parts on itself).

Incidents during the run were numerous. A Bollée went through a hedge and had to be ignominiously towed out by a cart. Another machine overturned and landed its occupants in a pond. Some machines broke down and were loaded on the train at Brixton. But at least fourteen covered the full distance and reached the Metropole Hotel at Brighton in time for tea.

Motoring was at last established in Britain, and despite the abuse that was heaped on it by a conservatively minded public, to say nothing of the jibes in *Punch*, for whom these new-fangled devices were a splendid joke, the motor movement grew steadily stronger. A show of vehicles was held at the Agricultural Hall in London and the 'Motor Car Club' was formed. In 1897 a number of further runs were organized, but what really put cars on the map in England was the 1,000 Mile Trial of 1900 which, consisting of a circular tour through England, up to Scotland and back to London, gave many country folk their first glimpse of a self-powered machine. By then the automobile had reached a stage when quite long journeys could be undertaken with a reasonable amount of confidence that the destination would sooner or later be reached, and the charms of getting about the countryside as well as the novelty of the pastime had begun to convert a growing number of enthusiasts to the delights of motoring. After a hesitant start, Great Britain had joined the motoring scene, and the first English cars – such as Lanchester, Napier and Daimler – were being produced. As early as October 1897 Henry Sturmey drove a 2 cylinder Coventry-built Daimler from John o'Groats to Land's End at an average speed of 10mph (16kph). For all this, motor racing as such was still confined to France.

It was left to an American to give the sport its international status. In July 1899 James Gordon Bennett, the Paris-based owner of the *New York Herald* (who had incidentally been responsible for sending Stanley after David Livingstone in 1869 and ten years later sponsored the De Long Arctic expedition), offered a silver trophy – allegorically depicting the Goddess of Victory in a racing Panhard, driven by the Genius of Progress – to be contested not by individual drivers, but by teams of three cars from each manufacturing nation, the cardinal rule being that every part of the competing cars had to be made in the country which it represented. The idea, it seems, stemmed from a transatlantic bet. For Charron had hardly won the Paris–Bordeaux race in May 1899 than he received a challenge from Alexander Winton of Cleveland, Ohio, who had just completed a successful drive from New York to Cleveland in a vehicle of his own make. The match was to be over a distance of 1,000 miles (1,609km). Charron accepted the wager, depositing a sum of earnest money at the Paris office of the *New York Herald*. As it happened the encounter never actually took place, but Gordon Bennett's Challenge Cup did.

At first nobody took it very seriously. The initial race in 1900 organized by the Automobile Club de France over a 353 mile (568km) course from Paris to Lyons attracted only five entrants – three Panhards from France, a Snoeck Bolide from Belgium, and the Winton from America. It was won by

Clifford Earp's Napier after its crash during the eliminating trials for the 1904 Gordon Bennett race. A rarity for those days was the

aluminium monobloc cylinder casting (with four automatic inlet valves per cylinder). This actual car is now in the Harrah Museum at Reno.

Charron in the Panhard at an average of 38.6mph (62.12kph) despite a damaged rear axle and an alarming encounter with a St Bernard dog a few miles outside Lyons. He was followed nearly an hour and a half later by Girardot in another Panhard. The remaining three cars, including Alexander Winton's, fell by the wayside.

The following year public interest was centred on the ACF's major race from the French capital to Berlin, in which 110 machines took part, and hardly anyone noticed the three French cars which competed for the Gordon Bennett Cup as a sort of side-show in the Paris–Bordeaux race. The event would have disintegrated into a fiasco, in fact, had it not been for a challenge from Britain in 1902. This time it was being run in conjunction with the Paris–Vienna, and to S. F. Edge and his Napier went the honours (as the only finisher) not only of being awarded the trophy, but also of chalking up England's first international victory in the new sport – while to Great Britain went the responsibility of staging the 1903 event.

Since public opinion would never have tolerated the idea of a continental-style race on the roads of Britain, it was held over a closed circuit at the Curragh in Ireland; and the field at last had a reasonably international flavour, since three British Napiers were challenged by three Mercedes from Germany, two Panhards and a Mors from France, as well as by two Wintons and a Peerless from the USA. And by all accounts, the organization was highly professional. A grandstand holding 1,000 spectators was built astride the start at Kilrush; bookings were handled by Thomas Cook; and a special train was laid on from Dublin. The *Motor* sent a staff of sixteen reporters and the *Autocar* organized a captive balloon above the finishing straight. The elaborate marshalling system involved twenty-seven stewards at each of the seven control posts, and the French contingent, not to be outdone by such cross-channel efficiency, chartered the *Ferdinand de Lesseps* which they converted into a floating workshop contain-

Werner's Mercedes (right) gets off to a smoky start in the 1905 race. The spectators were well kitted out for an event which began at six o'clock and lasted over seven hours. Darracqs reconnoitering the 85 mile (137km) Auvergne circuit at Mussagettes (below) for the 1905 Gordon Bennett race.

PNEU
LE GAULOIS
LE GAULOIS
MICHELIN
OBSTACLE

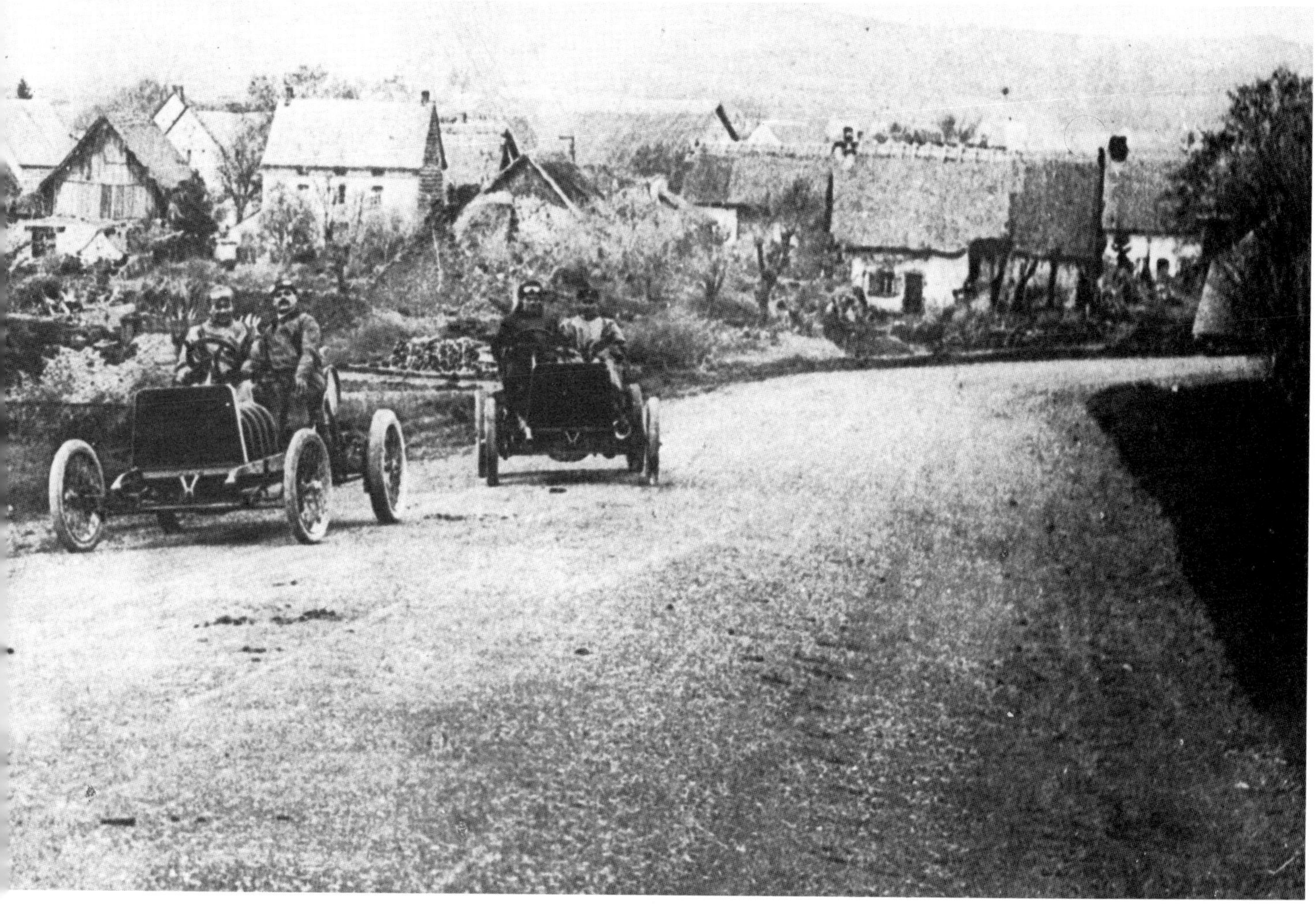

ing twenty-two cars and a staff of a hundred.

In his scholarly book on the Gordon Bennett series, Lord Montagu of Beaulieu quotes a spectator's report which aptly describes the feel of this first British circuit race:

> As soon as you saw the cloud of dust through the trees three and three-quarters miles away you caught sight of a small black, low thing rushing along the centre of the ribbon of road stretched out at your feet. As it came along the light yellowish cloud rose right up behind it in a dense, impenetrable mass, showing the little black body up in greater relief. A mile or so away, you caught the sight of two human heads topping the screen in front of the body of the car, and you then began to see that, as they came tearing along, it was with a swaying movement. It would lurch with the dip or rise of the road, to one side, then to the other. The greater the speed, the more violently the nose of the machine seemed to sway from side to side. Then you heard the hum, and the tearing thing that was coming straight for you took shape.

Camille Jenatzy won on the Mercedes at an average speed of just under 50mph (80kph), followed by the three Panhards, a Mors, and Edge's Napier. And so while Germany carried off the Gordon Bennett trophy, France took home the prize presented by Lord Montagu's father.

Jenatzy himself is reputed to have made £8,000 out of the race, which, considering the value of money, compares quite favourably with the winnings of a GP driver seventy years later. For racing had now become big business, and (in contrast to its early fiascos) the Gordon Bennett now emerged as the top event of the 1904 calendar. Manufacturers who had so far turned their noses up at the sport now hastened to join in the game. Along with numerous others, F.I.A.T. of Turin and Opel of Rüsselsheim appeared on the scene. 'Racing is the curse of the automobile trade,' snorted the chairman of Hotchkiss. But his company entered the lists all the same.

Part of the Darracq team (above) for the 1905 Gordon Bennett race. The marque built a team of specially light cars for this event which unfortunately failed the eliminating trials.

As a consequence of the Mercedes victory in Ireland, the 1904 Gordon Bennett was held in Germany and Kaiser Wilhelm II, himself an enthusiast, was determined to turn it into a prestige affair. The course chosen was an eighty-seven mile circuit in the Taunus mountains north of Frankfurt, close to the fashionable resort of Homburg, starting from the romantic medieval castle of Saalburg. With battlemented grandstands, a programme of 'illuminations', opera, ballet and no fewer than eighty military band concerts, the atmosphere was heavily Wagnerian. Moreover, to pre-empt their chances of retaining the cup against the challenge from England, France, Belgium and Italy, Mercedes entered a second 'shadow' team of cars built in their Wiener Neustadt factory under the black and yellow colours of Austria. But even this hedging of their bets did not prevent Théry in the Richard Brasier from finishing ten minutes ahead of Jenatzy's Mercedes at an average speed of 52·9mph (85kph) over the tricky, twisting circuit, to

Anticipating modern practice, Clifford Earp (above right) fitted bigger section tires on the rear than on the front of his Napier for the 1905 Gordon Bennett race. This was the only Napier in the race and was considered better on sprints than on the mountainous circuits where, with only two forward speeds, it was at a disadvantage.

bring the now coveted trophy back to France.

Now that the organization of the 1905 event was once again in French hands, the ACF published regulations which decreed the number of cars that any nation could enter according to the size of each country's industry. Since France had by far the largest motor industry, she allocated to herself a quota of eighteen. Britain and Germany both got an allowance of six cars, and other manufacturing nations – such as Austria, Belgium, Italy, Switzerland, Holland and indeed even the USA – just three cars each. What is more, to spike Mercedes' guns, the regulations added that no single make could enter more than three machines.

Understandably, this high-handed piece of Gallic logic was hardly to the taste of any other country. Protests poured in, but although the differences were resolved (by postponing the controversial regulations for a year) in time for the Gordon Bennett to be held at Clermont-Ferrand, it was to be the last of the series. Théry, earned his nickname of 'Le Chronomètre' by repeating his victory in the Richard Brasier ahead of the F.I.A.T.s of Nazzaro and Cagno, which apparently gave more pleasure to Turin than to Paris. For whereas the King and Queen of Italy visited the Corso Dante to congratulate the F.I.A.T. team, the French washed their hands of the whole affair, announcing that the following year they would stage a Grand Prix. Thus the Gordon Bennett Cup foundered, in the words of D. B. Tubbs, on 'politico-nationalistic-commercial grounds', and instead, the first French Grand Prix was run on the new Le Mans circuit in 1906.

The Early Land Speed Records [1899–1906]

A 1902 racing Oldsmobile (left) poses for the camera on a typical American short, dirt-covered track. In 1903 a special version of the Curved Dash two-seater covered a mile in 42sec at Daytona.
Right: a Serpollet steam car. The photograph is inscribed by Léon Serpollet to Roger Wallace. In 1902 Serpollet held the land speed record for a brief time, reaching 75.06mph (120.8kph), before this was topped in August of the same year by Vanderbilt at 76.08mph (122.44kph).

> We declare that the world's splendour has been enriched by a new beauty, the beauty of speed. A racing motor car . . . is more beautiful than the Victory of Samothrace. We shall sing of the man at the steering wheel . . .
>
> Filippo Marinetti *Futurist Manifesto* 1909

A FEW DAYS before Christmas 1898 the pioneer motoring journal *La France Automobile* announced that it would be holding a 'concours de vitesse' in Achères Park just north of Paris. Timekeepers with stop-watches were stationed at the beginning and end of a measured kilometre and cars of various sorts were put through their paces. As it happens, a Jeantaud electric car driven by Comte Gaston de Chasseloup-Laubat had the legs of its petrol-engined rivals, and covered the flying kilometre in 57sec. The world's first official land speed record had been set up at a speed of 39.24mph (63.16kph).

Almost immediately, however, the Comte was challenged by the Belgian, Camille

To Mr Roger Wallace as a souvenir of some very big jumps

Jenatzy, who, interested like himself in the electric cab business, proposed an encounter the following month. The match took place on 17 January 1899 and Jenatzy, in an electric machine of his own design, clocked up 53sec for the flying kilometre. For the first time, the land speed record had been beaten. But ten minutes later Chasseloup-Laubat sped off to lower it again with 51.2sec, or 43.69mph (70.3kph). Two new records in a day!

The duel between the rivals continued. Ten days later Jenatzy returned for another attempt, and lowered the time again to 44.8sec, a speed of 49.92mph (80.32kph) which inevitably impelled Chasseloup-Laubat to retrieve his lost record. On 4 March he was back with a more streamlined version of the Jeantaud and covered the flying kilometre in a full 6sec less, to set a new record of 57.6mph (92.7kph).

But Jenatzy did not take long to reply. On 29 April he appeared with a cigar-shaped creation called 'La Jamais Contente'. Built by his own firm, and powered by two electric motors driving directly to the wheels, his blue *bolide* brought the flying kilometre down from 38.8 to 34.0sec, breaking the 100kph barrier, and lifting the land speed record to 65.79mph (105.88kph).

This time it was game, set and match to 'The Red Devil' and Jenatzy's record remained unbroken for a full three years. C. S. Rolls had a go at it on a Mors, without success, and William K. Vanderbilt made an attempt with a 35 Mercedes, but although he exactly equalled Jenatzy's speed he could not better it. In fact, the electric car's record was finally captured by a steam-driven machine during the Nice Speed Week at Easter in 1902, when Léon Serpollet's canoe-shaped device, nicknamed 'Oeuf de Pâques', whistled down the Promenade des Anglais through the flying kilometre in 29.8sec, a speed of 75mph, or 120.7kph.

By now the heat was on. William K. Vanderbilt and Henri de Rothschild both tried to improve on Serpollet's record with a Mercedes-Simplex, but with no success. Finally, Vanderbilt switched to the 60hp Mors that he had driven in the Paris–Vienna race and took it through a measured kilometre on the Ablis–St Arnoult road in 29.4sec, to establish the first LSR with a petrol-engined car.

This provoked Henri Fournier, the winner of the Paris–Bordeaux and the 1901 Paris–Berlin, to have a go himself, and on 5 November he knocked a fifth of a second off Vanderbilt's time on the ACF's new course at Dourdan, only to be confounded when an amateur driver named Augières borrowed the same car from the Mors factory a fortnight later and did the run in 29sec flat, setting a new record of 77.13mph (124.1kph).

If 1902 had seen four new records, all within four fifths of a second of each other, the following year witnessed two new records by the same car and driver. At the Ostend Meeting in July 1903, Arthur Duray took his massive, top-heavy looking Gobron-Brillié through the kilometre in only 26.8sec, and later that year, aiming for the 140kph mark, actually achieved 84.73mph (136.36kph) at Dourdan in November.

So far, all this activity had been in France. But two months later the challenge came from across the Atlantic. In January 1904, no less a figure than Henry Ford braved the elements and slithered his Ford 'Arrow' (which was simply a huge 16.7 litre engine fitted in a steel reinforced wooden chassis *sans* gearbox, differential or springs) over the icy surface of Lake St Clair near Detroit at 91.37mph (147.05kph). It was a pretty desperate run. 'When I wasn't in the air I was skidding,' he recalled afterwards; 'but somehow I stayed topside up . . . making a record that went all over the world.'

Well, not quite, as it happened. Because less than two weeks later, in the warmer and jollier atmosphere of the Florida Speed Week, William K. Vanderbilt bettered this figure, with his big white Mercedes on Daytona Sands, by two fifths of a second. And also because, although both of these attempts were timed by the AAA, the snobbish ACF (who alone could officially ratify them) declined to recognize either the non-metric measurement or the AAA as the American national authority. So these records remained in the limbo of non-events for a couple of months until Louis Rigolly settled the LSR issue, again during the Nice *Semaine de Vitesse*, by thundering down the Promenade des Anglais on his space-framed Gobron-Brillié with its huge 4 cylinder double-piston engine at 94.78mph (152.53kph).

But even he didn't keep it for long. In May, the Baron Pierre de Caters, a well known Belgian sportsman, chopped three-fifths of a second off Rigolly's time on the road outside Ostend, 'just to annoy the Parisians a little', as he put it; which he obviously did, because during the July Speed Trials at Ostend, Rigolly put paid to such pleasantries with a resounding 21.6sec, thereby 'topping the ton' for the first time at 103.55mph (166.65kph).

Yet, if record breaking was a millionaire's

Barney Oldfield (above) at the controls of the famous '999', twin to the 'Arrow' racing car with which Henry Ford (right) set up a record speed of 91.37mph (147.05kph) on the frozen surface of Lake St Clair, Detroit, in January 1904.

Camille Jenatzy's 'La Jamais Contente' (below), an electric car which reached a speed of 65.79mph (105.88kph) at Achères in April 1899. Altogether Jenatzy held the record three times that year.

pastime, it was also the manufacturer's bread and butter. 'Win on Sunday, sell on Monday', goes the saying; and the land speed record was a certain stimulus to sales. In November 1904, therefore, a whole circus of Darracqs made their appearance at Ostend in search of records, and Paul Baras with the 100hp Gordon Bennett type clocked the flying kilometre in 21.4sec, to notch the LSR by a further 1mph.

Only a few weeks later, what is more, a British contender showed his paces at the Florida Speed Week. Driving a 90hp Napier, Arthur Macdonald covered the flying mile at 34.4sec, representing a speed of 104.65mph (168.42kph) – just thirteen-hundredths of a mile faster than Baras.

This new LSR had barely been announced by the Florida authorities than it was shattered, minutes later, by Herbert Bowden in a remarkable machine called the 'Flying Dutchman'. (It had two Mercedes 60 engines fitted into a stretched Mercedes chassis.)

Bowden bounced across the Daytona Sands to put up a run of 109.75mph (176.62kph) – over 5mph faster than the Napier. But, inexplicably, the authorities disqualified the car on the grounds that it exceeded the maximum permitted weight for the Speed Week Events.

Predictably, too, the ACF refused to ratify any attempts made on American soil. The year 1905 opened, therefore, with the strange situation that an American had manifestly set up the world's land speed record; an Englishman had been attributed it; but a Frenchman officially held it. It was just as well, therefore, that Darracqs produced a 22.5 litre V8 Special, with which Victor Hémery was able to add exactly 5mph to Macdonald's figure and restore the LSR to France.

Even so, Hémery's speed was one-tenth of a mile per hour less than Bowden's attempt, and the American brothers, Francis and Freeland Stanley, decided that something must be done about this. Their company, which manufactured a solid range of steam cars, had also gone in for the records game with a variety of machines, sporting nicknames such as 'Wogglebug' and 'Teakettle'. The maroon-coloured Stanley 'Rocket' took a year to devise and appeared at the 1906 Florida Speed Week, as did the 200 hp Darracq that officially held the record.

In the hands of Louis Chevrolet, the Darracq beat its own record with 19.4sec for the flying kilometre, but Fred Marriott, aboard the 'Rocket', promptly knocked a whole second off this, covering the measured kilometre at an astonishing 121.57mph (195.65kph) and the measured mile at 127.6mph (205.35kph). About miles the Paris authorities were as unco-operative as ever, but they accepted Marriott's performance over the flying kilometre as a new land record. And there for the next three years it stood.

Peking to Paris

IT MIGHT STILL be largely a rich man's toy, but by now the motor car was growing up, and its pioneers were ranging far afield. In 1902 E. E. Lehwess left London in a Panhard (optimistically named 'passe-partout') to drive round the world, and although he gave up at St Petersburg it was nevertheless a notable achievement. The following summer an American, Charles Glidden, drove his Napier up to the Arctic Circle, and a year later in America, Australia, New Zealand, China and even Japan. In 1905 R. L. Jefferson left Coventry in a Rover to plough through the roadless plains of Hungary and Bulgaria and give the Ottoman Empire its first glimpse of an automobile. A little while after this my father, Edmund Flower, shipped a Napier to Egypt at the age of twenty-one and drove it from Cairo to Alexandria, capping this with a dash across the desert from Cairo to Suez in an Opel. What's more, he relates, his friends at

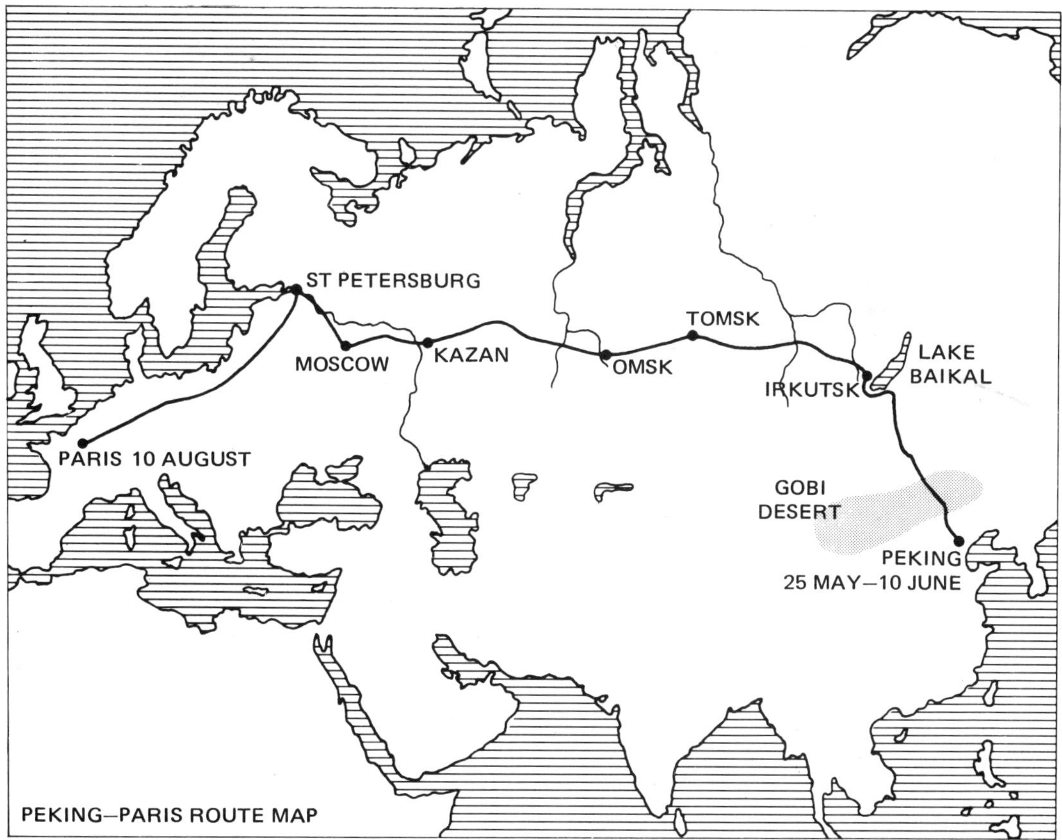

Above, waiting for the start: an autographed picture of Prince Scipione Borghese and Luigi Barzini with the Itala in Peking. There had been some considerable delay before this while the competitors waited for the Chinese to grant passports through Mongolia. A route map of the Peking to Paris race (right). The tent (above right): 'a shelter for man and machine'.

The Itala a few moments after its fall when a wooden bridge collapsed beneath its weight, and being hauled out basically unharmed (below).

Gezira Sporting Club pulled his leg about it. 'That Suez run of yours is nothing,' they taunted, 'You couldn't go up to Luxor – there's no road.' Then and there Prince Bentheim of Bavaria and Count Schlick of Austria bet him and Baron Richard Vachelerwizec the sum of £100 that they would not drive to Luxor in Upper Egypt in seven days.

Needless to say, the challenge was accepted. The Fagnier-engined Opel was fitted up with a bench seat and a pick-up type box for food and camping equipment, as well as with slings which had leather shoulder straps and ran under the hubs to enable four men to carry the car. Early in October the two hopefuls set out, driving along the banks of the irrigation canals. They reached Beni Suef the first night, Assiut the second, and finally made Luxor on the evening of the fifth day. Back in Cairo, Shepheard's was buzzing. In the grill-room a banquet for fifty was laid out round a table covered with sand, toy animals and farmyard scenes. There was much toasting of *Brüderschaft*, and all in all it must have been a memorable binge.

Such exploits were numerous in the early, salad days of motoring; but they were small beer compared to that most romantic of all long-distance events: the famous Peking to Paris race of 1907.

It came about when a prominent French newspaper, *Le Matin*, sprang a challenge with the following headline: 'Will anyone agree to go, this summer, from Peking to Paris by motor car?' Among the host of replies (many of which wrote off the project as utterly impossible) was a terse telegram from Prince Scipione Borghese, of the celebrated Papal family, entering his name for the race. Others did likewise, with the result that the Prince's modified 40hp Itala, along with a 15hp Spyker (not dissimilar to the 1905 model driven by Kenneth More in the

Bumpy at the best of times (and worse if a train turned up): the Peking-Paris race-winning Itala (above) driving on the track of the Trans-Siberian railway. Right: both man and horsepower were needed to get the cars through the mud. According to a report in the *Autocar* (27 July 1907) 'no less than 150 coolies were employed' during the first stage of the race.

Colignon's De Dion (above) fording a river in Mongolia. Bridges were untrustworthy or non-existant throughout Asia and all the competitors relied heavily on mules and horses appearing at the right time.

film *Genevieve*), two 10hp De Dion-Boutons and a 6hp Contal tricycle, made their appearance early that June in the capital of the Chinese Empire.

Admittedly, in the eyes of Luigi Barzini, who was accompanying Prince Borghese and his chauffeur Ettore as a special correspondent for the *Corriere della Sera* and the *Daily Telegraph*, the approaching competition appeared as unreal as a dream. 'The very presence of a motor car in that ancient town seemed more absurd than would the sight of a palanquin going over London Bridge' he asserted, adding that, 'The civilization of the Chinese race achieved once a kind of perfection and, fearful of losing that, it refused to move further. One thing alone moves now in China, and that is Time.' Be this as it may, the start was given at 8am in the morning of 10 June, and the five cars chased each other through a labyrinth of narrow streets and past the Imperial enclosure at a speed which must have seemed magical to the watching crowds. The 'hundred greatest days in automobile history' had begun, and *Peking to Paris*, Luigi Barzini's homeric account of the journey, has its honoured place on the bookshelves of every Italian household, second only to Dante's *Divine Comedy* (and Artusi's cookbook, *l'Arte di mangiar bene*).

Viewed dispassionately, the Peking to Paris race turned out to be not so much an epic of danger and suspense (since no one came to any harm) but rather of endurance against difficulties and prolonged discomfort. It was, above all, the first time that automobiles were being subjected to a long arduous transcontinental trial over deserts, plains, forests and mountain passes, with only primitive tracks to follow.

After the Nankow Gorge, a narrow slit between two crags, and beyond it the Great Wall of China, blending like a 'prodigious architectural moulding' on the crests and sides of the peaks, the road became a river bed full of broken stone, boulders and pools; and from here on over the mountain range to Kalgan the machines had to be manhandled by mules and coolies through points where a pick-axe was sometimes necessary to clear sufficient room for the cars to pass. The Mongolian prairies followed, and then five hundred torrid miles across the parched monotony of the Gobi desert, marked only by whitening bones and the endless line of telegraph poles. Their progress in the burning heat seemed to Barzini to be 'at once an

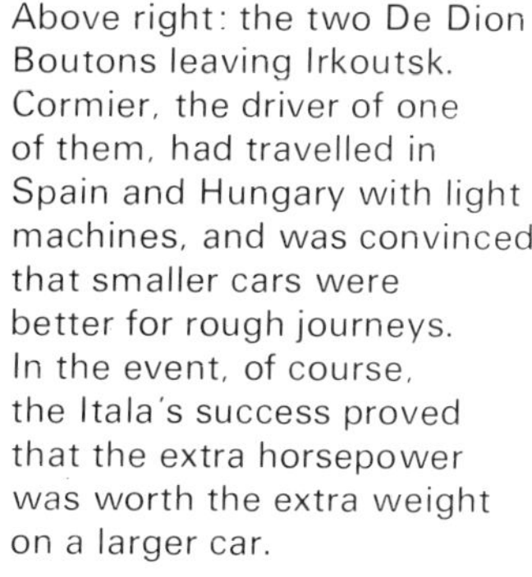

Above right: the two De Dion Boutons leaving Irkoutsk. Cormier, the driver of one of them, had travelled in Spain and Hungary with light machines, and was convinced that smaller cars were better for rough journeys. In the event, of course, the Itala's success proved that the extra horsepower was worth the extra weight on a larger car.

assault and a flight'. But it presented less problems than the subsequent caravan route between Urga and Kiakhta where the heavy Itala was suddenly engulfed in treacherous slime.

'The soil under our feet was heaving,' relates Barzini. 'It was as if we were walking over floating cork . . . we realized that the mass of mud would swallow up our car if we did not succeed in saving it at once.' To make matters worse, a trekking Buriat tribe appeared on the scene but after one look at the sinking car refused to do anything to help. It was no use, they said.

Providentially enough, however, some Mongolian horsemen also rode up, and they set to work. Yet even by putting planks under the wheels and getting oxen to pull, they failed to drag the car out of the mud. Finally someone had a brain-wave and started the engine. 'At the sudden noise, the four terrified beasts pulled desperately,' recalls Barzini, 'and suddenly the car came out of its furrow with one bound . . .'

After this unnerving experience, the Itala crew treated the marshy plains with respect, carefully reconnoitering any suspect ground before driving over it. Finally they reached the river Iro, where once again the help of local oxen, was necessary to ford the car through waist-high water, after the magneto had been removed, and the engine covered with grease. Here in a sandstorm they took their leave of the Celestial Empire – 'our faces literally black with dust, and over our clothes a thick crust of the different kinds of mud with which we had come in intimate contact all along our way: the black mud of the bogs, the yellow mud of the Chara-gol, the white mud of the Iro' – to be whisked into the office of the chief of police of Kiakhta, frontier post of the Russian Empire, who handed them *podorojnes* from both the minister of the interior and the governor general of the imperial police. Without these telling documents, as it turned out, they would never have circumvented the Russian bureaucracy, let alone crossed Siberia.

Admittedly Trans-Baikalia – until the advent of the railway a whole year's journey from Moscow – was fertile and prosperous compared with the parched plains of Mongolia, something like Scotland, thought Barzini, with its wooded hills and wild scenery. But, alas, the weather was Scottish, too, for although midsummer it rained all the way across Siberia – which in an open car without roof or windshield was far from pleasant.

Normally, the great inland sea of Lake Baikal was crossed by ship, but thanks to his impressive documents from Moscow Prince Borghese got permission to skirt it by driving on the track of the Trans-Siberian railroad. For some miles they progressed along it with a sort of galloping gait, with the left wheels of the car between the rails and the right wheels on the wooden ties outside. Then a train was signalled and they were deviated over a short stretch of road to the next level-crossing. But half-way across an old wooden bridge over a small torrent there was a frightful crash as the planks gave way. The car slowly turned a somersault and plunged into the abyss, carrying its passengers down in a debris of splintered woodwork. Miraculously a single beam saved them from catastrophe, and the car's fall was to some extent cushioned by the four spare tires strapped on the rear. No less miraculously the sturdy machine, once it had been hauled inch by inch back on to the road by the neighbouring population, proved (as the Siberians put it) to be 'still alive'. And hardly had they regained the relative security of the railroad than it again escaped annihilation by seconds from a passing freight train.

For 6,000 miles across Siberia and Russia, it was a continuous struggle against the elements, sometimes bumping along forest tracks, but more often sliding over soapy peat and getting hopelessly stuck in the squelching mud. 'What a lot of different people we had seen at work around our car, pushing it, pulling it, raising it!' sighed Barzini on one of the occasions that they were being dug out of trouble: 'In how many tongues had the same ideas been expressed with panting breath; how many human wills had joined their efforts to ours!' The wonder of it was that the engine, transmission and suspension stood up to such non-stop pounding, and that the crew themselves did not succumb to sheer fatigue. There was a deadening monotony about the Siberian villages, each indistinguishable from the one before, with each house resembling its neighbour. But for all this, there were memorable moments, too, such as the *mujic* carpenter in a hamlet between Perm and Kazan who quoted Latin tags while repairing a wheel, and the telegraph operator in Nijni-Novgorod who sent off the text of Barzini's cables reading vertically downwards.

Prince Borghese's crew reached Moscow while the other competitors were still in Siberia. So warm and enthusiastic was their welcome that they could hardly refuse to make the long detour up to St Petersburg (what, it was argued, were a couple of extra days after so many?) and from the Imperial Russian capital onwards their progress through Germany, Belgium and the north of France was nothing short of a triumphant procession, flanked by well-wishers and, towards the end, three sparkling new Italas sent out by the Paris agent.

It had taken them twelve days to cover the first 600 miles through China, and forty-one days to cross the empire of the Czar; the last 600 miles were knocked off in two and a half days, despite a good deal of time lost in social engagements, and Scipione Borghese finally drew the Itala up in front of the offices of *Le Matin* in Paris on 10 August, exactly two calendar months after the start from Peking. The De Dions and the Spyker, which had similar experiences, though less graphically recorded, followed three and a half weeks later, having completed the expedition in just under one hundred days. (Of the Contal tricycle, nothing more was heard.)

Half a century later the Fiat Company, at the suggestion of Barzini's son, contemplated a commemoration run over the same terrain, from the Great Wall to the Seine, but the Chinese government refused to give permission for it to be held.

Would a modern car stand up to such a trial any better? Who knows. At any rate, there seems little cause to take issue with the technical summing up of 1907:

On the whole the Peking to Paris race has

Prince Borghese drives the Itala triumphantly into Paris. The victors were accompanied to the finishing post at the *Le Matin* offices by a

cavalcade of cars, two mounted patrols of the Republican Guard, and 100 cyclists.

proved conclusively that the motor car is a much stronger and more resilient machine than has so far been thought, and that the usual inconveniences of automobilism, and the frequent breakdowns from which tourists suffer, the breakages and repeated disasters to the machines, are due rather to carelessness or want of skill in chauffeurs than to any congenital weakness of the car itself. It may therefore be said that this industry has arrived near its perfection . . .

At any rate, *Le Matin* felt encouraged the following year to join with the *New York Times* in sponsoring what was probably the longest and almost certainly the zaniest motoring contest ever held. Their idea was nothing less than a race around the world in which competitors, after a short journey by steamer up the British Columbian coast, would disembark at Scagway, drive through the Klondike and Alaska, and cross the Bering Strait on the ice.

Although expert opinion such as the *Motor* dismissed the whole project as 'mad-brained', nonetheless three French cars – a De Dion, a Motobloc and a Sizaire Naudin – along with a German Protos, an Italian Züst and an American Thomas Flyer, eventually lined up for the start outside the Seventh Avenue offices of the *New York Times* on 12 February 1908 and were cheered off by a crowd of some 50,000 spectators. (The Kaiser himself had sent greetings to the German team.)

But hardly were the cars out of New York than they found themselves bogged down by mud and snow. The Motobloc retired after seventy miles (112km) and the Sizaire Naudin fell out an hour or two later. Battling over vast expanses of snow with hardly a visible track, and sometimes running along the railway line, the remainder of the field only got as far as Chicago after three weeks of motoring. But somehow or other (allegedly by being hitched to a train and even transported on a sledge) the Thomas reached San Francisco on 24 March and sailed for Alaska. There a short reconnoiter showed clearly that the Arctic crossing was impossible, and they retraced their steps only to find that the Protos, after being bogged down in the mud in Wyoming had come from Ogden by train, had slipped out of Seattle aboard the *Glenlogan* while the De Dion and the Züst had taken a boat to Japan. *Le Matin* announced a modified route for the race and the *Autocar* commented: 'Seeing that the organizers are endeavouring to simplify the race as much as possible, it may be suggested whether, after all, it would not have been more satisfactory to ship the cars from New York to Le Havre, and then proceed by road to Paris.'

Certainly an element of farce was beginning to creep into the whole proceedings. The De Dion was sold to a Peking merchant on the pretext that since the Asiatic route had been covered the previous year there wasn't much point in doing it again. After struggling through thick mud at the rate of ten miles a day, the Thomas struck the Trans-Siberian railway and bumped across the Imperial Russian Empire on the ties until its gearbox broke and the Protos got past. The occupants of the Züst were nearly drowned on what they thought was dry land, and at one point, with true Italian flair, improvised a new crankshaft bearing from a cough-drop tin, mud, wood, and some bullets. In the end, sixty-nine days and two hours after leaving Vladivostok and 170 days after the start, after covering 12,116 miles (19,509km), the Thomas team reached Paris to a star-spangled welcome and were declared the winners even though the Protos had actually got there first (there was, after all, a little matter of having missed out Japan). The Züst, which probably did more actual motoring than any of the others, was still at Omsk, where the crew were seized as spies when they tried to send a cable in Italian. When it finally finished the course, it was taken over to England only to be destroyed by fire in a railway station. The K-6-70 72hp 6 cylinder Thomas, on the other hand, was shipped back to Buffalo and continued to be used until it eventually became a prize exhibit in Harrah's

Borghese (above) and the crew in the Itala on reaching European soil after four months crossing Asia and Russia. Although the clutch and some of the springs had to be replaced in Moscow, the car had stood up to its battering remarkably well. The New York to Paris motor race of 1908 (right) – the Italian Züst, which finished third behind the American Thomas and a German Protos.

collection at Reno (where my colleague, Alex Low, drove it recently).

Commenting on its remarkable technical performance, an American newspaper declared soberly in 1908: 'The demand today is not for cars that can run from New York to Paris, but faster and more economical substitute for the horse on ordinary roads and city streets.' To which another journal added: 'A wonderful achievement, but apparently we do not yet need to write the epitaph of the horse.'

Early Rallies and Hill Climbs

De Laventhal's Mercedes (above) preparing for the ascent at the Gaillon hill-climb on the Paris-Rouen main road. An unusual feature of this particular event was the flying start – cars took a run at it. Competitors form a long queue (right) for one of the special hill-climbs in the Scottish Reliability Trials in June 1906. The number of cars, quite remarkable for any competition at this period, clearly shows the popularity of this branch of the sport.

YET ALMOST BEFORE the first decade of motor sport was over, the early champions were beginning to withdraw, and Charles Jarrott was already writing in 1905 that

> The curse of commercialism is the ruin of sport, and the degeneracy of motor racing as a sport is due to the financial issues now involved in every race . . . the charm disappears, and I can see in the near future, and before the racing of cars dies the death that is yearly predicted, the sporting element obliterated altogether by the all-devouring monster of commercialism – the curse of the twentieth century.

Even if seventy years later this prophecy has all too familiar a ring about it, there is no doubt that as cars became more numerous the sport itself began to branch into a number of well-defined and specialized events.

Out-and-out enthusiasts continued to concentrate on the great new circuit races which – after the ban on unrestricted road racing – had replaced the old city-to-city marathons, setting their sights on such major events as the Tourist Trophy (first run in the Isle of Man in 1905), the French Grand Prix which was inaugurated on the Le Mans circuit in 1906, and the Targa Florio which made its debut the same year.

Gentler souls, on the other hand, showed a

4-29
RS-234
4-8
TS-78

preference for reliability trials, of which the best-known precursor was probably the International Touring Car competition. This started off in 1905 as a leisurely road run of some 500 miles from Frankfurt to Innsbruck, beefed up by a hill-climb at Semmering and a speed test over 3.4 miles (5.5km) at the finish. As a prize the winner was entitled to have his portrait painted by Professor Hubert von Herkomer, the German artist who sponsored the event. Among the competitors, as it happens, was Prince Henry of Prussia, younger brother of the Kaiser, and from 1908 onwards the trophy carried his name. It was intended to be mainly a social affair and trade entrants were barred. Nevertheless, a number of professional drivers managed to dodge through the rules (including a youngster called Ettore Bugatti, who is reputed to have fallen asleep at the wheel of his Deutz and to have crashed into a tree) and long after the series ceased in 1911 Prince Henry's name was perpetuated by such famous cars as the Vauxhall Prince Henry Tourer, and the equally celebrated Prince Henry Austro-Daimler, designed by Dr Ferdinand Porsche.

From these aristocratic jaunts sprang the Austrian Alpine Trial, which grew into the major touring event of Europe and subsequently developed into the International Alpine Rally – or, as it is now known, the Coupe des Alpes. The first Austrian Alpine, held in June 1910, was run over a relatively modest route in the Alps, although it included the Katschberg and Tauern passes. By 1912, however, it had been extended to cover 1,488 miles (2,394km) over 13 difficult passes, and lasted seven days. (Of the 84 starters, 72 finished of whom no fewer than 25 were unpenalized.) In 1913 the 1,630 mile (2,670 km) route spanned 19 passes, and only 9 cars finished with clean sheets; while in the last of the great Austrian-organized trials, run in 1914, the 75 starters were required to battle over nearly 1,850 miles (2,977km) of alpine roads during eight days of motoring, including some timed hill-climbs and a 5km speed test – thus setting, in fact, the pattern for all the later Alpines and even the AC de Savoie's vicious little Evian–Mont Blanc Rally.

Fritz Erle's powerful Benz (above), with a capacity of 7,479cc, was winner of the gruelling Prince Henry Trial in 1908.
Water was provided at Inverness for cars (above left) in the Scottish Reliability Trials in 1907. In Britain, where the government frowned on racing from the start, this less hair-raising side of the sport quickly gained ground.

Overpage: a 15hp Marlborough climbing the Greenan Hill during the Irish Reliability Trials in 1909.

These international trials, with their emphasis on reliability rather than on sheer speed (though some dicing was undoubtedly involved by competitors who had to make up for any lost time), soon became an established part of European motor sport, and it is hardly to be wondered that the principality of Monaco, with its vaunted Winter Season – of which the high spot was the 'Monte Carlo Week' in January – should have decided to get into the act. In the autumn of 1910 M. Alexandre Noghès, President of the Automobile and Cycle Club of Monaco, announced a Monte Carlo Rally for the following January, open to private cars of every description, which would be allowed a schedule of seven days to reach Monte Carlo from a number of starting points. The *Motor* greeted this news coldly: 'With the object of attracting visitors to the Riviera, the Muncipality of Monte Carlo has instituted a "gathering of the clans" for the month of January next.' As it turned out, most of the twenty-three competitors in this first event set off from Paris. The others selected Berlin, Vienna and Brussels, and the winner was Henri Rougier in a 25hp Turcat-Méry – despite a complaint from Captain van Esmarch, who started from Berlin in a Dürkopp, that apart from exceptionally

Y88

bad weather conditions he had been unfairly held up on the French border (thus establishing the tradition that a good protest was all part of the game).

But the challenge of grappling with winter conditions – which in those days without four-wheel brakes, snow tires, anti-freeze, heaters and only the most rudimentary sort of all-weather equipment were a very real hazard – appealed to the sporting spirit of many an intrepid motorist, and in 1912 no less than eighty-seven competitors started from such places as Paris, Vienna, Berlin, Geneva, Brussels, Le Havre, Amsterdam, Boulogne, and Turin; while there was even one stalwart (Nagel in a Russo-Baltique) who set off from St Petersburg. The average speed required was 15.5mph (25kph), and although Chalet did the 416 miles (670km) from Geneva in his 12hp Schneider at an average of almost 31mph (50kph) the outright winner was Beutler in a Berliet who had come from Berlin. Comfort counted towards the winning marks, and while such cars as Count de Malavia's splendid Rolls-Royce sedanca were obviously beyond reproach, the fact that the points awarded to each car were not divulged caused some unhappy scenes at the finish.

Successful though this second event had been, no further 'Montes' were held until 1924, and the residents of the Riviera had to be content with the annual hill-climbs of La Turbie and Mont Ventoux.

Indeed the delicate artistry of sprinting up a corkscrew course against an accurate chronometer (like the Cresta run at St Moritz in the inverse direction) had very early on attracted a strong following to hill-climbs, and the famous Mont Ventoux, which ascends 5,250ft in 13.5 miles (1,600m in 21.5km) is today the oldest surviving climb, having been in continuous use for competitions since 1902. At the other end of the scale, Shelsley Walsh in England, first held on 12 August 1905, is only 1,000yd (914m) in length, but the narrow track which climbs sharply between high banks to the famous S-bend has held an irresistible challenge for several generations of *aficionados*. In 1905 E. M. C. Instone negotiated the ascent in 77.6sec in his Daimler to establish the first recorded best time; which over several decades has been steadily reduced, and now stands at 30.72 sec (put up by M. Brain in a Cooper-Chrysler in 1969).

La Turbie, above Nice, is marginally older than either of these, but has now lapsed. It was a dangerous course, full of twists and sharp turns, with a drop on one side of thousands of feet, and both muscle and nerve were needed to race the big bangers up it.

A. F. C. Hillstead, who was one of the original 'Bentley Boys', remembers that as a child he was taken by a school friend to Count Eliot Zborowski's Regency house on the top of Putney Hill, where he was shown the magnificent 60hp Mercedes that the count was to drive in the La Turbie hill-climb in 1903. Zborowski, the veteran of so many city-to-city races, was determined to win the event at all costs.

A few days later, while they were trying to fathom the mysteries of simple arithmetic, the headmaster of the school came up to his friend Louis and led him from the room. News had just come through that his father, Count Zborowski, had been involved in a fatal crash at the very beginning of the climb and had died immediately. It is reputed that his sleeve had caught in the hand throttle at the first corner.

Yet such is the compulsion of motor sport that Louis Zborowski appeared at Brooklands after World War I with a fantastic car known as Chitty-Bang-Bang. Indeed legend has it that when he also was involved in a fatal crash with his Mercedes at Monza in 1924, he was wearing the same cuff-links that had caused his father's death.

Boillot's Peugeot (above) storms up Mont Ventoux to win the 1912 hill-climb. The event was already of ten years standing and is now the oldest surviving hill-climb in the world.
R. T. Hartmann's Benz (right) coming up Kop Hill during the Essex Motor Club's open hill-climb in 1914. This was the year in which Hornsted broke the official land speed record in a Benz at Brooklands at 124.10mph (199.72kph).

Continental Racing, the Tourist Trophy, and Brooklands

FOR THE HARD CORE of the racing fraternity, of course, interest was centred on such major events as the French Grand Prix, the Circuit des Ardennes, the Targa Florio, the Kaiserpreis, the Tourist Trophy in the Isle of Man, as well as the Vanderbilt Cup in the States; and from 1907 onwards the first specialized racing track to have been built – Brooklands.

Many of these races were spin-offs, to a large extent, of the Gordon Bennett series. The 1906 French Grand Prix, for instance, which involved six laps of an immense 64 mile (103km) circuit at Le Mans on two successive days, retained most of its regulations, including the weight limit of 1,007kg, while dispensing with the controversial restrictions on national entries – with a resultant line-up of twenty-five French cars against an opposition of only nine German and Italian machines. Yet while French honour was presumably satisfied by Szisz's win in a Renault (though with Nazzaro's Fiat in second place) it was generally agreed that the course was far too long and that its poor road surface had put a premium on tire changing. The Renault's detachable rims, in fact, had proved the deciding factor in its victory.

Tacitly, the 1907 Grand Prix at Dieppe recognized these shortcomings: it was run on a single day over ten laps of a 48 mile (77km) circuit, and a fuel consumption restriction replaced the limit on weight, which had tended to encourage the design of over-powerful machines with dangerously flimsy chassis. And indeed the entry was far more representative, since twenty-four French cars

The undulating straight of the Sarthe circuit (above) between Bouloire and Saint-Calais, site of the first French Grand Prix in 1906. The race was run over six laps of 64.12 miles (103.19km) on each of two days. Porporato (right) on a Berliet during the Salon Cup contest of 1905. In 1908 he came fourth in the Targa Florio and followed this up by winning the Targa Bologna.

Ferenc Szisz, winner of the first French Grand Prix in 1906, made a spectacular appearance on his ninety-fifth birthday. The motorsport fraternity was impressed but puzzled by his controversial statements–only to discover later that it had been hoaxed by Szisz's younger brother (above) who couldn't resist a belated share in Ferenc's glory.

Scene in the paddock (left) before the start of the 1907 Kaiserpreis in Germany. Car No 32A is Beutlers' Swiss Martini–he finished twelfth while Beck, also in a Martini, came fifteenth.

Plenty of manpower was available (bottom left) to pull out this ditched De Dion during the Irish Reliability Trials in May 1908. The De Dion Company more or less gave up racing after 1899, but their cars continued to be very popular in this kind of event.

Nazzaro (overpage) on the winning Fiat, thundering through the village of Petralia during the 1907 Targa Florio. Forty-four cars took part that year and the race was run over the Grande Circuito.

were matched by fourteen foreign entries wearing the colours of six countries – including a Dufaux Marchand from Switzerland and a Christie from the USA. But this time the previous result was reversed and Nazzaro's Fiat finished six minutes ahead of Szisz's Renault to 'wrest the blue riband of automobile sport from the grasp of France' (as a non-supporter of the French gleefully put it). To the further dismay of the ACF, the 1908 Grand Prix, again held on the Dieppe circuit, resulted in a sweeping German victory, Lautenschlager's Mercedes heading a procession of two Benzes, another Mercedes and an Opel, divided only by a lone Clément-Bayard in fourth place. So stinging, in fact, was this second blow to Gallic pride that they did not stage another Grand Prix until 1912.

The Vanderbilt Cup (about which more later) was also run on Gordon Bennett lines, and the Kaiserpreis, which attracted eighty-four entries in 1907 but was never repeated, used part of the same Taunus circuit as the 1904 Gordon Bennett. On the other hand, the Belgian Circuit des Ardennes, held from 1902 until 1907 over several laps of a closed road course, can reasonably claim to be the ancestor of circuit racing.

The Targa Florio, of course, was very much the creation of Count Vincenzo Florio (of a prominent Sicilian family renowned for its Marsala wines) who while still a youngster had already sponsored the Coppa Florio on a circuit near Brescia. Run every year since 1905 over variations of the rugged Madonie circuit in Sicily (except during the war years and in 1912–14 when it appeared as the Giro di Sicilia) the Targa Florio became the oldest-established race in the international calendar, and certainly one of the most glamorous.

Back in Britain, to be sure, the government's refusal to allow public highways to be closed for racing (to say nothing of the 20mph (32kph) speed limit which remained in force until 1925) meant that Englishmen had to cross the sea for their sport. Fortu-

nately, however, the Isle of Man was not only autonomous in such matters, but (with a weather eye open to the tourist trade) was actively prepared to promote competitive events on the island. In 1904 the Gordon Bennett eliminating trials were staged on a circuit running from Douglas along the coastal roads, and on 14 September 1905 the first Tourist Trophy for 'touring cars' was held over this 52 mile course. Almost all the current British machinery was represented, and technical talk in the Douglas bars revolved chiefly around such critical subjects as petrol consumption (the 25mpg limit first stipulated by the regulations was relaxed to 22.5mpg just before the race) and how to pare surplus weight down to the permitted 1,600lb. Official indulgence, what is more, went so far as to close the five level-crossings on the route against the trains (which were allowed thirty seconds to steam through, but only when no car was in sight!).

Tamagni (above), on a Junior, awaits the start of the 1908 Targa Florio. This race in the Sicilian mountains was won by Trucco on an Isotta-Fraschini.
Georges Boillot (above right), described as epitomising 'the spirit of France in motor racing', at the wheel of a Lion-Peugeot.

Christian Lautenschlager (right) won the French Grand Prix at Dieppe in 1908 on his Mercedes at nearly 70mph (113kph), despite eleven tire changes. This was his first major success, his next victory in the French GP being in the famous 1914 race.

Practice, by all accounts, was both fast and furious. A Swift, an Argyll and one of the White steamers all made inadvertent attempts to reshape the local architecture, which was mostly of granite; a Gladiator had a frightening encounter with a herd of cattle, and a Wolseley left the road for an agricultural session. At the start of the race itself Charles Rolls, failing to double-declutch, achieved the dubious distinction of being the first driver (and possibly the last) to strip the gearbox of a Rolls-Royce. Six hours and nine minutes later, John Napier brought his 18hp twin-cylinder, Scottish-built Arrol-Johnston (which he himself had designed) home into first place at an average speed of 33.9mph (54.5kph) and just ahead of the other Rolls-Royce driven by Percy Northey.

The following year, on a shorter 40 mile course, the positions were reversed. Northey allowed error to creep in by smacking the parapet of a bridge, and Charles Rolls took the flag nearly half an hour in front of Bablot in a Berliet, and a full hour and a quarter ahead of Napier's Arrol-Johnston in seventh position.

All great races have their own special character and flavour, and those who have competed in the TT will surely agree with Richard Hough's description of its Quixotic personality and 'that indefinable charm and air of inconsequence, bred perhaps from its mainly Irish locale . . .' Certainly, for those first five rumbustious years in the Isle of Man, before the opening of Brooklands, the Tourist Trophy was the centre of British racing development.

A product of the spacious Edwardian age, Brooklands – the first permanent racing circuit in the world – was built by a rich enthusiast called Hugh Locke-King on his estate at Weybridge in Surrey. An army of 2,000 men cleared 30 acres of woodland, diverted the river Wey, and used 200,000 tons of cement to construct the 2.75 mile, pear-shaped circuit, 100ft wide with two main straights leading to steeply banked curves. The whole project, including grandstands, tunnels under the track and a splendid clubhouse, took only nine months to complete, and even before it was officially opened Selwyn Edge had booked the track for an attempt on the American-held world twenty-four hour record. Single-handed at the wheel of his green 60hp Napier, though paced by two similar models, he drove through the night by the illumination of hundreds of lanterns to cover 1,581 miles at an average of 65.9mph (106.05kph) – nearly 500 miles further, in fact, than the previous record.

From the first meeting to be held there on 6 July 1907, the ambiance of Brooklands was curiously redolent of the Turf: brief horse-racing style sprints were held, and drivers were identified by coloured jockey-type smocks. But at least this tradition of running a number of races of short duration, usually handicapped on an individual basis, gave many 'bank-holiday' enthusiasts the chance to prove themselves; and women's races, as well as events for the services and journalists, all helped to cast the net of motor sport wider. Moreover, on non-race days, the track was open to all and sundry for a small fee (with the result that landaulettes were driven high up on the banking at little more than a snail's pace, dropping in the process their lamps, acetylene generators, tool kits, and anything else that could be shaken off).

Small wonder, therefore, that Brooklands captured the imagination of a whole generation of motorists. In those patrician days, admittedly, the great sporting figures were mostly rich men or their chauffeurs – few other people had the opportunity to sit behind the wheel of a racing car – but the Gents versus Players aspect was unobtrusive, possibly because dicing around the circuit was an adventure where life and limb hung somewhat delicately in the balance. Certainly by all accounts the atmosphere of Brooklands during the first decade of its existence had an almost undergraduate sort of light-heartedness, whether in Mrs Billing's Bluebird café housed in one of the aeroplane

The opening ceremony at Brooklands (above) 17 June 1907, with Dame Ethel Locke-King leading the cavalcade of cars. Dame Ethel maintained a keen interest in the track after her husband's death in 1926 and lived to the ripe old age of ninety, dying in 1956. H. F. Locke-King (left), founder and owner of the famous Brooklands track in Surrey. The course, which soon became the centre of motor sport in Great Britain, was initially built as a testing ground for manufacturers.

sheds, where practical jokes were traded with such early aviators as Jack Alcock, A. V. Roe and the Pashley brothers, or in the posher precincts of the clubhouse bar where the importance of *supercarburante* was appreciated as much as in the Paddock. If Brooklands became a legend in its time, it was largely because of the varied nature of its activities, which included serious research by manufacturers as well as record-breaking runs, and international trophy races as well as club events; and undoubtedly by giving so much enjoyment to thousands of people from 1907 until 1939, this great circuit did as much as anything else for the cause of motor sport in Great Britain.

Over to America

A PHOTOGRAPH taken before the start of the Paris–Madrid race shows William K. Vanderbilt, impeccably turned out in wing collar and bowler hat, at the wheel of his 70hp Mors. For all his family's traditional leanings towards the Turf, 'Willie K.' had set his youthful sights on the new sport of motoring, forming first the National Automobile Racing Association and then organizing a hill-climb at Newport (which he won himself in a Cannstatt Daimler along with the slightly unconvincing title of 'champion of America') before getting down to the speed game in earnest for a couple of seasons in Europe. In 1902 he concentrated on record attempts, covering the flying kilometre at 76.08mph (122.44kph) in a Mors – the fastest yet for a petrol-engined car. In the Circuit des Ardennes he finished third, behind Jarrott's Panhard and Gabriel's Mors, and although he fell by the wayside in the Paris–Madrid it was with a good deal of competitive muscle as a driver (unlike Gordon Bennett, who never drove a car himself and favoured a four-in-hand carriage for his personal transport) that he launched the Vanderbilt Cup in America in 1904.

Run over a triangular course on Long Island, under regulations not dissimilar to the Gordon Bennett races, the first Vanderbilt Cup attracted huge crowds who swarmed ecstatically on to the track as the local favourite George Heath took the flag in his Panhard just 2.5sec ahead of Albert Clément's Clément-Bayard, with Lyttle's Pope-Toledo in third place two laps behind. The following year a number of Europe's top drivers crossed the Atlantic – no doubt some of them with beady eyes already focused on the export potential of the American market – for the 1905 event, which was won by Hémery's Darracq; and in 1906 another Darracq, this time in the hands of Louis Wagner, kept the lead throughout while Vincenzo Lancia in a 140hp Fiat and Arthur Duray in a de Dietrich diced neck to neck for second place. (Lancia finally crossed the line just 16sec ahead of his rival – close

A desperate moment in the 1906 Vanderbilt Cup race at Long Island, New York, when the Belgian driver, Arthur Duray, nearly lost both mechanic and spare rim from his 18.1 litre 130hp de Dietrich. He finished third behind Wagner's Darracq and Lancia's F.I.A.T. All three averaged over 60mph (96kph) for the 297 mile (477.97km) race.

going for those days.)

Yet, thrilling though these races undoubtedly were, the problems of crowd and track control grew worse each year, and casualties escalated to such a degree that Vanderbilt was forced to give up the public roads and build a closed circuit – the Long Island Motor Parkway. Here the 1908 Cup went to George Robertson's 1906 Locomobile ('Old 16') at the head of a virtually all-American field.

For undoubtedly the magic had now switched to Savannah, where the first Grand Prize of the Automobile Club of America was being held over sixteen laps of a twisty, 25 mile circuit, and the best European drivers and machinery dominated a race which turned out to be one of the most exciting of all the early classics, with Wagner's Fiat taking the flag 56.4sec ahead of Hémery's Benz, and another Fiat, driven by Nazzaro, in third place. (For the record, it also saw the appearance of an 11.2 litre Chadwick tourer, the first car to race with a supercharger, though without any noticeable success. Superchargers only came back into fashion in the twenties.)

The next Grand Prize was held in 1910 over a new course at Savannah, built largely, it appears, by convict labour. It was won by David Bruce-Brown in a factory-entered Benz, just a whisker ahead of his team-mate Hémery in a similar 120hp model. Bruce-Brown was still up at Yale at the time and legend has it that his mother arrived at Savannah in a special train to prevent him from starting – only to lead a cheer squad when she realized that he was in the lead. In 1911 this brilliant young driver won again in a Fiat, but unhappily was killed when his car overturned during practice for the 1912 event.

For all this, the interest of the American public was so increasingly orientated towards track racing that a group of Indianapolis businessmen, headed by Carl G. Fisher, decided to build a permanent speedway just outside their city – at that time the pioneering centre of the American automobile industry. Even so, they can hardly have foreseen that this rectangular, 2.5 mile track with its two 1,000yd straights and four identically banked turns would become not only a national institution but the oldest racecourse in the world to have been operated continuously since its construction.

Yet oddly enough, when the Indianapolis bowl opened on 19 August 1909 with a programme of short races, it was very nearly a flop. The gravel surface of the track soon began to disintegrate; accidents multiplied, and there was talk of giving up racing there altogether. But at this point the promoters took some basic decisions. First, they re-

A scene during America's famous Indianapolis 500 Miles Race (above), taken in 1914. Fifteen of the forty-five entrants were European, and the winner was René Thomas in a Delage.

Goux changing a wheel (right) on his Peugeot during the 500 Miles Race at Indianapolis in 1913. He won at 75.92mph (122.18kph) from a Mercer and a Stutz. Peugeot's other chief driver was Boillot and the two complemented each other, Goux being the better over longer distances.

Overpage: a wheel comes off Pullen's Mercer at 'Death Curve' during the 1914 Vanderbilt Cup race at Santa Monica. Pullen won the Grand Prize in a Mercer at Santa Monica the same year, the first time an American car was successful in this event.

Johnny Marquis's Sunbeam (above) overturning at 'Death Curve' during the International Grand Prize at Santa Monica in March 1914. The accident occurred during the thirty-fifth lap and both driver and passenger were injured.

The 1914 Vanderbilt Cup (above right) at Santa Monica. The first starter, Grant, on an Isotta-Fraschini, gets away.

surfaced the entire course with some 3,200,000 paving bricks. Next, having come to the conclusion that frequent racing would spoil the market, they announced that only one race would be held each year – on Memorial day, 30 May. And, after careful consideration, they opted for a 500 mile (805km) event which could be run during the hours of daylight. From this moment on, the 'Brickyard' never looked back.

A crowd of 80,000 spectators watched the fastest machines from America and Europe contest the first '500' in 1911. Midway through it the Americans took the lead and a duel developed between Ray Harroun's Marmon Wasp and Ralph Mulford's Lozier. Harroun eventually won by 1min 43sec at an average speed of 74.59mph (120.04kph), somewhat less, in fact, than half the qualifying pace of today. But the formula was right and the razzmatazz even better, and the following year, in what was grandly billed as 'the World's Greatest Spectacle', Joe Dawson roared home in his National to collect 50,000 dollars of prize money after the connecting rod of De Palma's Mercedes had broken within sight of victory just a lap and a half from the end. The year 1913 saw the Europeans over in force and Jules Goux attributing his victory in the Henry-designed Peugeot to the stimulating effect of a bottle of champagne at each pit stop. Indeed even as World War I put an end to racing in the Old World, its cars continued to triumph in the New World of Indianapolis – where Delage, Peugeot and Mercedes dominated the 'brickyard' until Gaston Chevrolet's impressive victory in a 3 litre Monroe-Frontenac special in 1920.

More Science and less Size

SO LONG AS motor sport was in its infancy constructors had designed their cars according to the simple rule of thumb that the larger the engine, the faster the car. Yet right from the beginning Léon Bollée's little three-wheelers had pointed in the opposite direction, and the Renault brothers, amongst others, had shown that a small well-balanced machine often had the legs against brute force and muscle. The first appearance of a separate category for light cars (up to 400kg weight) was in 1898, and thereafter what was known as the *voiturette* class became part of the motor racing scene. In 1902, Renault won the Paris–Vienna outright with a 3.7 litre light car – a David in comparison with the Goliaths of 18 litre capacity, even if it would hardly be considered a tiddler today – and the following year was only just behind the leader in the Paris–Madrid when his fatal accident occurred.

A school of thought that favoured science rather than size was definitely emerging, and from 1905 onwards the influential French magazine *L'Auto* (now *L'Equipe*) accelerated this trend by sponsoring a special Coupe des Voiturettes to encourage the sporting light car. This event placed a limitation on both weight and engine size; though, oddly

The voiturette limitation on weight and engine size encouraged some eccentric machinery, such as the twin cylinder Lion-Peugeot (right), seen here doing 75mph (120.7kph) during record attempts at Brooklands with Georges Boillot at the wheel. The mechanic is hardly registering enjoyment! The Lion-Peugeot's curious shape did not prevent Jules Goux from winning the Coupe des Voiturettes in 1910 (below). In 1912 the Lion-Peugeots came to an end and the brilliant designs by Henry began to appear.

3

H. T. S. Morgan (above) during record attempts at Brooklands in 1912 with one of his three-wheelers. He did almost 60 miles (96kph) in the hour. His father, the Rev Prebendary A. G. Morgan, turned up to watch in a top hat.
By 1912 the Lion-Peugeot had become much more conventional in design and appearance. Here is René Thomas (left) with the last of the breed in the Grand Prix de France race for voiturettes up to 3 litres, held at Le Mans.

enough, in 1909 the restriction applied only to the bore and not the stroke of the pistons, with the result that certain mavericks appeared like the single-cylinder Lion-Peugeot which had a stroke of 250mm and, in consequence, such a ludicrously high hood (bonnet) that the driver could not see over it but had to peer round the side. All the same, such freakishness had its advantages since piston speeds were incredibly high for that time, and the Lion-Peugeot won the Grand Prix des Voiturettes, the Sicilian Cup and the Catalan Cup that year. Some forty other manufacturers also concentrated on the light car events and indeed the first successes recorded by marques such as Delage and Hispano-Suiza, that later achieved fame for their luxury machines, were in the voiturette races between 1906 and 1910.

About this time there was also a sudden craze, especially in England and France, for even lighter machines known as cyclecars. By offering really cheap motoring, these forerunners of Formula 3 with their motorcycle engines (Archie Frazer Nash and H. R. Godfrey marketed their GNs at under £100 ($240) and, like Charles Cooper thirty-six years later, fitted them with double-knocker JAP power units) soon attracted such a healthy following that in 1913 the ACF held two races for cyclecars, at Amiens and at Le Mans, in which motorcycle combinations and three-wheelers also competed. The Amiens event was won by W. G. McMinnies in a Morgan, with Frank Thomas as his mechanic, which considerably contributed to the fortunes of the little Malvern firm (even if Thomas habitually raced a GN with an oversize engine known as the 'Hippopo-Thomas'). Although some of these backyard devices gave the impression of having been put together with a knife and fork and were inclined to come apart with a loud snapping noise, the cyclecar fraternity obviously got a tremendous bang out of their racing. In fact Sir Francis Samuelson and his bride dedicated their honeymoon to driving a Marlborough at Amiens.

At the other end of the scale, to be sure, not only were race regulations changed in 1911 to exclude any unduly bizarre machinery, but after a decade of obeisance to thundering great pistons that took their time going up and down, a new and brilliant generation of designers were busy blueprinting ideas that would determine the shape of cars for decades to come. Ettore Bugatti, for instance, was producing a small 1,400cc of great flair and originality behind its horseshoe radiator; Ferdinand Porsche had just completed the famous 5.7 litre Prince Henry Austro-Daimler with its 86bhp 4 cylinder engine; Laurence Pomeroy at Vauxhalls and Marc Birkigt at Hispano-Suiza were both creating outstanding machines; while at Des Moines, USA two brothers were building 4 cylinder 5,752cc racing cars that were first known as Masons and, only after 1914, by their own name of Duesenberg. But of these young engineers perhaps the one who had most influence on the progress of scaling down and laid the foundations of modern Grand Prix design was Ernest Henry. In 1911, Robert Peugeot, whose independent Lion-Peugeot concern had just been united with the more orthodox Peugeot establishment in Audincourt, called in the twenty-seven-year old Henry, and gave him a drawing-board and a clean sheet of paper. The result was one of the most epochal racing cars ever produced. Georges Boillot drove the handsome new Peugeot, with its fast revving 7.6 litre ohv engine, to victory in the revived French Grand Prix at Dieppe in 1912 against the immense and archaic Fiats, and the following year won at Indianapolis, lapping the Brickyard at 93.5mph (150.47kph).

Largely distilled from the ideas and experience of Georges Boillot, Jules Goux and Paul Zuccarelli, the secret of Henry's design was high revolutions achieved by the use of two shaft-driven overhead camshafts and four inclined valves for each of the four cylinders. And since the chassis, too, was lighter and had far better road-holding qualities than the Edwardian monsters, the new Peugeot became, almost overnight, the hottest name in racing.

In 1913 Boillot took the honours again at Dieppe with his team mate, Goux, in second place. (Admittedly the race turned in their favour when Guyot, in the Delage, who was leading at half distance, had the misfortune to run over his own mechanic in the pits area.) All the same, since the French Grand Prix was the premier event on the calendar, the man who won it was indisputably world

In 1913 Goux brought one of the Henry-designed 7.6 litre Grand Prix Peugots (above), fitted with a special streamlined body, to Brooklands and took the world's one-hour record at 106.22mph (170.94kph). Lautenschlager (above right) roaring away from the Piège de la Mort hairpin in the 1914 French Grand Prix at Lyons. This tremendous victory was the climax of his career.
A rare bird from Belgium (right): Baron de Woelmont at the wheel of a 3 litre SAVA at the 1913 Belgian Grand Prix, a combined speed and regularity event held at Spa.

28

champion.

To Boillot and his Peugeot, therefore, fell the task of upholding the reputation of France the following July in a climate of intense national rivalry against the concentrated challenge of Fiat and Mercedes. For the Grand Prix of 1914, which pundits consider to have been the climax of a whole epoch of racing and the forerunner of a new era, the ACF had chosen a circuit of 23.38 miles (37.72km) in the hilly country behind Lyons, with its tortuous stretches along the river Gier and a fast undulating six mile straight culminating in a wild downhill plunge through two right angled corners to the notorious 'Piège de la Mort' hairpin. Run over twenty laps, it was calculated to test road-holding, brakes and engines to the full. Thirty-seven cars from six nations (France, Germany, Italy, Britain, Belgium and Switzerland) made up a scintillating field and the *Motor* thought that 'the preparations bore a striking similarity to the preliminaries of a battle'. Mercedes in particular had turned out in such strength that there seems some truth in the story of the board meeting at which the directors had solemnly agreed that 'for reasons of propaganda, Mercedes have decided to win the French Grand Prix this year'. In contrast, the Italian arrangements were somewhat haphazard, the British Vauxhalls were late for scrutineering, and the French were so over-confident that their star drivers, Boillot included, only got back from Indianapolis on the eve of the race.

They found Lyons in a state of pandemonium throughout the night before the race as a crowd of 300,000 spectators flocked out to the circuit. At eight o'clock in the morning the cars were started in pairs at thirty-second intervals. Boillot's Peugeot was the first round, having completed the lap in 21min, but, to the consternation of the crowds who were there to witness a French victory, Sailer's Mercedes passed the grandstands only 72sec later, which meant that on elapsed time he was leading by 18sec, and at five laps the German was out in front with a lead of 2min 45sec. On the sixth lap his run ended with a broken connecting rod, and Boillot's blue Peugeot led again; but both Lautenschlager and Wagner were harrying him from close behind and Salzer in the third Mercedes overhauled Goux in the second Peugeot. Boillot drove as he had never driven before, flogging his car mercilessly, and although bedevilled by tire trouble still managed to stay in front with a slender 14sec lead after six hours' racing. But, as they went into the last lap the German had a slight time advantage, and Boillot only three cylinders. Then, moments from the finish, his car expired and Lautenschlager roared down from the 'Piège de la Mort' to head Mercedes' 1-2-3 victory, the first in Grand Prix history.

In stunned silence the vast French audience heard the strains of *Deutschland über alles* ring out over the countryside before giving Mercedes professionalism a well-deserved applause. It had been the triumph of hard-headed management and team tactics over inspired individual effort. And as such it provided a magnificent and moving finish to the 'Belle Epoque' of motoring, for three weeks later, Europe was at war.

Dusty work (above): Witchell's 3.3 litre 4 cylinder Stracker-Squire in the 1914 Tourist Trophy on the Isle of Man. The race was run over 2 days with 8 laps totalling 300 miles (483km) on each day, and was won by Guinness in a Sunbeam, Witchell coming fourth.

The formidable Mercedes team (right) that scored a 1-2-3 victory in the French Grand Prix of 1914 with inset (left to right): Lautenschlager (the winner), Wagner, and Salzer.

The Sport Revives

In the 1921 French Grand Prix, Segrave (above left), in his Talbot-Darracq, came ninth after a race in which he had been dogged by troubles, among them no fewer than fourteen punctures.

BARELY HAD THE ARMISTICE been signed in November 1918 than manufacturers burst into print with advertisements heralding (as Morgan's, for one, put it) an 'early return to something like the Good Old Times', and hopefuls in Paris began lobbying for a resumption of the Grand Prix in Alsace Lorraine to celebrate its return to France.

But the dust and debris of war were not to be swept under the carpet as easily as all that, an official ban on motor racing in Europe was maintained for another two seasons. The only major races in 1919 and 1920, in fact, were the Indianapolis '500' and the Targa Florio.

So long as the United States had not been directly involved in the European conflict, racing had continued at Indianapolis, as well as on a number of board track speedways that had sprung up at various points of America, and over in the New World the classic rivalry between the Teutonic and Gallic marques had gone on, some 4,000 miles from Flanders, in a contest between Ralph de Palma's Mercedes (shipped over only days before hostilities began) and Dario Resta's Peugeot. The German car won at Indianapolis in 1915, and the Peugeot took the flag in the reduced 300 mile (483km) race in 1916 ahead of the field, after which the track suspended operations and became a military landing field.

Yet, however bleak the immediate post-war scene might appear on both sides of the Atlantic, enthusiasts were not to be discouraged. Early in 1919 Ralph de Palma set about breaking records at Daytona with a V12 Packard, and Ernest Ballot, already a specialist engine constructor (mostly marine, but also Delages, etc.), decided, only days after the Armistice (on Christmas Eve, as it happened), to build a team of 'materially superior' racing cars to compete in the first post-war '500' at Indianapolis.

Designed by Ernest Henry and completed in 101 days (to catch the boat to America they had to leave Paris not later than 26 April), it is hardly to be wondered that the four

Ralph de Palma (above) with the very fast V-12 Packard, a car successful both in races and record breaking in America from 1917-20. De Palma, born in Italy, came to America with his parents when he was ten, and became one of her most famous racing drivers.

Ballots that appeared at the Brickyard bore a strong resemblance to the pre-war Peugeots, although, probably because of Henry's experience building aircraft engines during the war *chez* Bugatti, their layout featured straight-eight engines, henceforth to become the fashion for racers (whereas the majority of cars at Indianapolis in 1919–20 were powered by four cylinders, in 1921 over half the entrants had eight cylinders).

As it turned out, these 101 day miracles, although fastest round the oval, ran into axle ratio troubles, and once again a pre-war Peugeot, in the hands of Howard Wilcox, took the honours ahead of Eddie Hearne's Stutz disguised as a Durant Special, another Peugeot driven by Goux and, somewhat further down the field, the Chevrolet brothers, Louis and Gaston (the latter of whom was to win the 1920 event in his Monroe-Frontenac, ahead of a Ballot and two Duesenbergs).

Meanwhile in Sicily, undeterred by the ban of the official body, the AIACR, Count Vincenzo Florio was busily planning the resumption of the Targa Florio, which eventually was run on 23 November in a snowstorm. Enzo Ferrari, driving his maiden race in a CMN, was first off; followed by Ascari, who soon overcooked things and ended up with his Fiat thirty metres down a ravine. But the hero of the day was André Boillot (the brother of the famous Georges) in a Peugeot. After at least six dramatic departures from the road, he ended up by crashing into the grandstand ten yards from the end, spun violently, and crossed the finishing line backwards. Since this would have

Count Masetti (top) winning the Targa Florio in a 4.5 litre Mercedes in 1922.
Bordino (above) in the 2 litre during the French Grand Prix at Strasbourg, 1922. He had to retire but his team mate Felice Nazzaro won the race for Italy.
Alessandro Cagno (right), on his 1.5 litre supercharged Fiat, was the winner of the Gran Premio Vetturette at Brescia in Italy in 1923.

8
3
5
4

meant disqualification, the car was manhandled round, and as the chequered flag fell, Boillot collapsed over the wheel of his car with the cry: 'C'est pour la France.' Obviously romance was not yet lost to racing.

Far from it, once the brakes were taken off in Europe the sport burgeoned through the vintage years of the twenties as never before. Alongside the French Grand Prix – up to this point regarded as *the* Grand Prix – came first the Italian GP, and subsequently, a whole series of national premier events of almost equal standing. Brooklands got back into its stride and was imitated, in one way or another, by other continental capitals. The famous Monza autodrome in the wooded grounds of a royal park outside Milan became the home of Italian racing, while its counterpart at the Château de Montlhéry, just south of Paris, soon developed into the supreme realm of speed. Ravages of war, notwithstanding, the Automobil-Verkehrs-und-Übungs-Strasse, planned at Grünewald on the outskirts of Berlin as early as 1909, was completed in 1920. (Fritz von Opel won the opening meeting of the AVUS in 1921 with a car of his own make.) And alongside the upper echelons of formula racing came such classic road events as Les 24 Heures du Mans and the Mille Miglia, the Coupes des Alpes and the Monte Carlo Rally.

The first post-war French Grand Prix, what is more, run at Le Mans in July 1921 under the 3 litre formula, proved to be an eye-opener. When Fiats withdrew because of industrial unrest in Italy, and the English part of the Sunbeam-Talbot-Darracq contingent was held up by the coal strike (nothing is new, to be sure, under the sun) it looked like being a French benefit. But then at the last minute, thanks to the intervention of Albert Champion, whose name has since become famous for sparking plugs, Fred Duesenberg brought over the first all-American team to challenge the Europeans on their own ground.

Held on the 10.72 mile (17.26km) Circuit Permanent de la Sarthe, which incorporated two of the main roads running into the southern part of the city, the race was run, in fact, over thirty laps of narrow, unpaved country roads from which the stones exploded like shrapnel. If in terms of sheer power output there was little to choose between the Ballots, Talbot-Darracqs and Duesenbergs, the beautifully turned out blue and white cars from the States had hydraulically operated four-wheel brakes, which gave the Americans an edge over their rivals. Jimmy Murphy, the Irish-American driver who was to achieve further immortality by winning at Indianapolis the following year, before being killed on a small upstate New York dirt track in 1924, crashed during practice and broke three ribs. But, heavily bandaged though he was, Murphy took the lead in what one of the competitors described as 'a damned rock-hewing contest' between Duesenberg and Ballot, braking late and cutting through the inside of the Pontlieue and Mulsanne corners; and although Chassagne's blue Ballot got ahead on the eleventh lap and held the Duesenbergs off for another six laps until a stone pierced its petrol tank, it was Murphy who brought the blue and white Duesenberg across the finishing line with two flat tires and water boiling out of a holed radiator. He had to be lifted out of his seat, but, for the first and only time an all-American car, driven by an American, had captured the highest European prize – and this at a time when European cars had been virtually unchallenged at home, and even in the States, for two decades. Forty-one years, indeed, were to pass before another American, Dan Gurney, was to win the French Grand Prix again (at Rouen, in a Porsche).

In 1922, the first year of the new 2 litre formula that brought a brief, but brilliant, phase to GP racing, the veteran, Nazzaro – who had triumphed at Dieppe in his Fiat way back in 1907 – achieved Fiat's last victory in the French classic. But next year it was the British turn to cheer. 'Tours 1923' has a special place in British racing lore, for, after an epic struggle against the Fiats,

H. O. D. Segrave in action (above), winning the 1923 French Grand Prix on his No 12 Sunbeam. Marinoni's supercharged 1500 Alfa Romeo (right) has its tires changed in the pits during the 1928 Targo Florio.

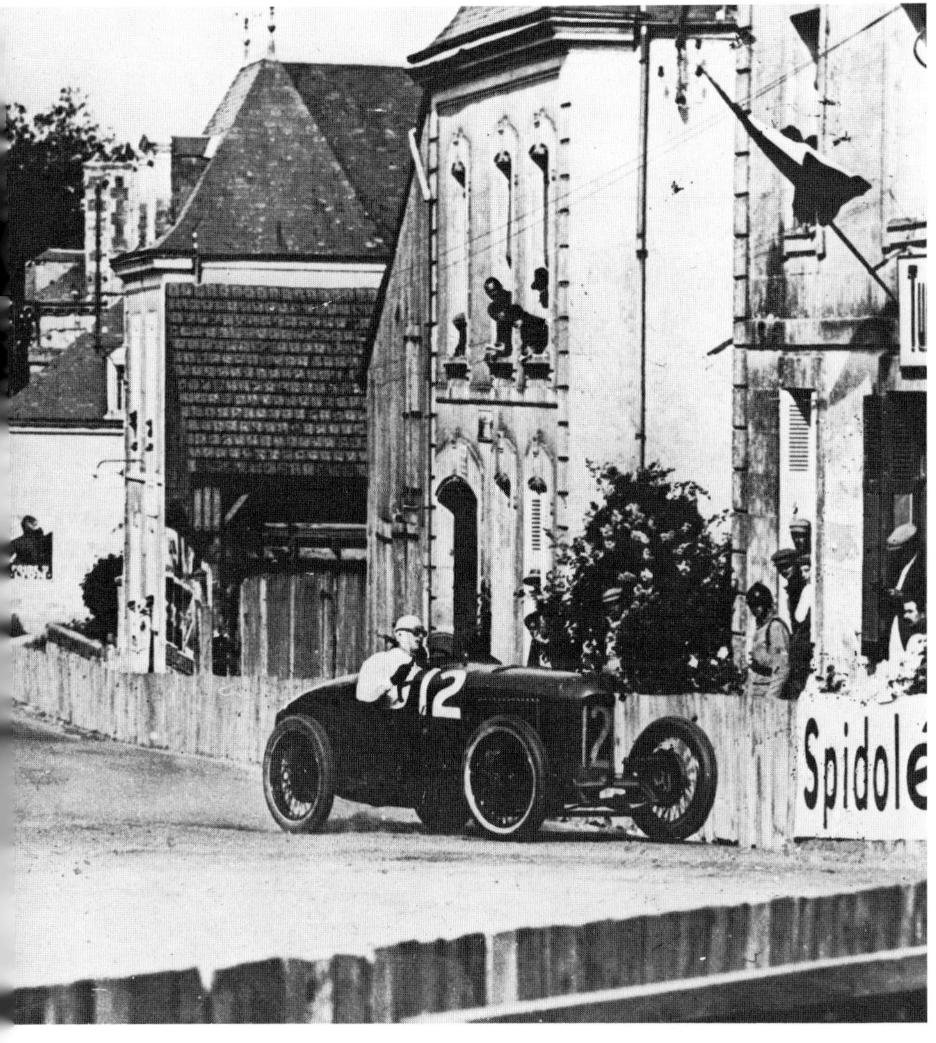

Henry Segrave brought his Sunbeam slipping clutch and all home, to victory.

The Fiats, with their 15bhp advantage, had started as favourites and had slashed to the lead, but as grit and road metal were sucked into their unshielded Wittig superchargers, one after another fell by the wayside to give Sunbeam the chance of a 1-2-3 victory.

Segrave recalls his excitement as he came across Salamano's red car by the side of the road only minutes from the finish.

> Letting everything go and making a funnel of his hands close to my ear, Dutoit (my mechanic) shouted: 'C'est le 14 qui est en panne. Nous sommes en tête!' . . . I could scarcely believe my ears – for the first time in history an English car was leading in the Grand Prix with only one lap to go . . . How can I ever forget those last few miles – every noise in the engine seemed magnified a hundredfold, every corner seemed impossible, my brain refused to work in complete co-ordination with my hands and feet. But luck was with us . . .

Even if the perfect team finish was lost when Kenelm Lee Guinness stalled at Membrone on the last lap and let Friderich's Bugatti slip into third place by a slender margin, it didn't seem to matter. The green cars from Wolverhampton had come in first, second, and fourth. Designed by Vincenzo Bertarione, who had been brought over from Turin, the Sunbeams may have been 'Fiats in green paint'. But they were green all the same, and their victory was no less impressive.

Brooklands between the Wars

YET MOTORING, undeniably, was still the sport of the few. Mass production was in its infancy, and practically all cars (T-model Fords apart) were handcrafted jobs. Indeed, since the framework of the grandest landaulet and the humblest saloon alike had to be constructed of wood by skilled coachbuilders, most cars on the road were open tourers, with a top folded back behind the rear seats ready to be put up if the weather turned nasty. Such things as windshield wipers were hardly yet a gleam in the designer's eye, so that when it rained it was necessary to open the top half of the windshield to see where one was going. Needless to say, there was a great deal of wrapping up in rugs, and ladies kept their hats and hair in place with a veil tucked under the chin, even if some of the smarter touring models had an additional windshield to protect the passengers in the back. Few cars outside the United States boasted an electric starter, which meant cranking the engine with a handle (a doubtful pleasure at the best of times), and the great majority had brakes operating on the rear wheels only. Water cooling systems were so atrocious, what is more, that radiators boiled on anything but the gentlest of hills.

But they looked the part. Perpendicular rather than horizontal, with more than a lingering trace of their horse-drawn ancestry, the products of the early twenties were, on the whole, better designed than their predecessors (thanks to wartime experience of light alloys and high tensile metals) and better finished than those that followed them. And, for all their idiosyncrasies, they offered the sheer pleasure of driving with the sun on the face and the wind in the hair, along with a special glow of satisfaction as you neatly double-declutched your gears.

In those salad days of motoring, to be sure, the road was blessedly one's own. There were no halt signs, traffic lights, one-way streets or parking problems; the modern nightmare of traffic snarls and noise was almost unknown; you could picnic anywhere in the country in peace. The whole business of motoring was a sport in itself.

Nowhere, as it happens, was it more delectable than at Brooklands – now alas as remote as chariot-racing, with the clubhouse turned into Vickers-Armstrong offices, the Byfleet banking partially demolished to allow planes to land, and trees growing through the concrete under the old Members' Bridge. For Brooklands between the wars was a hive of motoring activity where exciting things were happening, not just on race days but at almost any moment of the week.

Count Louis Zborowski (above left), at the wheel of his famous 23 litre Maybach aero-engined special, Chitty Chitty Bang Bang 1. Its fastest lap at Brooklands was 113.45mph (182.58kph). The start of the first 200 Miles Race at Brooklands in 1921 (above). Discernable

are: Archie Frazer Nash's GN (No 2); A. V. Phillip's Deemster (No 4); Topping on a Baby Peugeot (No 5); Dixon on a Coventry Premier (No 8), and Wood's Temperino (No 10).

Tucked away in the green of Surrey, yet conveniently close to Mayfair, it was, on the one hand, a smart country club where you could watch the latest models go through their paces while sunbathing under the rhododendron bushes on Members' Hill (or playing tennis, if you wished) and trade jokes with the drivers in the bar before dining and dancing. But, above all, it was the place where Grand Prix cars mixed, on a handicap basis, with fast Tourist Trophy type tourers and standard models tuned by enthusiasts who raced for the hell of it and didn't care much whether they won or lost.

During World War I, Brooklands had been taken over by the Royal Flying Corps, whose heavy trucks with solid tires had played havoc with the track. It was never properly repaired, so that drivers had to put up not only with teeth-shattering bumps, but also the physical strain of being airborne off their seats on the steeply banked bridge over the river Wey.

Nevertheless, racing started again in 1920 with Malcolm Campbell winning the first event in his Talbot. A young Etonian called Henry de Hane Segrave soon made his mark with an Opel; Archie Frazer Nash drove a GN called 'Kim', and Kenelm Lee Guinness set up a land speed record in the 350 V12 Sunbeam which can now be seen at the Montagu Museum.

Giants and eccentrics abounded. Count Zborowski, who had a penchant for aero-engined cars, built four 'specials' on pre-war Mercedes chain-driven chassis, fitting them with Maybach, Benz, Mercedes and Liberty engines. The best known of these, with its 23 litre Maybach airship engine (as used in the Zeppelins), had a lazy exhaust that rumbled softly: 'chitty-chitty-bang-bang-chitty-chitty-bang-bang' and was henceforth known as Chitty I. Louis Zborowski used to drive up in it from his estate near Canterbury with a crew dressed in oversize check caps and black shirts. Unluckily, though, as he was 'taking the cement' (in Brooklands parlance) towards the end of the 1922 season, a tire blew on Members' Banking. Hitting the parapet, the huge machine spun off in circles and went backwards through a timing box beside the track, removing several of the timekeeper's fingers as he dived for safety. (The same unfortunate official was killed later by a motorcycle that dived over the banking.)

Zborowski never drove Chitty I again at Brooklands, though he continued to race Chitty II, the White Mercedes, and the

Racing at Brooklands (above left) was nothing if not varied. Fifty light cars, for instance, took part in a high speed reliability trial in 1925 over a distance of 100 miles, using private link-roads, the test hill, and a section of the track.
Here, the passenger of Vernon Ball's Amilcar does some counter-balancing to avoid the fate of car No 8, in the 100 Miles High Speed Race at Brooklands.
You can almost smell the Castrol R! The start of the 1500cc class in the 1929 500 Miles Race at Brooklands (above) with (left to right) an OM, three Bugattis and Archie Frazer Nash's 'the Slug'.
Duel of the Titans (right): J. Dunfee's Speed Six Bentley lined up against John Noel's big, white, aero-engined Mercedes for the start of the BRDC's first 500 Miles Race in 1929.

Higham special (which, after his death at Monza in 1924, was taken over by Parry Thomas and re-christened 'Babs'). But the ebullient count had started a fashion for aeroplane-engined machines. For while new cars were expensive and hard to come by in the immediate post-war period, surplus aero engines were cheap and the pre-war long-wheelbase chassis, into which they could often be coaxed, were readily available.

One hopeful enthusiast built his dream-racer around a 20 litre Clerget aero engine and promptly killed himself. Someone else put a Sunbeam 'Arab' engine into a small TT Humber. Ernest Eldridge acquired Nazzaro's venerable 1908 Fiat 'Mephistopheles' from John Duff (who had blown it up, smothering himself and his mechanic with hot metal and oil), lengthened the chassis by a foot, and installed a 300hp 6 cylinder Fiat aero engine to produce a shatteringly fast machine that broke the land speed record in 1924. And 'Viper I', built at the Wolseley works by Alistair Miller with a Hispano-Suiza V8 aero engine, nearly came to grief in the hands of Kaye Don as he managed to 'phenomenally avoid' a trip over the top of the banking.

Among other legendary figures were Parry Thomas, the brilliant Welsh engineer from the Leyland Motor Company, who developed his 7 litre straight-eight Leyland into one of the fastest cars on the circuit and won race after race. Few episodes at Brooklands, indeed, were recalled more gleefully than his spectacular duel with Eldridge's Mephistopheles for a bet of £500 (which represented more like £5,000 in our devaluated currency): both cars shed treads with cracks like twin pistol shots as they diced neck and neck towards the finish, and Thomas just managed to pass Eldridge – who had led all the way lapping at over 125mph (201.17kph) – as the Fiat slid sideways at the Fork.

Then there was Sir Henry Birkin who, like W. O. Bentley before him, raced a DFP and subsequently a touring Rolls-Royce, until he got involved with the 'Blower' Bentleys; and Tommy Hann with his curious tandem-seated Lanchester special named 'Hoieh-Wayareh-Gointoo' that he eventually discarded for a yellow and black two-seater called 'Softly-catch-Monkey'. Though for psychedelic colouring no one could better Kensington Moir's zig-zag black and white striped Straker-Squire.

And alongside the aero-engined bangers (that were in some ways the precursors of today's dragsters) and the sophisticated machinery of the 'Bentley Boys' was ranged the 'back-yard' ingenuity of the early GNs and Morgans and the sporting flair of 'half size' racers such as Calthorpes, Hillmans, side-valve Aston Martins, chain-drive Frazer Nashes, and the almost dainty French Amilcars and Salmsons. If Louis Coatalen's brilliant little 4 cylinder twin ohc 1½ litre Talbot Darracqs, with their differential-less back axles, so dominated the voiturette scene that 'they never lost a race' (except, of course, in sports car and handicap events) the announcement by Herbert Austin of his Seven ('the finest Meccano set ever produced') came as manna to the tuning-up fraternity. Innumerable sporting successes were achieved by the racing Sevens developed by Gordon England, and their super sports derivatives, which with polished aluminium bodies and staggered seats, sold at £265 complete with a Brooklands' certificate guaranteeing 75mph

Malcolm Campbell (above) taking a bend at speed in his Bugatti during the Brooklands Easter meeting in 1931. The programme included nine races and a gliding display.
Spectators examining in the paddock (right) at the first race meeting of the season at Brooklands in 1930. Closest to the camera is a Grand Prix Bugatti, with its famous alloy-spoked wheels.

6
8

(121kph). Whereupon, at Morris garages in Oxford (just opposite Magdalene College deer-park) Cecil Kimber breathed heavily on a bull-nosed Morris Cowley to create the first MG, and subsequently transmogrified a Minor into the earliest of the Midgets. Austin and Morris thus brought not only motoring, but motor sport to the millions, and many were the big names who first tried their hand at Brooklands in an Ulster replica Seven or an M Type MG.

To accommodate this mixture of unequals it was necessary to introduce a form of handicapping, worked out for each car and the skill of its drivers, and effected in the manner of the Turf by adding ballast, though this developed into handicap by time. But, although short handicap races were popular, the enterprising Junior Car Club (founded in 1912 as the Cyclecar Club, and today the British Automobile Racing Club) established the first major event at Brooklands in 1921: the 200 mile (322km) race for voiturettes – an international affair in the continental manner – and followed this up four years later with a One Hour High Speed Trial for members in their everyday sports and touring cars. In 1926 the RAC held the first British Grand Prix at Brooklands (won by Sénéchal and Wagner in a Delage) and in 1929 the British Racing Drivers' Club, which grew out of the exclusive Brooklands Motor Club to become one of the most prestigious fraternities of the motoring world, held its first 500 mile (805km) event for racing cars, run over the outer circuit on a class handicap basis. The first of this series, which was, in fact, the fastest of all long distance races at that time, was won by Jack Barclay (of Berkeley Square fame) and F. C. Clement in a $4\frac{1}{2}$ litre Bentley.

But these were not all: the Essex Motor Club organized a 'miniature Le Mans' with a Six Hour Endurance race in 1927, which the JCC followed up with a Double-Twelve hour race for sports cars, and later a series of International Trophy races, rather ingeniously handicapped by channelling cars into corners of varying severity. The Light Car Club held an annual Relay Race, and in 1930 the newly formed Veteran Car Club began to hold races for veteran cars at Bank Holiday Meetings. Whatever you wanted, Brooklands had it.

Not surprisingly, too, there were several ladies who were as much at home on the concrete as in the clubhouse. Jill Thomas, Elsie Mary Wisdom, Gwenda Stewart and Kay Petre, for instance, all lapped the outer circuit, bumps and all, at over 120mph (193.12kph) – and, like their male counterparts who had done likewise, had a badge to prove it.

Rodney Walkerley (to whom I am indebted for this particular reminiscence) recalls that Kay Petre, a pretty slender girl with a blue ribbon in her hair, who looked too fragile to drive a V12 10.6 litre single-seater Delage, staged a Bank Holiday duel against Gwenda Stewart and her 1,660cc supercharged 8 cylinder front wheel drive Derby-Miller for the unofficial title of what the Press engagingly called 'Fastest Woman in the World'.

The girls were unleashed one at a time and everyone was so agog, says Rodney, that they even turned out of the club bar to watch. Kay went out first and lapped at 134.24mph (216.04kph) and 133.88mph (215.45kph). But, on the fourth lap the filler cap opened, fountaining high octane all over the tail; so, prudently enough, she called it a day. Gwenda then made 133.67mph (215.12kph), upon which an exhaust manifold split over a bump, gassing the driver with fumes, and leaving Kay Petre the winner. But the day after the encounter Mrs Stewart mended her exhaust system and went out again. After a frightening slide on the banking (frightening at least to the onlookers) she lapped at 135.95mph (218.79kph) and snatched the women's lap record back from Kay.

Of such stuff – like the 300mph de-restriction sign beside the entrance – was the mystique of Brooklands made up.

Raymond Mays (opposite) winning the International Trophy race at Brooklands in 1937 on his 2 litre Zoller-supercharged ERA. The previous year he had been beaten into second place by Prince Chula of Siam, also in an ERA. Together with Humphrey Cook, Peter Berthon and aided by Reid Railton, Mays conceived the ERA in 1933-4, and it proved to be one of the most successful makes of the late thirties.

Dark-haired, petite Kay Petre (right) was one of the most popular figures at Brooklands during the thirties. Badly injured in September 1937 when her car somersaulted on the Byfleet banking after colliding with another car she was back again at the wheel of a supercharged 1.5 litre Riley by the following March.

Bentleys at Le Mans

IF, IN BRITISH EYES at least, a sports car meant a Bentley, so a Bentley meant Le Mans. This French provincial city had been a centre of motor sport since the beginning of the century – the first Grand Prix was held there in 1906, and again when racing recommenced in 1921. But the real reason for its fame was the sports car race – *Les 24 Heures du Mans* – that still stands supreme as the international test of speed and endurance.

A race right round the clock was by no means a complete novelty when Charles Faroux and Georges Durand conceived the idea in 1923, for twenty-four hour events had, in fact, been held on American board tracks such as Brighton Beach on Coney Island, and, indeed, on a small dirt track outside Indianapolis. But Le Mans immediately caught the public fancy.

The first race started on the Sarthe Circuit at four o'clock in the afternoon of 26 May 1923 in a hailstorm. The corners were illuminated by army searchlights and acetylene lamps to assist drivers during the dark, and in case spectators got bored, additional entertainment in the shape of a cinema and jazz concert were laid on in a makeshift 'village'. It was mainly a French affair and Legache and Léonard won in a 3 litre Chenard-Walcker after covering 1,372.94 miles (2,209.53km) at an average of 57.2mph (92.05kph), but John Duff established the Bentley presence by setting a lap record for

Before manufacturing cars in his own right, W. O. Bentley (above) was the London agent for the French DFP car, which he also raced. 'W.O.' is seen here with the 12.1hp DFP in which he took class B records at Brooklands in February 1914.

Start of the 1928 Le Mans 24 Hours (right) as three Bentleys thunder into the lead along with a Chrystler roadster. The Bentleys were driven by Clement/Benjafield, Birkin/Chassagne and Barnato/Rubin.

sports cars at 66.69mph (107.33kph), and covering the greatest distance, before running out of petrol and finishing fifth.

The following year no such error crept in and although delayed by a wiring staple that jammed the gear change, Duff and Clement won the 1924 race in their 3 litre Bentley at the lower overall speed of 53.78mph (86.55 kph).

In 1925 the field included two American-entered Chryslers along with the British contingents, and this year inaugurated the 'Le Mans start' in which drivers were lined up and had to sprint across the track and erect their folded tops before starting the engines and roaring off. It also, unhappily, saw the first fatal accidents (André Guilbert in his Ravel, and Mestivier who spun off the straight in his Amilcar). Neither of the two Bentleys finished on this occasion – one caught fire, in fact – and Courcelles and Rossignol took the flag in their 3½ litre Lorraine-Dietrich. The 1926 event, in contrast, started as a three-cornered tussle between the Lorraines, the 3.8 litre Peugeot, and the Bentleys. At eight o'clock on the Sunday morning, number one Bentley was three laps behind the leading Lorraine when it retired with a broken rocker, and twenty minutes from the end Sammy Davis slid the second Bentley into a sandbank at Mulsanne, enabling the Lorraines to finish with a 1–2–3 victory ahead of two OMs.

It was the 1927 race, in fact, that really gave substance to the Bentley legend. Sammy Davis, who was driving 'Old No 7' recalls how only twenty-four cars lined up for the start (partly because the Tracta team had

Change of drivers as the Clement/Chassagne 4.5 litre Bentley (above left) comes in for a pit stop during the 24 Hours of Le Mans in 1929. It was placed fourth behind three of its team mates in a 1-2-3-4 Bentley triumph. The winner of the Le Mans 24 Hours in 1928 was the 4.5 litre Bentley (above) driven by Woolf Barnato and Bernard Rubin. The new 4.5 litre models (the first of these had been introduced to the Le Mans race the previous year, but had been knocked out by the famous multiple crash) gave 110bhp as opposed to the 3 litre's 88bhp.

gone joy-riding the night before, ending up in a crash which put most of them in hospital) and after the getaway those manning the pits settled down to the monotonous routine of clocking lap times. Every eight minutes and forty-five seconds, or thereabouts, the Bentleys rushed by, their exhausts growing from a distant murmur to a fierce crescendo as they passed the pits and the grandstand to dwindle again in the direction of Pontlieue.

But suddenly, an hour after dusk, the time-keeper stiffened. Not one, but all three Bentleys were overdue. Minutes dragged by and there was no sound, nor even the flicker of a headlight. Then some smaller cars went by. The entire Bentley team had disappeared on a single lap.

Finally, from far away, came the sound of an engine, and into the blaze of the grand-stands crept No 7. Its lamps were out, a front wheel wobbled drunkenly, and a twisted wing pointed straight over the hood.

What had happened, relates Davis, was that when darkness fell he had fallen back a bit to avoid dazzling his team mate with his headlights. He saw the Bentley ahead rush down the hill, jump the little bridge, and disappear round the bend.

> As I swung around that right hand turn, on the road was a scatter of earth, a piece or two of splintered wood. The thing flashed an immediate warning . . . but even then it did not occur to me to do more than slow down a little and be ready. The car swung round White Corner almost at full speed. I jammed down the brake pedal, tried to spin the wheel and skidded broad-side on, for, white and horrible in the

headlights' beam an appalling tangle of smashed cars appeared right across the road in front! With the rending crash of riven metal, we slid right into the mess, with a shock that threw me hard against the wheel. All the lights went out.

Half climbing, half falling out, he saw that the mess ahead was one of the Bentleys on its side, while right on top of it was the other. Callingham, in the leading 4½, had come storming through White House Corner to find a Schneider broadside across the track. Crashing into it, he had spun and rolled across the road into the far side ditch. Seconds later, Duller in the 3 litre managed to avoid the Schneider but smashed into the 4½. Sammy Davis did likewise. Of the three Bentleys only his, disentangled with catastrophic rending noises, was able to continue. And as he limped off, another car crashed into the wreckage.

Back at the pits the damage was inspected. The frame was bent, the axle back on the springs, the headlamp twisted to bits, but the car could still run. To win was hopeless, but Sammy was determined to go on.

Chassagne and Laly in the Aries were far ahead, and it was raining. But gradually 'Doc' Benjafield, now driving the stricken car, reduced their lead, catching up a whole lap, in fact. And then, with less than an hour to go, the Aries stopped by the wayside and the Bentley, its mudguards flapping in the wind, swept by. As No 7 flew round the circuit, the Bentley hopes began to soar. But they were still over ten miles behind, and the next time round there was no sign of the Aries. It was still in the race – and ahead too.

Finally, mounting the rise before Mulsanne, Benjafield saw the long blue Aries again, with its hood open. 'Moments such as this are too full of emotion to describe,' recalls Davis. 'From now on Benjy knew that the unbelievable would happen, and that the old car would win.'

It was Sammy Davis who brought the battered machine over the line to be smothered in flowers and champagne by a delirious crowd. And afterwards, when one or two things in the steering were shown to them, they marvelled even more at their luck.

During the celebration dinner at the Savoy in London, Sir Edward Iliffe, who was in the chair, rose to state that a lady who was entitled to be at the dinner was outside, adding that he had invited her to enter. The folding doors were swung back, there was a deep engine roar, and with her one headlamp blazing, No 7 came into the room.

Thus grew the saga of the Bentleys at Le Mans. In 1928 against an American challenge by teams of 4.9 litre straight-eight Stutzes and 4.1 litre Chryslers, Woolf Barnato (who was now financing Bentleys) and Bernard

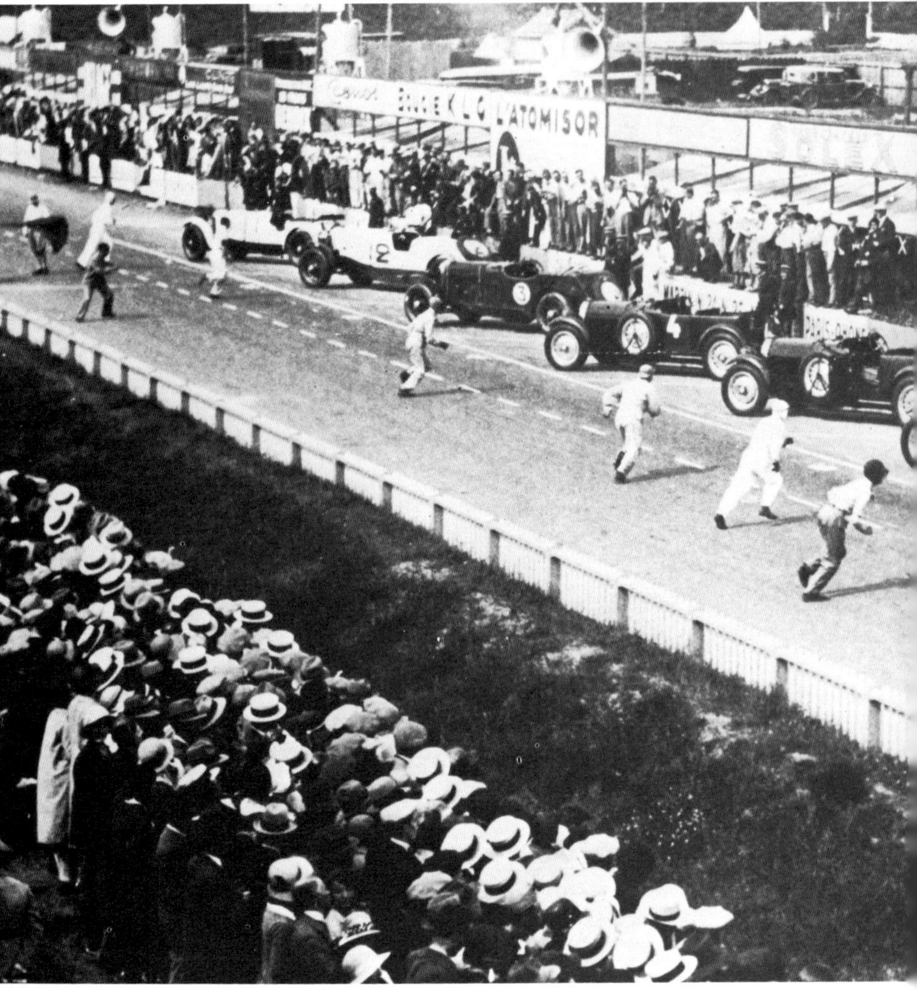

The classic Le Mans start was first introduced in 1925. The drivers sprint across the track for the start of the 1931 event (above) with a Mercedes and three 4.9 Bugattis prominent in the line-up. One of the fastest of the Brooklands Outer Circuit specials was Oliver Bertram's 8 litre Bentley-engined Barnato-Hassan (right), seen before the 1935 500 Miles Race. Second from the right is Wally Hassan, designer of the car.

Rubin broke the sports car record on the second lap of 74.1mph (119.25kph) and eventually took the flag in their 4½ litre Bentley, ahead of the Brisson-Bloch driven Stutz, with Chryslers in third and fourth position and Sir Henry Birkin's Bentley, which came fifth after pushing the sports car record up to 79.23mph (127.51kph) on the last lap of all.

By 1929 it was already Bentley versus the rest, and the result was an overwhelming victory; with Barnato-Birkin leading three 4½s home at an average of 73.63mph (118.5 kph) to achieve a 1–2–3–4 Bentley triumph.

In 1930 Caracciola and Christian Werner appeared with their 7.1 SS Mercedes to challenge the Bentley supremacy, and Bentleys themselves fielded two separate teams: the works entry of Speed Sixes controlled by W. O. Bentley, and Dorothy Paget's three 'Blower' 4½s managed by Kensington Moir. Among the rest of the field were the Stutzes, two Lagondas, Earl Howe's 1750 Alfa Romeo, the first 846cc MGs, and the first ladies too – Mmes Mareuse and Siko in a 1½ litre Bugatti. The race got off to a fast start with the White Mercedes leading and hounded almost neck to neck by the Bentley team, until it finally blew up at 2.30 am. One of the Stutzes burnt out at Mulsanne, and the other broke its rear axle, while the Blower Bentleys themselves fell out with broken valves and cooked pistons. Finally the two works 6½ litres, driven by Barnato-Kidston and Clement-Watney, took the flag in team order, Old No 1 winning for the second time. But, sadly enough, it was the last race for the Bentley works team. By the following year financial troubles had exceeded even Woolf Barnato's ample resources – in the opinion of his accountants, at least. W. O. Bentley's gallant firm was sold to Rolls Royce, to begin a splendid new lease of life away from the racing scene.

The old order had passed, and for *aficionados* it was the end of an epoch.

Grand Prix Racing: The Twenties

FOR THE HIGHER ECHELONS of racing, 1924 stands out as the peak season of the decade. Juiced, as it were, by the new Two Litre Formula that had been introduced in 1922 to boost the development of efficient small engines, a wave of outstanding machinery lifted Grand Prix racing into a scintillating new phase.

The Italians, to be sure, were the pace-makers. By enabling their engines to breathe and turn freely without lubrication failure, and then by blowing them (forcing, that is, the petrol-air mixture into the cylinders instead of relying on atmospheric pressure) the Fiat racing department sparked off an Italian renaissance with first the Type 804 and then the supercharged 805. What is more, apart from building the fastest cars – Bordino set up a new lap record in each of the major events of 1922–3 – they had the best drivers and the most efficient pit organization. Small wonder, therefore, that Fiat dominated the racing scene as never before. The cars that were jauntily driven over the Alps to Tours for the French National Event were the first GP machines to be fitted with super-chargers, and although on this initial outing they all retired, once the trifling design error had been rectified they pulverized all opposi-tion (including the twin ohv straight-eight

Antonio Ascari's Alfa Romeo P2 (above) after his fatal crash in the 1925 French Grand Prix. He was leading on a damp track when he ran too close to a paling fence. His hub cap became entangled, and the car capsized.

A wet start to the Free-for-all race held at Montlhéry (right) in support of the 1927 French Grand Prix. The race was won by Divo's Talbot. The Talbots failed in the GP itself, only one car finishing, and the firm withdrew from racing at the end of the year.

BOSCH
L.M.C.
S.E.V.
S.E.V.

Henry Segrave (opposite), seen in conversation with King Alfonso of Spain after he had retired in the 1926 Spanish Grand Prix at San Sebastian. The race was won by Constantini on a Bugatti.
The 2 litre supercharged Mercedes at the start of the Solitude race in Germany in May 1925. Otto Merz, the winner, is at the wheel of car No 15 (above), and Karl Sailer is in car No 14. The Solitude Ring covered a network of closed public roads around Schloss Solitude, near Stuttgart, and was used for the last time in 1965.

Millers and Dr Rumpler's *avant-garde* Benz) at Monza three months later. Indeed, if the Italian GP of 1923 was the first international race to be won by a supercharged car, only one subsequent event of this status – the Targa Florio, as it happens – was won without a blower until 1939 (except, of course, on those occasions when supercharging was disallowed by the regulations).

All of which meant, perhaps inevitably, that some covetous eyes were focused on Turin, and so many of their top designers were lured away by tempting offers to plagiarize (and often, in fairness, to improve on) the Fiat expertise that the directors of the great Piedmontese firm decided to withdraw from racing at the end of 1924. Perhaps they felt they shouldn't try to push their luck too far and that it didn't make commercial sense anyway. Certainly it was galling to run the risk of being beaten by designs that had originated on their own drawing-boards. Yet, even as Fiat began to bow out, a splendid new successor was ready in the wings.

Nicola Romeo had moved into the old but ailing Societa Anonima Lombarda Fabbrica Automobili during the war, renamed it Alfa Romeo, brought in Enzo Ferrari to direct operations and Vittorio Jano as chief designer (from Fiat, of course) and the result was a marvellous 8 cylinder double ohc 2 litre supercharged model known as the P2. Indeed, from this point onwards, right up to 1951, save only for the interval in the thirties when Mercedes and Auto Union chased everything else off the roads, Alfa Romeo was to make the biggest waves in European racing.

The year 1924, then, was a vintage one. Duesenberg set up a new record at Indianapolis; Mercedes re-entered the GP arena and won an exciting Targa Florio; Segrave pulled off the Spanish Grand Prix on the Lasarte circuit at San Sebastian; the Swiss GP made its debut (as a voiturette race); new circuits were opened at Montlhéry and Miramas, and the French Grand Prix was a scorcher.

Fittingly enough, it was run again at

Overpage: a sleeve valve-engined Peugeot in action during the 1925 Targa Florio. The famous Sicilian race was won that year by Bartolomeo Costantini.

PIRELLI
27 APRILE 1924
RIO
ANSALDO
PIRELLI
MICHELIN
MICHELIN

Although Fiat had retired from the Grandes Epreuves in 1924, Bordino (above) made a demonstration tour in South America in 1925. He is seen here in Argentina, at the wheel of a Tipo 805 with single-seater bodywork. One of the great drivers of the early 1920s, Antonio Ascari (left) reached the peak of his fame in the 8 cylinder P2 Alfa Romeo with which he won the 1924 Italian Grand Prix, and the 1925 Grand Prix of Europe at Spa. Here he leads at Spa, his last victory before his fatal crash at Montlhéry.

Lyons over part of the famous 1914 circuit, with a field of twenty-two cars. For their last appearance at the GP, Fiat entered four supercharged 805s (only two of which were new, driven by Nazzaro and Bordino, and the others rebuilds); while Alfa Romeo made its debut with three P2s in the hands of Ascari, Campari and Wagner. The Planchon-designed V12 Delages were normally aspirated; their drivers were Divo, Benoist and Thomas. And, having junked barrel bodies and tanks, Ettore Bugatti brought his classic Type 35, the progenitor of so many famous GP machines and one of the most beautiful cars of all time, to its very first race.

The favourites, however, were Sunbeams, who were hoping to repeat their 1923 victory with improved blown versions of the Tours 'Sixes'. Unfortunately, it did not turn out that way. Laurence Pomeroy has given an intriguing backstage insight on what inevitably (with suitable apologies to the great German firm) became known as 'Sunbeam's Bosch shot'.

The British cars were so clearly superior to the others, he says, that Alfas, who fancied their chances as runners-up, approached the Sunbeam team manager to do a bit of horse trading. If he would agree to let Alfas take second and third position they would willingly let Sunbeams win without pressing any of the cars too hard. 'This "offer" was probably made with a light heart over a mutual glass of wine,' recounts Pom.

It is certain that Sunbeams went to the line confident of a second successive victory in Grand Prix racing, but this was not to be. The night before the race they were visited by the Bosch Company, who exclaimed upon the burnt contact-breaker covers of the magnetos, which were placed at the rear of the engine facing outwards the exhaust pipe. These particular instruments had remained untouched since the previous year, and no doubt the addition of the blower caused the piping to get much hotter and caused the burning to start. Bosch mechanics made a replacement with some magnetos of the lastest type that had just arrived from Stuttgart.

During the race the Sunbeams suffered from constant misfiring. Their superior speed was confirmed by unofficial timing during the race which gave Sunbeam 130mph (209kph), Alfa Romeo 124mph (200kph) and Delage, running unsupercharged, 114mph (183kph); but nobody could account for the irregular running of the cars which constantly held them back. Sunbeams' ill-luck thus gave Alfa Romeo the rare distinction of winning the French Grand Prix with their first entry for the event . . .

In the middle of the night following the race the Sunbeam development engineer, Captain Jack Irving, leapt from his couch, rushed to the sheds, put back the old magnetos and the trouble vanished. By such a small incident were the Wolverhampton Company deprived of the rare honour of winning the French Grand Prix for two successive years.

But this was only part of the drama of a race that is generally rated as the 'greatest Grand Prix', surpassing even the excitements of the 1914 event. Five drivers and three marques led at different stages of the thirty-five laps; Ascari's Alfa blew up when all set to win just three laps from the end, thus opening the way for Divo's Delage which was urged on by a frantically cheering crowd; but once again the French hopes were dashed as Giuseppe Campari's Alfa crossed the line only a minute ahead of the blue car after seven gruelling hours. For a new marque, it was a propitious start. But the story of Alfa Romeo and of Enzo Ferrari is almost synonymous with racing from that August afternoon over half a century ago right up until now.

For the others there were compensations, though. Henry Segrave made up for his Bosch shot at Tours by winning at San Sebastian six weeks later. Antonio Ascari took the flag with his Alfa Romeo at Monza to close the 1924 scene, and moreover,

Divo in the Talbot, car No 4, (above left), and Benoist in the Delage (car No 6) fight for the lead at the start of the 1927 French Grand Prix at Montlhéry. Benoist was the eventual winner, followed by two more Delages.

opened the 1925 season by repeating the performance in the Belgian Grand Prix at Spa. But unhappily it was the last victory for this immensely popular driver who habitually went flat-out from the startline in a manner that the Italians approvingly call *garibaldiano*. For in the French Grand Prix at Montlhéry that July he crashed to his death when leading in the wet. The Alfas (which looked unbeatable) were immediately withdrawn in sympathy and Divo (and Benoist) went on to win in the Delage, ahead of another Delage and Masetti's Sunbeam.

These four seasons (1922–5) saw the Italian genius at its peak, to be sure. Power outputs nearly doubled and maximum road speeds increased dramatically. Later cars certainly held the road better and braked more efficiently, but for many years few were faster. Which indeed was just what worried the organizers.

Concerned that the 2 litre cars were dangerously swift (by 1926 they were topping 130mph or 209kph) the AIACR introduced a new formula which restricted engine capacity to $1\frac{1}{2}$ litres. The immediate result was a fiasco. Only three Bugattis lined up on the starting grid at Miramas to compete in the French Grand Prix. One of them retired, another was flagged off, and the senior motor race on the international calendar devolved into the spectacle of Goux's solitary machine chasing itself around that featureless track.

The next year at Montlhéry was hardly any better: seven cars started, and Delage achieved a 1-2-3 victory, ahead of a single Talbot. By 1928, indeed, the great French classic was demoted to a sports car event. Yet if from a competitive point of view the new formula was something of a lemon, it nevertheless inspired some brilliant machinery. And, once manufacturers like Alfa Romeo and Sunbeam had withdrawn to the wings, it brough a resurgence of *gloire de la France*. In 1926 Bugatti introduced a blown version of the Type 35 and swept the board with successes at Rome, in the Targa Florio, at Monza and the Spanish GP (to say nothing

Christian Werner (above) crosses the finishing line to win the 1928 German Grand Prix at the Nürburgring in his Mercedes, in partnership with Caracciola. The previous year, Werner had won the inaugural race at the Ring. André Boillot (right), brother of the celebrated Georges Boillot, who carried on the Peugeot racing tradition, after winning the Coupe de la Commission Sportive at Montlhéry in 1927. He was suffering from severe toothache at the time!

Nuvolari (above) in action at the RAC international Tourist Trophy on the Ards circuit near Belfast. Alfa Romeos won the first three places in the 1930 event, with Nuvolari taking the flag. Caracciola's 2.3 litre Alfa Romeo (left) storms past Michaelangelo's 'David' in the Piazza Michaelangelo, above Florence, during the 1932 Mille Miglia.
The ten-year Italian hold over the race had been momentarily shaken the previous year by his victory, together with Sebastian, in a Mercedes.

of the abortive French GP at Miramas); while the 1½ litre double ohc Delage straight-eights with their low raked radiators carried all before them in 1927. Delage, indeed, ran twenty cars in seven races during these two seasons, out of which, largely thanks to Robert Benoist, they won five (with a grand slam in two) and suffered only three retirements due to engine trouble. Pomeroy considered them to be nothing less than a 'technical tour-de-force both in design and construction' – a judgement that was reinforced ten years later when Dick Seaman ran one for a season and won three races in a row without touching the engine.

But mass motoring had now reached a point where sales to the public were no longer much affected by racing successes. Popular cars, after all, were a different breed from the Grand Prix machines. One after another the manufacturers withdrew. Both Delage and Talbot gave up at the end of 1927 leaving Bugatti to keep racing alive as the only major works team, although Alfa Romeo made an occasional appearance along with a new contender, Maserati. For 1929 the AIACR produced a formula that was even more unpalatable than before, so that the French and Spanish GPs were the only 'approved' international events. All the rest were run under *formula libre*.

Oddly enough, just as the technological burst that had carried the GP car to such a high level began to run out of steam, or rather money, so the public's interest in the sport seemed to grow. The calendar was suddenly full of secondary races, with a succession of events every week-end from May to September. Many of these, breaking away from the mainstream of GPs, were aimed specifically at sports cars, and the great sports car events, such as Le Mans and the Mille Miglia, were what hit the headlines.

If classic racing had fallen on evil days, it was a golden period for the gifted amateur. Independent drivers such as Tim Birkin, William Grover Williams, René Dreyfus, Phi-Phi Etancelin and Count Czaykowski were able to pit their skill against the top professionals, with considerable *panache*. It was the great era for Bugattis, too. W. F. Bradley, enthusing over the Type 35 with its long pointed tail and polished axle, ahead of the narrow horseshoe radiator, thought it so beautifully finished that it was 'the kind of toy which an enthusiast had only to see to buy'. Toy or not, Bugatti won more races than any other make between the wars – in fact more than all the others added together. Indeed, from 1924 to 1926 Bugatti cars achieved a total of 1,045 victories and registered 806 wins in 1927 alone. And during the next three years the 35B had matters more or less its own way, the point being, of course, that it was a catalogued model that could be bought by amateur drivers. (Which they did with such effect that many races, especially in France, became little more than a Bugatti benefit.)

Heyday it may have been for the amateur driver and dog days for the others, but two events of top importance mark these non-vintage years. The Nürburgring with its eighty-nine left hand bends and eighty-five right-handers over a length of 17.56 miles (28.26km) was built in one of the loveliest settings in Germany, and Anthony Noghés devised a circuit through the streets of Monte Carlo that, by running wholly on Monagasque soil, could claim to be a national event and which because of its carnival character became the most durable and romantic of all Grand Prix.

The Heyday of International Rallies

The spirit of amateur hill-climbing in the twenties (left): an AC at Shelsley Walsh. The record for the period was set by B. H. Davenport in a Spider at 48.8sec in 1926.

During my first term at Oundle I remember watching agog from the dormitory window as Old Boys, up for the Cricket week-end, improvised a round-the-houses race, snarling through the narrow streets with the windscreens of their J4 Midgets and Le Mans type Singers folded flat, while the village police and the school authorities turned an indulgently blind eye, for young gentlemen were expected to be riotous on such occasions.

To youthful eyes this was glamour indeed, just like later that summer when I watched the 1934 Alpine Rally cars dice past Samaden Golf Course into the check post at St Moritz, and crept out of bed at dawn to witness the same mudstained competitors flagged off again, at two minute intervals, from outside the old Grand Hotel . . .

THERE WAS A WHIFF of Dornford Yates about the cars and equipages that set off, silver flasks and all, for the great winter adventure of the Monte Carlo Rally, while Bulldog Drummond, one feels sure, would have been in his element storming up the Stelvio in the Alpine Rally. For if GP racing was normally a professional business, rallies were still the domain of the amateur. The majority of competitors in the Monte and the Alpine were well-to-do sportsmen who took part for the sheer exhilaration of it all.

For several years after the war administrative difficulties – such as a newfangled need for passports and visas – precluded the organization of international rallies. It was not until 1924 that the first tentative Monte was held again and even then it was overshadowed by the Paris–Nice Trial. But by 1925 something of the old spirit had returned and the winner, Repusseau in a 45hp Renault, set out from Tunis.

Next, in 1926, the Hon Victor Bruce took the honours from John o' Groats (at the northern tip of Scotland) in an AC – a notable feat since he was the only British entrant, and it was the first time a British

A British Sunbeam (left) deep in the snow en route during the Monte Carlo Rally of 1930. Originally, merely reaching Monaco was considered to be a tough enough trial of endurance, but subsequently special mountain and driving tests were incorporated at the end of the event. The control point in Monte-Carlo is inset.

car had triumphed – and the following year his wife won the newly initiated *Coupe des Dames*.

By now the idea of driving to the Riviera in the middle of the winter had caught on, and it is sobering to reflect that Europe in the wicked old days still offered the possibility of starting from Tallinn up in Estonia (via Riga, Kaunas, Konigsberg and Berlin), which provided the winners in 1933, or Bucharest (via Cluj, Kosice, Olomouc and Prague). The weather factor, as unpredictable as ever, often meant the difference between failure and success. Competitors setting off in the sunshine of North Africa were often washed away in Spain, and it was many years before anyone managed to get through from Greece, although in four of the six last rallies before the war the outright winner started from Athens. Scandinavia was a favourite choice: Dr Van Eijk took first place with his Graham-Paige from Stockholm in 1929; Donald Healey did likewise in his 4½ litre Invicta from Stavanger in 1931 and was only just pipped at the post the following year by Vaselle's Hotchkiss which, like him, had started at Umea in northern Sweden.

Bonus points were awarded for the more difficult starting points – Athens, for instance, rated 1,000, Bucharest 935, Tallin 910 and John o' Groats 850 – and originally merely to reach Monte Carlo was test enough. The bar of the Metropole Hotel was always abuzz with post-mortem chat: of how the Bucharest contigent, snowbound, had paid astronomic bribes to the local peasantry to be hauled out by oxen; of how a Bentley, a Crossley and a

Start of the 1931 Tourist Trophy race (above) in Ulster. Norman Black's little 750cc supercharged MG Midget, No 42, was the eventual winner. The Ards circuit, where the race was run from 1928 to 1936, was formed of a triangle between Dundonald, Newtownwards and Comber, east of Belfast.

36/220 supercharged Mercedes had all gone off the road at the same place outside Glasgow, and after surgery by the local blacksmith, had caught up the lost time; of how Whalley's Ford had just missed hitting a train in Denmark but Donald Healey's Triumph hadn't. To say nothing of Louis Chiron who had skidded into a ditch and after hours of hard work got the car back on to the road, only to be promptly shunted into the same ditch again by another competitor. Such things were all part of the fun. Yet, in fact, it was the final regularity trial over the Col de Braus, which competitors were required to cover at the same speed as they had averaged on the rally, that decided the outright winner. Also a curious little test on the promenade known as the 'Wiggle-Woggle'.

Since a second or two here could be the deciding factor, much time and effort was spent bending the regulations – often to a ludicrous degree – until the Monte became a battle of wits between competitors and organizers. How to win without actually cheating, as Stephen Potter would have said; the ploy being to scrutinize the regulations for any possible loophole, exploit it fully and then dream up a counter protest if anyone objected.

At the other end of the calendar, since it was held in midsummer, the International Alpine Rally, whose origins stretched back to the pre-war Austrian Alpine Trials, was revived in 1928 by a consortium of national motor clubs. It was intended, in the words of the *Autocar*, to be 'The trial of trials, fulfilling the double object of testing both man and his car to the full.' And this, over a route that varied from year to year but always included the highest passes in the Alps and the Dolomites, it most certainly did.

For one thing, cars had to be standard production models. For another, certain parts – such as radiator caps – had to be sealed, which meant that even topping up with water en route was barred. Against this, there was no outright winner. Anyone who finished without loss of marks was awarded a coveted 'Coupe des Alpes', which went also to the team with the best performance.

Not surprisingly, the professionals soon appeared alongside the amateurs. In 1929, for instance, Caracciola and Werner turned up with supercharged Mercedes from the works, while Nazzaro, Salamano and Cagno were all hired for the event by Fiat. Yet none of this top ranking talent made the grade, as it happens. Nazzaro, faced with a lorry or a wall in a narrow Bolzano street, chose the wall, and Caracciola's Mercedes lost power to the point that spectators could walk up the hill beside him. But the challenge of the Alps and prestige of the rally remained a magnet for the big boys.

Every sporting event has its ups and downs. For the Alpine, 1934 was a vintage year. The route started at Nice and went via Aix-les-Bains, Interlaken, St Moritz, Venice and Zagreb to finish at Munich. 1,812 miles (2,916km) in six days through the mountains of six countries.

Competitors had left Nice at five o'clock on a marvellous day, reported the *Autocar* correspondent, and had headed inland through the valley of the Isère towards the blue mountains of Haute Savoie. Each curve was taken on the skid point with tires screaming, the spare drivers waving cheerily as they were swung into blind corners. In the van were the big Ford V8s, the fast blue Delahayes, and Trevoux in his Hotchkiss; these were followed in the 3 litre class by the green Talbots of Tommy Wisdom and Mike Couper and also the SS1 team (ancestor of the Jaguars) which were opposed by the 2 litre FWD Adlers. In the 2 litre class were the Riley Sixes with Gamecock bodies competing against the Wanderers and Opels, and in the 1½ litre class the TT replica Frazer Nashes, BMWs, Aston Martins and MGs. Finally, in the smallest class of all came the 'Southern Cross' Triumphs, the Singers and the 995cc Adler Trumpf-Juniors.

Over the Cayolle they went, rough and alive with hairpin bends and the muddy river far below that seemed to the *Autocar* reporter to be 'shining like silver paper in a shadow', on to the even more twisty Col d'Allos and the still looser and steeper Izoard (the Galibier had been cut out because of a washed-away bridge). Up the Glandon, Pätzold's V8 Ford ran out of road and overturned. By the end of the first stage, three other Fords and a Hotchkiss had been forced to retire, but any personal disappointments were made up by the warmth of the reception at Aix-les-Bains, which included a cabaret.

Next day, at the frontier atop the Petit St Bernard, carnets were stamped as quick as a pit stop. Black-shirted Fascists marked the dangerous corners and handed out fruit and bottles of San Pellegrino at the Aosta filling stations before the cars roared up the long, bare, bleak Grand St Bernard. Then came the run down through Switzerland with 'the mountains standing out as blue shapes against the brilliant green of the meadows', and villages full of those wooden chalets with low overhanging roofs, painted shutters and flower boxes that one knows so well. Nor was the second stage without its incidents. One of the two remaining Dutch Fords was reported to have turned over, but managed to

A British 6 cylinder supercharged K3 MG (top) passes through Parma during the 1933 Mille Miglia, Italy's famous 1,000 miles race over public roads. The car was driven by G. E. T. Eyston and Count Lurant and won the 1,100cc class.

The Ladies' Cup winner (above) in the 1935 Circuit de l'Aiglon rally event, with her very sporting Peugeot and an armful of trophies.

get going again; an SS1 had clouted a boundary stone but nevertheless continued; the Singers were having tire troubles, and one of the Frazer Nashes with a holed sump was using more oil than petrol.

Interlaken was lost in the mist, making the early morning start difficult, and soon the rally cars were cloudbound up the Grimsel and the Furka among the glaciers of the Rhône. Swiss postal buses had to be given right of way, sometimes a disconcerting procedure on open hairpins with a sheer drop into the heaving mist below. Zigzagging down the Bernardino pass, Wieleman's Ford V8 crashed head on into another car and Magnus' Ford retired with gearbox trouble. As the competitors raced into St Moritz, the position of the various teams at half distance was that in the top class Delahaye had lost no marks; in the 3 litre class Talbot, Adler and SS1 were still clean, as indeed were Wanderer, Opel and Adler in the 2 litre, and BMW in the 1½ litre class. Rileys had lost 67 marks by refilling a radiator, but Triumph led the tiddlers with a clean sheet. The Germans were flogging their cars to the limit, keeping well ahead of time, watched with interest by the British to see if they could stay the pace (which most of them did).

After the dawn start from the Grand Hotel at St Moritz the fourth day of the trial included a timed climb of the Stelvio as well as a speed test on the Autostrada, and many of the cars beat their set average easily. In every Italian village the police kept back the crowds and saluted or urged the competitors on to go even faster. By contrast, the gondola trip at Venice to the hotel and a hot bath seemed interminable to the weary drivers.

But the following morning was worse: they had to struggle out through the smelly canals in whatever craft they could find at a very early hour (two of the SS1 team overslept), and after the long straight Italian *statale* roads, conditions in Yugoslavia seemed nightmarish. The higher the speed the more the dust surged and, whitened as if with flour, the thirsty crews crept into Zagreb clamouring for baths, greatly in excess of the Yugoslavian supply.

But in the mountains, though, it began raining. Austria was in a permanent state of cloudburst, so that the Turracher Höhe (thought the *Autocar* scribe) was 'like a long edition of Beggar's Roost'. In fact some cars were said to have gone up in reverse, only to find, as they breathlessly arrived at the check post, that it wasn't there.

In Germany, the road to Munich was lined with SS troops. Their horns screeching, the weary drivers and exhausted cars clattered over the tramlines to a rapturous military welcome between rows of Heil-Hitlering police.

For six days they had escaped from workaday routine to dice over some of the most dangerous roads in the world. Happiness had meant the chance to pit themselves and their machines against the might of the mountains. It had called for deftness, endurance, and at times courage as well. Which, all said and done, is what international rallying is all about.

World Land Speed Records [1922-1939]

APART FROM ALL ELSE, there was a sudden revival of interest in the world land speed record during the twenties. Kenelm Lee Guinness started the ball rolling again when he realized that his lap speed at Brooklands was not far short of the official pre-war record set up by L. G. Hornsted in the Blitzen Benz. Admittedly, 'Cupid' Hornsted's time of 124.1mph had been significantly bettered by both Ralph de Palma in the Packard and Tommy Milton's Duesenberg at Daytona, but neither run had been officially recognized. On 17 May 1922, therefore, Guinness took the 350hp Sunbeam, with its modified 'Manitou' V12 aircraft engine, out on to the concrete at Weybridge and set up a new LSR of 133.75mph (215.25kph) down the railway straight. This record remained for two years before being shattered at Arpajon in a celebrated duel between René Thomas and Ernest Eldridge.

René Thomas, who moved from Ballot to become Chef de Service Courses at Delage, had shown the paces of his sophisticated new V12 (virtually an oversize GP car) at the Gaillon hill-climb near Evreux and up the Route de Fernex during the Geneva Speed Trials. Eldridge, in contrast, had simply lengthened the chassis of Mephistopheles (Nazzaro's 1907 Fiat) and installed in it a 21,714cc 6 cylinder 24 valve Fiat aero engine that produced 300bhp. Brains and brute force met at the Moto Club de France's meeting held in July 1924 down the perilous

In March 1910, Barney Oldfield (top left) achieved a speed of 131.75mph (212.03kph) on the famous Blitzen Benz at Daytona. Malcolm Campbell (above) watches as Bill Perkins, his mechanic, makes final adjustments to the Sunbeam before the record attempt at

Pendine sands in Wales, September 1924. Car and driver were brought to the starting point on the wet sands (above left), which 'slashed up from the front wheels, obscuring my goggles and making vision difficult', as Campbell commented after his successful attempt.

In February 1927, Campbell (above) went again to Pendine sands to win back the speed record from Parry Thomas. Here, wet sands and all, Bluebird made it at 179.88mph (289.49kph). Bad weather conditions spoilt Parry Thomas' first attempt on the record with Babs, (above left), (note what the wet sand did to the tires), but in April 1926 he set up a new LSR of 171.02mph (275.23kph) in the Liberty aero-engined car. Segrave's 4 litre Sunbeam (left) thunders down the sands at Southport at 152.33mph (245.15kph) to beat Campbell's record for the first time.

tree-lined N20 at Arpajon between Paris and Orleans.

Thomas made the first attempt to clock a two-way mean of 143,31mph (230.63kph) and bring the LSR back to France for the first time in twenty years, only to have it snatched away again when Eldridge thundered through with Mephistopheles at 146.8mph (236.25kph). But Thomas spotted a technicality: Mephistopheles had no reverse gear. His protest was upheld and his opponent's attempt disallowed.

Faced with this quandary, Ernest Eldridge ingeniously jury-rigged a reverse gear by crossing the chains, and, snaking from side to side of the narrow road, retrieved the record for Britain (albeit with Italian machinery) at 146.01mph (235.12kph).

Watching these developments with a predatory gaze, to be sure, were the two men who were to turn the LSR into a world spectacle. For, even as British cars were being outclassed by Italian, French, and subsequently German machinery on the GP circuits,

Henry Segrave and Malcolm Campbell kept Britain the fastest on wheels; and the clash of their ambitions, together with the rivalry between John Cobb and George Eyston in the late thirties, is overwhelmingly the story of the world land speed record between the wars.

Captain Malcolm Campbell (an underwriting member of Lloyds who had served in the Royal Flying Corps and was one of the top figures at Brooklands) started by buying Kenelm Lee Guinness' 350 Sunbeam, which he re-named Bluebird, and – after two disappointing attempts at the Fanoe speed trials in Denmark – finally topped Eldridge's record by 0.15mph on Pendine Sands in Wales. Then, in March the following year, he raised this figure to 150.76mph (242.63kph). Describing the run he said,

> I had to brace myself in the seat all the time, to be sure that the throttle was held wide open. In fact the sensation of speed was more intense than anything I had ever known. The marking flags seemed to be rushing to meet me instead of, as at more moderate speeds, appearing to be approached by the car. The pressure on my eardrums was very heavy and the air felt solid, like water when one is coming to the surface after a dive. I was conscious of some bumps and little patches of soft sand occasionally checked the car slightly. When this happened the wet sand slashed up from the front wheels, obscuring my goggles and making vision difficult.

But, by now, the limitations of the gallant old aero-engined car were apparent and Campbell already had plans for building a land speed record car from scratch.

In the meantime, Major Henry O'Neale de Hane Segrave, the Baltimore-born son of an Anglo-Irish father and an American mother, who had earned Sunbeam's gratitude for his wins in the French and Spanish GPs, had a new baby from Wolverhampton to play with. Having a capacity of only 4 litres (made up of two obsolete GP engines mounted at 75 degrees on a common crankcase with a single

crankshaft and fitted with a Roots-type supercharger) the engine of this contender from Sunbeams was less than a quarter the size of Campbell's monster. Nevertheless, on the beach at Southport, Segrave registered 152.33mph (245.35kph) to snatch a new record before the blower exploded.

While both Campbell and Segrave were pondering their next moves, a new contender moved in. John Godfrey Parry Thomas, Chief Engineer of Leylands, had bought the Higham Special after Zborowsky's death, for £125. Re-naming the car 'Babs', he gingered up the 400hp Liberty aero engine, hid it under a streamlined white body, and took it off to Pendine where, no doubt to the surprise of all concerned, he beat Segrave's six-week-old record by nearly 20mph, notching up 171.02mph (275.23kph).

Segrave reacted immediately. 'I went to see Coatalen again and asked him if he thought it would be possible to build a machine which would attain a speed of 200mph (322kph) on land,' he recalls. At that time it was generally thought that the wind resistance could not be overcome over 180mph. 'Let's take a 1,000hp engine,' was Coatalen's riposte. But the trouble, of course, was to fit it into the chassis. And there was the tire problem, too.

The shrewd French engineer decided to use not one, but two, redundant 22.5 litre V12 wartime units, one at the front and the other at the back. Dunlops, for their part, got down to the job of designing the tires, finally guaranteeing $3\frac{1}{2}$ minutes' life at 200mph for each tire. Even on the test bed the 1,000hp Sunbeam was an awe-inspiring sight. 'When I stood in front of it I doubted human ability to control it,' Segrave confessed, and insisted that the twenty-three mile Daytona beach in Florida, with its ten mile dead straight, was the only possible place for his attempt.

But, meantime, after a full two years' work, Malcolm Campbell's splendid new Bluebird, with its 450bhp Napier Lion aero engine, was ready at last. Shortly before Segrave sailed for the States, Campbell rushed his light blue car to Pendine. The weather was bad, yet he was determined to seize the LSR honours before it was too late. Which indeed, wet sands and all, he did, shooting through the flying kilometre at only three fifths of a second

In 1928, after rebuilding Bluebird (top), Campbell recaptured the LSR at Daytona in February, only to see it broken two months later by Ray Keech in the Triplex Special. To wrest back the record, Bluebird was again rebuilt in 1929 with a new streamlined body, massive front wheels, and dual steering control (above). Bluebird makes an appearance in a parade of historic vehicles in London in November 1929 (right).

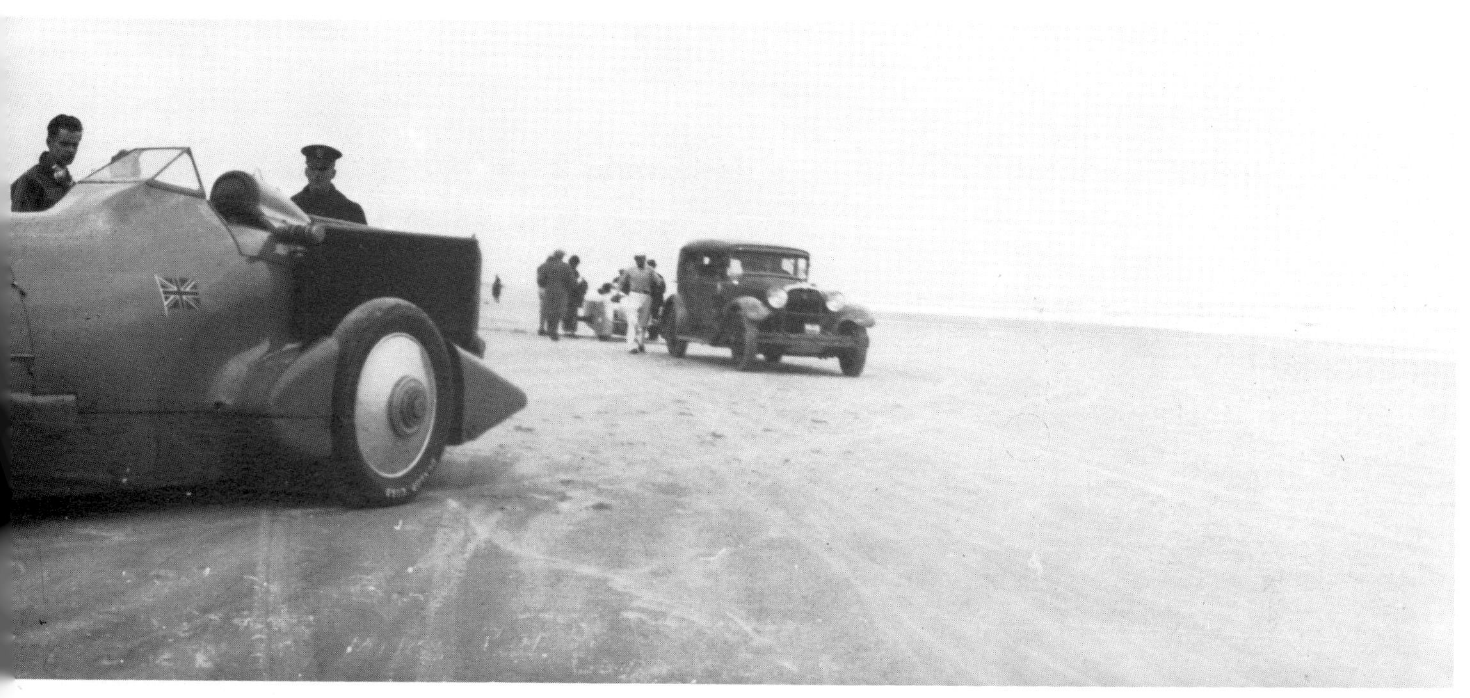

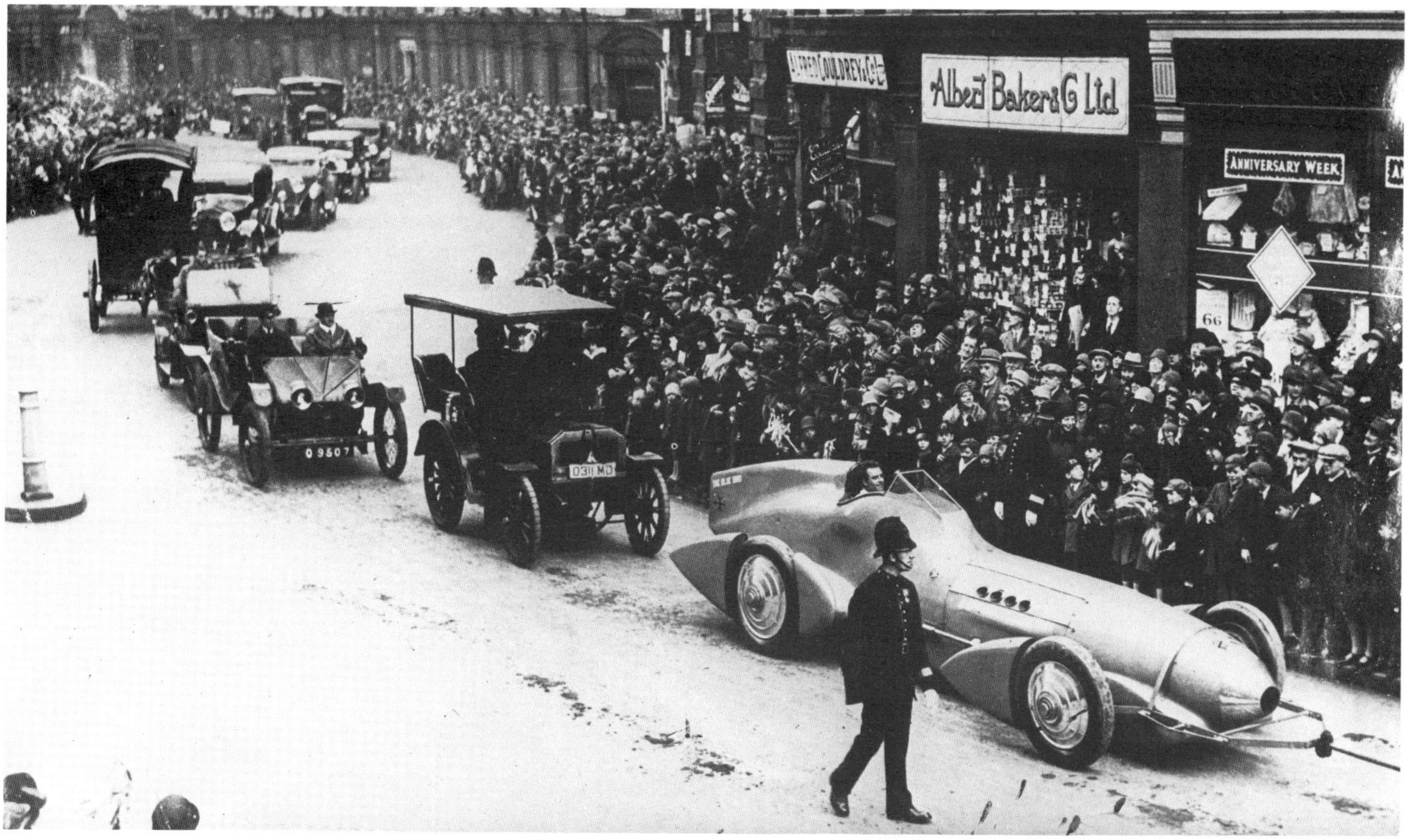
Albert Baker & Co Ltd
ANNIVERSARY WEEK

short of 180mph, to clock up 179.88mph (288.07kph).

Cogitating this new target aboard the *Berengaria* in mid-Atlantic, Segrave heard that Parry Thomas, returning to Pendine with Babs to retrieve his lost title, had overturned during the attempt and been decapitated on the spot. Such distressing news can hardly have contributed to his peace of mind, especially as the huge red Sunbeam had not yet run on its own wheels. Yet, on 29 March, in front of a vast crowd of spectators who had camped out all night, Segrave accelerated away like a bullet down the dry smooth beach at Daytona. Caught in a cross-wind, he skidded for some 400 yards and ended the run, amid a high spout of water, in the sea itself. Fortunately it was shallow, and after changing the tires, he was off on the return run, blasting up a curtain of sand behind him. But he made it. Bettering Campbell's speed by more than 28mph, he pushed the record up to 203.79mph (327.97kph).

'Damn good show', cabled his discomfited rival, who set about rebuilding Bluebird with a beefed-up Schneider Trophy Napier Lion engine that gave close on 900bhp. Meanwhile, other would-be 'record men' were entering the lists to challenge the British monopoly. Prince Djellal Eddin of Egypt's Djelmo was wrecked when it overturned at Pendine, luckily without injury to the driver, Giulio Foresti. And when Malcolm Campbell took his new-look Bluebird to Daytona for the Florida Speed Meet in February 1928, he found opposition in the shape of Ray

In 1930 Kaye Don took the 24 litre Sunbeam-built Silver bullet (above and right) to Daytona. But unfortunately the result was not as impressive as the car. Silver Bullet was sold, and Don turned to the water speed record for the rest of the season.

Keech's Triplex Special and Frank Lockhart's Stutz Black Hawk.

Surprisingly, for Florida, the weather was bad, and the first time out Campbell hit a bump that threw the car into the air for fully thirty feet, breaking all the shock absorbers and damaging the undershield. But on the next run, three days later, despite a terrifying skid, he put up a mean of 206.96mph (333.07kph).

Neither the fearsome Triplex, with its springless truck chassis and three Liberty engines, nor Frank Lockhart's elegant white Miller-engined Stutz Black Hawk, were able to match this speed: in fact Lockhart plunged into the sea on his first attempt and was lucky to be rescued from drowning by spectators. Yet, two months later, Ray Keech bettered Bluebird's time by under 1mph, to seize the record for America for the first time since 1906; while, sadly enough, young Lockhart, the immensely popular Indianapolis winner of 1926, crashed to his death when a tire burst and the Black Hawk somersaulted end over end at around 210mph (338kph).

But by now an astonishing machine was being produced to regain the title from across the Atlantic. Golden Arrow was powered by the same 24 litre 'broad-arrow' 12 cylinder 925hp Napier Lion engine as the Supermarine seaplanes. What's more, with its separately faired wheels and engine cowl fitting snugly round the three cylinder blocks, along with a vertical tail fin, it had a passing resemblance to the Schneider Trophy aircraft. To achieve a target speed of 240mph (386kph) the designer, Captain J. S. Irving, was determined to cut down wind resistance to an absolute

In March 1929 Henry Segrave regained the land speed record for Britain in the magnificent 930hp Napier-engined Golden Arrow (bottom right), raising it well beyond Sir Malcolm Campbell's reach with a speed of 231.45mph

However by constantly improving Bluebird, Campbell set up five consecutive land speed records between 1931 and 1935, finally achieving his goal of 300mph (483kph). Seen here are: a demonstration at Brooklands (above); a tire inspection (top right) after one lap on the concrete, and a diminutive Donald Campbell (above right) looking out from the cockpit of his father's car in 1933.

minimum.

Early in 1929, Segrave took Golden Arrow to Daytona. Like the vast crowd of spectators that thronged the dunes, he had to wait the better part of a fortnight for gales to subside. Finally, on 11 March, amid a welter of sand and spray, the great car shot down the beach, covering the measured mile in 15.55sec. Six minutes later, it thundered back again, just one fiftieth of a second slower. Golden Arrow had raised the land record to 231.45mph (373.38kph) and back in a jubilant Britain Henry Segrave was knighted for his achievement. From now onwards, he renounced cars for boats.

Not so Campbell. Encouraged by the South African government, he decided to try for the record on the dried-up lake of Verneuk Pan, 450 miles north of Cape Town. But after a frustrating month, he could only reach 217mph (349kph).

Clearly, Bluebird was no match for the Golden Arrow (any more than Kaye Don's vast 4,000hp Sunbeam Silver Bullet, which had turned out to be an expensive white elephant). Back in England, therefore, with the help of Reid Railton of Thomson and Taylor at Brooklands, Campbell had the car completely rebuilt with a supercharged Napier Lion racing engine. While the work was in progress, came the news that Sir Henry Segrave had lost his life while attempting the water speed record on Lake Windermere.

Nevertheless, on Thursday 5 February 1931, the re-vamped Bluebird was back at Daytona and, in barely five minutes for the whole performance, pushed the record up to 246.09mph (396.04kph) for the two-way average, which earned a knighthood for Campbell too.

Even so, Sir Malcolm was not satisfied, and in a new attempt in 1932, he topped the 250mph (400kph) mark with 253.97mph (408.72kph). It was now becoming almost an annual trek to Daytona. In 1933, with a 36.5 litre 2,300hp Rolls Royce V12 supercharged engine (similar to that which had won the Schneider Trophy in 1931) Bluebird again lifted the record to 272.46mph (438kph).

But Campbell's goal was 300mph (483kph). During 1934, Bluebird was rebuilt again. On the return to Florida in January 1935, she was 4mph faster than before, but the ridged surface of the beach was becoming hazardous at this speed, and caused wasteful wheelspin, too. It needed little persuasion from George Eyston and John Cobb (who had been at Bonneville setting up long-distance records) for Sir Malcolm to move to the immense salt flats in Utah. There, early in the morning of 3 September, he made his first attack. On the first dramatic run he was almost overcome by fumes, and a front tire burst, nearly causing the car to catch fire. But he clocked up 304.3mph. On the return, with his foot hard down, his instruments showed that he had peaked the 300 mark. So, when the official time of 299.87mph was announced, it came as an intense disappointment. But, fortunately, on recheck, the timekeepers discovered an error in their calculations. It was actually 301.13mph (484.62kph).

'When I have reached the 300mph mark, I shall leave the arena,' Campbell had vowed. He had now taken the land speed record no less than nine times. But if he hung up his motoring helmet at last, it was only – at the age of fifty – to start attacking the water speed record.

His place was taken by two brilliant new contenders. Captain George Eyston, who raced motorcycles under an assumed name while still at school (he was also an Olympic yachtsman), had already taken dozens of records at Brooklands, Montlhéry and Bonneville, in everything from an MG Midget to the 25 litre Speed of the Wind. It was logical, therefore, that he should try for the greatest prize of all.

The car that he took to the Utah salt flats in 1937 was a mammoth seven-ton monster with three axles, eight wheels and two supercharged Rolls Royce Schneider Trophy engines, with a staggering capacity of 73 litres. Although Thunderbolt was virtually untested, Eyston immediately topped 300mph, but clutch troubles intervened and he was content to push the record up to 312.00mph (502.12kph) in a two-way run, completed only minutes before the weather broke and snow began to fall. When he returned, it was to face a formidable adversary.

John Cobb, by profession a furbroker and a member of Lloyds, held almost as many records as Eyston, including the Brooklands outer circuit; and now to attack the absolute title, he commissioned Reid Railton (who had re-vamped Bluebird for Campbell) to produce a land speed record car from scratch. The result was a technically brilliant unconventional machine – since the Napier Lion engines driving all four wheels were located at different angles and the driver was placed right up in the streamlined nose – but a very elegant one, too, clothed in a smooth and completely detachable aluminium shell.

These two splendid cars met at Utah in the summer of 1938. Eyston went out first and bettered his own record by a sensational 33mph, to bring the LSR up to 345.5mph (554.42kph). The Railton, on its first outing, was just 3mph slower. Three days later, after some tweaking by its attendant designer, Cobb made another attempt. 'John's got it,' commented Eyston as the Railton flashed by. Which, at 350.20mph (563.59kph) he had.

But Thunderbolt had been subjected to some expert breathing on its machinery, too, and Eyston was out the following morning to cover the mile in only 10.1sec and snatch the record at 357.5mph (575.34). And that, for the moment, was that.

Nevertheless, Cobb had the last word. In August 1939 he was back at Utah, and a week before World War II, he rocketed down the sands at 369.70mph (591.76kph) to make, as a French magazine, *L'Auto*, called it, 'a last rare English gesture before the blackness of war fell upon the world'.

While Campbell, having reached his aim, turned to the water record, Captain George Eyston's giant 'Thunderbolt' (above and right) was being built behind the guarded doors of the Bean works at Tipton. Designed to travel at 350mph (563kph), Thunderbolt reached 312mph (502.12kph) on its first outing.

In a great duel with Eyston, John Cobb (below), in his Railton, took the record on 15 September 1938 at 350.2mph (563.59kph), and again on 23 August 1939 at 369.7mph (594.97).

Grand Prix Racing: the Magnificent Thirties

AFTER THREE YEARS of doldrums the *Grandes Epreuves* got off to a fresh start in the thirties as first the blue, then the red and latterly the silver cars thundered victoriously round the circuits, raising both dust and records. For while racing is an adventure that calls for courage and virtuosity, the impetus that nourishes this most dangerous of sports is more complex than simply the thrill of speed and of competing man against man. Just as the rivalry of individuals had soon given way to the struggle of manufacturers who used racing as a means to advertise the qualities of their cars, so commercial considerations were now swamped by political ambitions. Convinced that to win races was good for the image of a revitalized Italy, Mussolini gave all possible support to Alfa Romeo, which was indeed nationalized in 1933, and once the red cars began to dominate the circuits again and boost Italian prestige it was not long before the propaganda chiefs of Nazi Germany began to get into the act as well. On direct instructions from Hitler himself, no expense or effort was spared to put German cars on top and demonstrate the technical superiority of the Third Reich. The business of winning races was conducted like a military operation, and when the goal was achieved (with the help, be it said, of foreign drivers) it was trumpeted from the housetops by all conceivable means. Motor sport, in fact, became the space race of the totalitarian states – which made for good entertainment, if nothing else.

During the 1931 season Bugattis still had things all their own way. But the following year Alfa Romeo's P3 monoposto appeared. On its first outing, in the hands of Nuvolari, this classic 2,654cc 8 cylinder twin supercharged brainchild of Vittorio Jano won the Italian GP at Monza, and followed this up with a 1-2-3 victory in both the French and German Grands Prix. At the same time the 8C 2300 was fastest in sports car races, scoring at Le Mans, the Mille Miglia and the twenty-four hour race at Spa. For two seasons, in fact, Alfa Romeo won just about everything

Nuvolari (left) in a 3,000cc Maserati 8CM at Pescara in 1934.
In 1936 the 6 litre C Type 16 cylinder Auto Unions swept the board. Here they are at the start of the Italian GP at Monza (right), won by Rosemeyer. For 1937 Mercedes-Benz brought out the 5.7 litre W125 (below), the most powerful racing car yet built, with Manfred von Brauchitsch and Rudi Caracciola fighting nose-to-tail round Monaco highlighting a great racing period.

insight.

Then in 1934 the happy-go-lucky *formula libre* was replaced by a new regulation that allowed unlimited engine size but (in the hope of restraining top speeds) dictated a maximum weight of 750kg. At the same time, spurred on by a cash prize and other inducements from the German government, both Daimler-Benz and Auto Union (an amalgamation of Audi, DKW, Horch and Wanderer) produced sensational new cars.

Of the two, Auto Union's 16 cylinder rear-engined P-Wagen, designed by Dr Ferdinand Porsche, was the more remarkable, for although the engine-behind-driver layout is normal today, it caused a good deal of head-shaking forty years ago. The *Motor* thought it looked like 'an aeroplane fuselage on wheels, finished in frail aluminium covered with air-scoops and vents'. In contrast the Mercedes straight-eight W25 was more conventional, but likewise had independent suspension all round and a frightening scream from its blower.

These fearsome 'silver torpedoes' made their first appearance outside the Fatherland in the French Grand Prix held on the Montlhéry autodrome. But as the blue, scarlet and silver machines snaked round the circuit, passing and repassing in one of the most exciting and desperate races yet seen, Louis Chiron nevertheless held off the Teutonic attack. Try as they might, neither Caracciola's Mercedes nor Hans Stuck's Auto Union could throw off the flying Frenchman in his old style P3. One by one the Germans cracked up. And so, instead of being annihilated by Hitler's new juggernauts, the Alfa Romeo scored another grand slam victory.

All the same, the writing was clearly on the wall for the classical high-seated, cart-sprung machinery, beautiful though it was. Inevitably German science and money were reshaping the whole concept of a racing car. The Bugattis, Alfas and Maseratis that had dominated the circuits for over a decade were about to be relegated to back numbers. But before they bowed out, Nuvolari chalked up a final grandiose success for the P3 on the newcomer's home ground.

For the 1935 German Grand Prix at Nürburgring both Mercedes and Auto Union had signed up the top driving talent available. Caracciola, Fagioli, von Brauchitsch and Hermann Lang were at the wheel of the Mercedes; Achille Varzi, Hans Stuck, Bernd Rosemeyer and Paul Pietsch made up the Auto Union team. Competing against this phalanx of silver machinery were a trio of P3s driven by Nuvolari, Chiron and Brivio; two 2.9 litre Maseratis; a Type 59 Bugatti and a solitary ERA.

The starting positions were decided by ballot, and as Nuvolari, a slight figure in sky-blue trousers and a yellow sweat shirt, climbed into his scarlet Alfa Romeo in the fourth row he must have felt the weight of the odds against him. Yet when Caracciola shot off almost before the flag had fallen, Nuvolari swooped right round the outside of the squirming field, and at the end of the first lap as they came down the long undulating straight before the pits (where the Mercedes flashed past at 170mph (274kph), against the Alfa's 150) Nuvolari was only 12sec behind him. By the fifth lap both Chiron and Brivio were out with transmission troubles and Nuvolari was left alone to uphold the honour of Alfa Romeo and Italy.

Which, driving with an inspired and elemental genius, he did. Oversteering round each corner in a four wheel drift (a technique he is always credited with having invented) he snarled past Caracciola on the tenth lap, only to lose the lead through an agonisingly long fuel stop when the pumping device broke and the pit staff frenziedly sloshed the carburant in by hand. When he rejoined the race, it was in sixth position. But one by one the silver cars were picked off by Nuvolari to see the Alfa's red tail snake past and disappear round the corner ahead, until only Von Brauchitsch remained 69sec ahead. From the Mercedes pit Neubauer signalled frantically to the young Prussian to go faster. And indeed, rising to the occasion, he set up a new

Bernd Rosemeyer (above) with the Auto Union on the notorious 'Karussel' corner at Nürburgring in 1937, when winning the Eifelrennen for the second time. The Eifelrennen was always a lucky race for Rosemeyer: in 1935 he had come second to Caracciola in this event in only his second motor race. Kenneth Evan's 2.9 litre monoposto Alfa Romeo (right) pursued by a 750cc twin-camshaft Austin Seven on the sinuous Crystal Palace circuit in 1939.

lap record at 10min 30sec and at fourteen laps had increased his lead to 86sec. But for all this he was no match for the flying Mantuan on the peak of his form. Lap by lap Nuvolari reduced his lead – to 63sec, then 47, then 43, then 32. As they went past the pits into the final twenty-two kilometres, Brauchitsch pointed frantically at his near side rear tire. Coming out of a corner nine kilometres from the end, it collapsed, just as Nuvolari's P3 shot through to what the world's press hailed as 'a historic triumph of man over machine'.

With an obsolescent car that was fully twenty miles per hour slower than his adversaries the Italian maestro had annihilated both German teams in front of a quarter of a million of their compatriots. Yet, even if it was probably Nuvolari's finest achievement, it was nevertheless a swan-song. Mercedes won practically every other major event in 1935, and although Alfas produced a new streamlined V12 (with which Nuvolari pulled off a few more surprises in Hungary and Spain) there was little the red cars could do to dent the Teutonic onslaught. The German technological muscle was too strong: too much money was being lavished on the engineering departments of Stuttgart and Chemnitz. During 1936 Bernd Rosemeyer swept all before him in the C Type Auto Union (whose V16 engine had now been enlarged to 6.1 litres and developed 520bhp), winning the Eifel, German, Pescara and Italian GPs to gain the European Championship; and Varzi rounded off a stupendous year for Auto Union by collecting the honours at Tripoli on Italian colonial soil.

Mercedes, who had themselves been somewhat overshadowed by all this, responded with the most powerful racing car ever built: the amazing W125, which had a twin-tube frame, a De Dion rear axle incorporating a four speed gearbox, a 5.7 litre engine that gave no less than 646bhp at 5,800rpm, and a road speed of 185mph. Laurence Pomeroy called 1937 the 'year of the Titans' because of such 'incredibly high performance factors' and the spectacle of Caracciola, Lang, von Brauchitsch and Dick Seaman (a new recruit to Mercedes) duelling around the circuits against Rosemeyer, Fagioli and Stuck must certainly have been one of the all-time greats in motor sport. Old timers still recall with awe the British Grand Prix at Donington Park when a crowd of 50,000 saw the Germans in action, hurtling down the narrow bumpy straight at 170mph with Rosemeyer taking the flag ahead of von Brauchitsch and Caracciola.

Unfortunately (Rodney Walkerley tells me), someone sat on the record of the German national anthem at the finish of it, which caused musical silence and very nearly a diplomatic incident. Luckily this was smoothed over at the after-race dinner by Lord Howe (when the anthem was duly played) and also by the sporting gesture of the Derby Club in paying out winnings due to the Germans by bookmakers who had welshed. Some of them, it seems, in insular ignorance (or patriotic fervour) had been offering odds of six to one or thereabouts against Rosemeyer and company. These were naturally enough snapped up by their team members, who were surprised in the closing stages of the race to spot six of the eight bookies half a mile off, going well and making for sundry gaps in the outer defences.

For 1938–40 the GP formula was based on a sliding scale of weight according to capacity which in effect limited engine size to three litres. Both Mercedes and Auto Union resorted to 3 litre V12 engines, but even so they were getting over 400bhp at greatly increased revs (the Auto Union's three camshaft unit now peaked at 7,000rpm) and so, astonishingly enough, although engines were only half their former size, speeds scarcely diminished – in fact Lang won the Belgian Grand Prix in 1939 at a slightly faster average than he had in 1937.

Against this, Rosemeyer's tragic death during a record attempt on the Frankfurt–Darmstadt *Autobahn* in January 1938 was a serious blow to Auto Union, and although Nuvolari (having left Alfas in a bad temper,

Nuvolari sliding the 3 litre 12 cylinder Auto Union at Nürburgring during the 1939 Eifelrennen. He was credited with inventing the technique of cornering in a four-wheel drift with little or no braking, ending up with a perfect straight-line exit.

it is said) allowed himself to be parleyed into the Auto Union team, it took him a little time to get the hang of the rear-engined cars. At the end of the season he won both the Italian GP and Donington with the D Type Auto Union, but apart from this it was a Mercedes year. True, they had a shock at the start of the season at Pau, when in a round-the-houses race in a snowstorm René Dreyfus' 12 cylinder Delahaye got the better of Caracciola and Lang's W154, but after this Mercedes had 1-2-3 wins in the French and Swiss GPs, and R. J. B. Seaman, the first British driver to do so, won the German GP for Mercedes ahead of Caracciola and Lang, who respectively won the Coppa Acerba and the Coppa Ciano. In 1939, too, which started tragically with the death of Dick Seaman when leading on a wet track at Spa, the silver projectiles from Stuttgart were virtually all-conquering, capturing every title except the French Grand Prix (which went to Muller's Auto Union). And finally, three days after Hitler's less attractive projectiles invaded Poland and the afternoon that Neville Chamberlain declared war on Germany, Tazio Nuvolari slipped past von Brauchitsch in the streets of Belgrade to win the last Grand Prix in Europe and bring the age of the Titans to a close.

The Post-War Scene

HARDLY WERE THE GUNS silenced than racing recommenced in Europe, and within four months of VE day a meeting was held in the Bois de Boulogne to celebrate the mother city of motoring's liberation – which to the delight of the Parisians was won by Jeanne-Pierre Wimille on a 1939 4.7 litre Bugatti. Pre-war machinery that had eluded the Gestapo was brushed and combed, and despite a chronic shortage of fuel and tires some thirty races were run on the Continent under 'formula libre' conditions during 1946. Seven Alfa Romeo 158s and two 512s (which had been bricked up in a dairy farm at Melzo) won three of the major events, thus re-establishing the Alfa supremacy which was to last until their retirement from racing in 1951.

Once racing got into its stride again, the FIA (which now replaced the AIACR) produced a new formula. So overwhelming had the German domination of Grand Prix events been in the years before the war that both the French and Italian National Clubs had tended, in self defence, to de-rate their top events: the French ran them as sports car races and the Italians concentrated on the 1.5 litre voiturette formula. There were some potent 4.5 litre sports racing cars – such as the Delahaye and the Talbot – available in France whereas Alfa Romeo and Maserati had their new left-over voiturettes, as indeed did ERA and Alta in England. The 1.5 litre supercharged or 4.5 litre unsupercharged formula, with no weight or body size restrictions, was thus to everyone's taste when introduced in 1947.

All the same the opposition to the 158s was sufficiently slight for the Alfettas ('nice little Alfas' – a name resuscitated for the spunky little saloon that is currently being produced) to win just about every race that they entered for the next five years. Wimille, Varzi, Count Trossi and the works tester Consalvo Sanesi notched up a procession of grand slam wins in the Swiss, Belgian and Italian GPs of 1947 and again at Rheims and Monza in 1948, and only when the Alfa Romeos didn't appear – they were not raced in 1949 after

With the return of racing to France after the war, the Grand Prix de Rheims was held in July 1947, supplemented by another race for 1,100cc 'Petite Cylindrée' cars. This was won by 'Bira' (Prince Birabongse of Thailand) in a Simca-Gordini. In 1948 the French Grand Prix was once again held on the famous Rheims circuit.

the deaths of Wimille and Trossi – were the honours shared by Maserati, who had produced a new tubular-chassis version of their pre-war 4CLs (known as the San Remo after its first-time-out victory in the hands of Ascari), along with Chiron and Rosier's 4,482cc Lago-Talbots and a new contender called Ferrari.

Of all post-war developments, the emergence of a new marque under the insignia of the prancing horse was perhaps the most significant. Enzo Ferrari, who had directed Alfa Romeo's racing affairs for so long, began building cars in his own right at Modena in 1939. Like so many other fledgling Italian constructors, he used Fiat *millecento* parts, coupling and reducing two of these 1,100 engines to give 72bhp at 5,500rpm, and mounting them in tandem in a Fiat chassis clothed with a body by Touring. This was ingenious if hardly earth-shaking. But immediately after the war Gioacchino Colombo joined him from Alfa Romeo to design a V12 1.5 litre sports racing car that soon began to make its mark in Italian events. Biondetti, for instance, won the 1948 Targa Florio and the Mille Miglia, and then in 1949 Chinetti and Lord Selsdon chalked up Ferrari's first victory at Le Mans. But GP racing had always been nearest to Enzo Ferrari's heart and a *monoposto* with the same power unit was concurrently developed. This was competitive in races not contested by Alfa Romeo, Ascari winning the Swiss and Italian GPs in 1949, and Villcresi at Zandvoort. In due course Ferrari became convinced, quite rightly no doubt, that to beat the Alfas he must switch to a large unblown engine. Replacing Colombo by Aurelio Lampredi, he pushed ahead with an unsupercharged V12, first as a 3.3 and then as a 4.5 litre unit. At the British GP at Silverstone in 1951 Ferraris saw the Alfas off for the first time in a straight fight, from which moment onwards they were indisputably the top racing marque.

Meanwhile in England Raymond Mays and Peter Berthon, who had produced ERAs before the war, began work at Bourne on an ambitious project sponsored by the British motor industry as a whole. But unhappily the BRM, with its incredibly complex V16 centrifugally supercharged 1,496cc engine, was plagued with an unending series of problems. In fact the British Motor Racing Trust became so disillusioned with its bog-slogging progress that it sold out in 1952 to Sir Alfred Owen, whose Job-like patience was at last rewarded nine years later when Graham Hill became world champion in a BRM.

Of more immediate impact, to be sure, were the efforts of a small garage in Surbiton, where Charles Cooper (who had been mechanic and manager to Kaye Don before the war) began building 500s, 500cc racers that soon started re-shaping the sporting landscape. For one thing, having welded together two Fiat Topolino front ends, he put the driver in front and the engine behind – a layout that Rumpler had introduced in 1923 and Ferdinand Porsche had so convincingly developed for Auto Union. For another, he fitted his *Tropfenwagen* with a cheap speedway type JAP motorcycle engine. Coming at a time when cars were at a premium and beyond the reach of most young enthusiasts these economy racers were an instant success. More than all else they led to the extraordinary development of Formula 3, from which cut-and-thrust school graduated so many of the British drivers such as Stirling Moss, Peter Collins, Stewart Lewis Evans and Bob Gerard, who subsequently were to dominate the Grand Prix and sports-racing scene – just as the highly sophisticated Coventry-Climax engined Coopers were to win their laurels in Formula 1 and 2 and win the Manufacturers' Championship a decade later. Petrol may have been rationed to a few gallons a month in Welfare-State Britain, but nothing could contain the bounce and sparkle of the Formula 3 boom.

Among the entrants for the Prescott Hill Climb in May 1948, as it happens, was a cream Mark 2 Cooper with an eighteen-year-old driver at the wheel. On his first competi-

George Murray Frame won a Coupe des Alpes in the 1948 Alpine Rally with a 2 litre Sunbeam-Talbot saloon. He is seen here negotiating a hairpin on the St Gotthard Pass. Two years later the *Coupe des Alpes en Or* (Golden Alpine Cup) was instituted for those who had won two Coupes des Alpes in succession.

tive appearance, Stirling Moss put up a new class record of 50.01sec for the 880yd (805m) ascent. Since the fastest run in 1938 had been 50.70sec by Arthur Baron in a Type 51 Bugatti it was a good indication of what was to come from these diminutive machines in the hands of a new generation. Indeed that season Stirling scored ten class wins in sundry hill-climbs and races with the JAP engined Cooper, and in 1949 he walked off with the 500cc race at Zandvoort. Peter Collins, likewise, was only seventeen when he made his debut with a 500cc Cooper-Norton in 1949, notching up victories at both Goodwood and Silverstone.

With both Brooklands and Donington Park (which had been requisitioned by the Army) lost to racing, the RAC thought of turning disused airfields into new circuits. To avoid the complaints about noise that had bedevilled Brooklands, they chose an isolated aerodrome near Silverstone village in Northamptonshire, laying out a 3.67 mile circuit that used both main runways and sections of the perimeter road. Here the first post-war British Grand Prix was held in 1948. Three months later, the British Automobile Racing Club took over the Westhampnelt fighter base on the Duke of Richmond's estate at Goodwood and laid out a circuit round the perimeter track. Brands Hatch, in contrast, had been a motorcycle cinder track between the wars. Re-surfaced in 1949, it immediately became the focal point of Formula 3 activities. Subsequently Snetterton, Mallory Park, Thruxton, Castle Coombe, Oulton Park and Aintree were opened. By this time some 10,000 enthusiasts in Britain alone held competition licences.

Nor was the boom confined to racing as such. The Alpine Rally, revived in 1947 as a local event in the French Alps, had already regained its international character by 1949 and involved a hectic dice through five countries. The Monte Carlo Rally, too, was resurrected that year (without its more exotic starting points in Eastern Europe, now victims of the Cold War) and despite the problems of visas and carnets nonetheless attracted over twice as many entries as in the old days (308 in 1950 against 143 in 1938). The Lyons–Charbonnières Rally was first held in 1949, as was likewise the Evian–Mont Blanc; and the classic Liège–Rome–Liège (a non-stop race of some 2,800 miles, or 4,500km, from Liège through Germany, the Brenner and the Apennines to Rome and back via the French Alps) that had first been held in 1931 was back on the calendar in 1950. As before, it was a real car-breaker, the Belgian Club's ideal being to toughen it up each year to the point where there was only one finisher. In a friendlier vein, since it required no great feats of endurance to qualify as a finisher, the newly established Dutch Tulip Rally interspersed a scenic road section with split-second hill-climbs as an excuse for some rousing, dinner-jacketed Dutch merriment at the end; while the lengthy 'Tour de France Automobile', inaugurated in 1951, featured tests on many of the famous French circuits and hill-climbs. (In due course someone dreamed up a Rallye Gastronomique in France, though not strictly speaking within the context of motor sport.)

The Scandinavians, too, were soon in the act. Finland called her regularity trial the 'Rally of the Thousand Lakes'; the KNAK's 'Viking' Rally was a sensational dice round the loose gravelly tracks of central Norway in which local knowledge and a sense of humour were essential attributes for success. (Even Finn Sohol, who achieved distinction both as Norway's tennis champion and rally driver, found the going pretty rugged.) All the same, lashings of smoked salmon and schnapps along with the legendary Norwegian hospitality proved a consolation for foreign entrants who had experienced expensive retirements. Sweden's offering, the 'Rally of the Midnight Sun', held some advantage for home teams who could guess what the normally secret route would be and practise accordingly. But for visiting drivers, astonished to find the sun shining brightly at midnight as at midday up in the Arctic Circle, it was a splendid introduction to the elegance and efficiency of their Nordic hosts.

Each of these rallies had its own special flavour and its own devotees. Year after year, for instance, the old Alpine Rally hands snarled into Marseilles at the beginning of July with beautifully prepared cars, parked in the shady Cours Pierre Puget, and swapped jokes at the bar of the Automobile Club de Marseilles et Provence. After collecting their documents and rally plates, and enjoying a ritual feast of bouillabaisse in the Vieux Port, most of them escaped the heat of Marseilles for some sun and fun (and last-minute marking of maps) along the coast at Bandol or La Ciotat before scrutinizing and the inevitable *vin d'honneur* at the Mairie. The start usually took place in the evening, Mille Miglia style, from an arc-lit ramp in the middle of the Vieux Port. Amidst much clapping and popping of flashbulbs, competitors accelerated off at two-minute intervals through narrow walls of human flesh to hassle with the city traffic and heavy lorries before tackling the first special stage hill-climb up the famous Mont Ventoux beyond Carpentras and Bédoin. The heat was on right from the beginning and for the rest of the night and most of the next day they had to corkscrew at full chat, up and down as many of the French Alpine Cols as the organizers could dream up before skidding exhaustedly into Monte Carlo for the first rest halt, by which time the weaker brethren had begun to fall by the wayside and quite a few cars had a scrap-heap look. For the next stage, the rally veered off into Italy to join up with the Coppa d'Oro delle Dolomiti race and a quick belt round Monza followed by timed dashes up the Stelvio and the wickedly dangerous Vivione and Gavia passes with a thousand feet unguarded drop on one side of the narrow gravel track and jutting-out rocks on the other.

Tough on the nerves? Well, yes. Especially as cloud usually intruded and brake linings had by now worn thin. But against all this there was the marvellous detached yet corporate sensation of twisting and turning

Start of the Grand Prix de Lausanne (right) in October 1947, with the supercharged 1.5 litre 4CL Maseratis of Sommer (No 2) and Villoresi (No 4) taking the lead from Wimille (Simca No 14) and Chiron (Talbot No 10). Villoresi was the winner.

After a spell of racing Bianchi motor cycles, Alberto Ascari (below right), son of the famous Antonio Ascari, came second to Cortese in the Cisitalia race round Gezira Island in Cairo in 1947, and was invited to join the Scuderia Ambrosiana, who were racing works Maseratis. He came second to Villoresi in the British Grand Prix of 1948, where he is seen at the pits with a 4CLT/48 Maserati.

Count 'Didi' Trossi (far right) refuelling his 158 Alfa Romeo at Monza in 1948, where he came second to Wimille in the Italian Grand Prix. In the immediate post-war years, Alfas were virtually unbeatable.

through some of the loveliest scenery in Europe. When dawn came up over the Alps it was like being born afresh.

If the Alpine had its heroes, they were still amateurs who drove for the fun of it and not for the money, relishing the danger and also the blessed relaxation of a bath and the hilarious swapping of news at the rest halts in Cortina D'Ampezzo, St Moritz or Chamonix. True, manufacturers were beginning to realize the public value of a good win, and whether factories like Rootes gained their cachet from the Alpine or the other way round is pleasantly debatable. Certainly, the presence of Stirling Moss, Peter Collins and Mike Hawthorn in the sleek pastel-green works Sunbeam Talbots greatly added to the zest; and, factory sponsored or not, Ian and Pat Appleyard's familiar white XK Jaguar, NUB 120 (now at the Montagu Museum) more than deserved to win the first Alpine Gold Cup in history in 1952 after finishing 'clean' for three successive years, which was one for the book, to be sure.

Over in the United States, of course, motor sport still meant Indianapolis. Back in 1936 the Vanderbilt Cup had been resuscitated for a 300 mile race at the Roosevelt Raceway, New York. But although it had been something of an all star affair headed by Nuvolari's 12 cylinder Alfa Romeo, and the following year the German Mercedes and Auto Union teams had come over complete with Caracciola, Seaman and Rosemeyer (who won), public interest had nevertheless been lukewarm. Oval track racing was more to the American taste at that time. For all this, post-World War II brought with it the revival of racing amongst a small group of enthusiasts, most of them former members of the Automobile Racing Club of America, who started the Sports Car Club of America. While the SCCA's original aim had been to collect and restore vintage cars it soon became the spearhead of road racing in the States. Men like Briggs Cunningham, the Collier brothers, Charles Moran, George Rand and their friends raced an assortment of specials over country lanes and in private estates on the East Coast, and in 1948 Cameron Argetsinger, while still at Cornell University, talked the local authorities of Watkins Glen into holding a European style event at this little resort on Lake Seneca. Run over a 6.6 mile circuit of village streets and unpaved country roads, the inaugural Watkins Glen was won by Frank Griswold in an 8C2900 Alfa Romeo (similar to my Cairo one, though with a coupé body) ahead of Briggs Cunningham in a Buick-Mercedes Special. A supercharged MG TC took third place. In the 1950 Watkins Glen GP Sam Collier, driving a Cunningham-owned Ferrari (one of the first barquettas to reach the US), crashed fatally while in the lead, and the following year Miles Collier died too. Lack of crowd control in the village was becoming dangerous and the venue was moved to a 4.6 mile circuit above the town and subsequently to the present 2.3 mile closed course where the SCCA 'nationals' were held in the late fifties and the US Grand Prix in 1961.

It was after acting as a steward at these early races and manager for Briggs Cunningham's team at Le Mans in 1950, that Alec Ulmann conceived the notion of holding a Le Mans type endurance race, albeit on a smaller scale, in the States. Charles Faroux (the great French journalist and organizer) had expounded the virtues of a David versus Goliath battle between the small and big cars put on an equal footing by some form of handicap. (Le Mans had the Index of Performance Cup as well as the out-and-out winner.) Ulmann seized on the idea, therefore, of a purely handicap race. A survey of the Hendrick B17 bomber airfield near Sebring in Florida disclosed, he felt, the type of geography that with goodwill and a pinch of salt could simulate the Mulsanne and Arnage corners and Hinaudières straight of Le Mans. And so it was that, organized by a small group of SCCA enthusiasts and sponsored by the Sebring Fireman's Association, the first race took place at Sebring on 31 December 1950. Twenty-eight cars, ranging from a

This painting by Roy Nockolds of the author's special MG TD Mk 2 on the Gavia pass in Italy gives the atmosphere of the International Alpine Rally in its great days after World War II.

Ferrari Berlinetta and a 4,422cc Cadillac-Allard down to a curious little contraption called a Crosley, lined up for a Le Mans type start – and six hours later, to everyone's surprise, the diminutive 724cc Crosley emerged gamely as winner on handicap. In March 1952 Sebring grew to a fully fledged twelve hour 'Noon to Midnight' event, and America had rejoined the mainstream of international racing.

The Romantic Fifties

An uncharacteristic picture of Fangio (left) pushing a recalcitrant Simca-Gordini in the 1949 GP du Bois de Boulogne.
The last of the bucaneers (below)—Mike Hawthorn.

WITH THE MID-CENTURY, racing entered its last great romantic decade. Professionalism was growing, of course, but competitive motoring remained a sport rather than purely show-business, and many of its devotees raced more for pleasure than for money. The shadow of Madison Avenue was still only a cloud on the horizon, bigger perhaps than a man's hand, but by no means all enveloping. If subsidies were given, they were at least offered by people concerned with the sport, such as oil companies, or tire and component manufacturers. It was the age of Fangio, Ascari and Gonzalez; of Briggs Cunningham and Ecurie Ecosse; of an exciting new generation of British drivers such as Stirling Moss, Mike Hawthorn and Peter Collins. It was a spectacular period and above all it was fun.

To start off with, the World Championship for drivers and constructors came into being in 1950. Alfa Romeo returned to the fray after a year of absence and immediately scooped it up, Farina, Fangio and Fagioli (the famous three 'Fs') winning eleven Grandes Epreuves in a row. Dr 'Nino' Farina, whose father had helped found the Pininfarina

Juan Manuel Fangio and Peter Collins (above) at Silverstone during the 1956 British Grand Prix.
'Nino' Farina (right) leaves the pits in the Alfa Romeo during practice for the Italian Grand Prix in 1951.

Coachworks, and who epitomized the sportsman-driver of the period (surviving untold accidents in his sixteen years of racing) became the first world champion. But for all this the 1.5 litre supercharged Alfas were a pre-war design and Ferrari was making enormous strides with his 4.5 litre unblown cars. In 1951 Alfa Romeo won four of the major races to Ferrari's three, and Fangio took his first world championship title. But Ascari was only a few points behind, and at the British Grand Prix at Silverstone Froilan Gonzalez shattered the long string of Alfa Romeo victories. The first German post-war GP at Nürburgring was equally disappointing for them, since Ascari beat Fangio by half a minute, and when Ferrari took the first two places in the Italian Grand Prix at Monza the lesson was clear. Although Alfa Romeo had won the championship again, the 159 'Maggiorata' in its final 200mph (322kph) form was at the end of its useful life. It could not be breathed on any more, and since the cost of developing a new engine for the remaining two seasons of the 1.5/4.5 litre formula, due to expire in 1953, was prohibitive, Alfa Romeo beat a dignified retreat.

Their retirement, along with the non-appearance of the BRM, took the steam out of Formula 1. Organizers, only too aware that a series of Ferrari walk-overs would hardly draw in the crowds, preferred to apply the Formula 2 rules, which specified a maximum capacity of 2 litres unsupercharged, or 500cc supercharged (though the latter was impracticable). Here at least there was some competition. Reflecting the upsurge of interest in racing in England, a number of British cars appeared on the starting grids. But although the HWMs, Connaughts and British-engined Coopers, as well as the Gordinis and even Maseratis, were outclassed by the Type 500 Ferrari, with which Alberto Ascari won almost everything in sight both in 1952 and 1953 – taking in his stride a double world championship – they did at least give drivers like Bira (Prince Birabongse of Thailand, who drove a Gordini), Lance Macklin and Peter Collins (on HWMs) and of course Stirling Moss (Cooper-Alta) and Mike Hawthorn (Cooper-Bristol) the chance to show their paces. So impressive in fact were Hawthorn's performances both at home and abroad on the Cooper that Ferrari offered him a works drive for 1953.

At the French Grand Prix at Rheims the blond Englishman justified their choice. In front of a frenzied crowd he battled wheel to wheel with Fangio's Maserati. 'Lap after lap, I couldn't shake him off in spite of every trick in the trade', Fangio recalled in his autobiography. 'We were still side by side, scarcely more than a yard apart.' On the final lap the two red cars passed the pits almost level, and finally, coming up to Thillois for the last time, Hawthorn delayed his braking so long that Fangio thought he would run out of road. But somehow he flipped round and beat Fangio on acceleration up the straight to win the Grand Prix de l'ACF by a second, with Gonzalez's Maserati in third place only four-tenths of a second behind his team-mate. 'England has a new and worthy champion,' commented Fangio afterwards.

In other directions, too, the Anglo Saxons were giving their continental counterparts some food for thought. In 1951 Peter Whitehead and Peter Walker drove the C Type to the first of Jaguar's five victories at Le Mans, and in addition Jaguars had a triumphant rally season with outright victories in the Rally Soleil, the Tulip, the Morecambe, the Scottish, the Liège–Rome–Liège, and the Alpine. The following season Stirling Moss won the twelve hour sports car race at Rheims in a C Type at 98.2mph (158.04kph), and Sidney Allard scored the first British victory for twenty-one years in the Monte Carlo Rally in a car of his own make, just ahead of Moss's Sunbeam Talbot. In the same year Peter Collins and Pat Griffiths drove a DB2S Aston Martin to victory in the Nine Hours race at Goodwood, while 1953 saw the struggle between Jaguar and Cunningham at Le Mans.

Briggs Cunningham had put in his first

Ascari leads his Ferrari team-mates Villoresi and Farina in the 1953 Dutch Grand Prix.

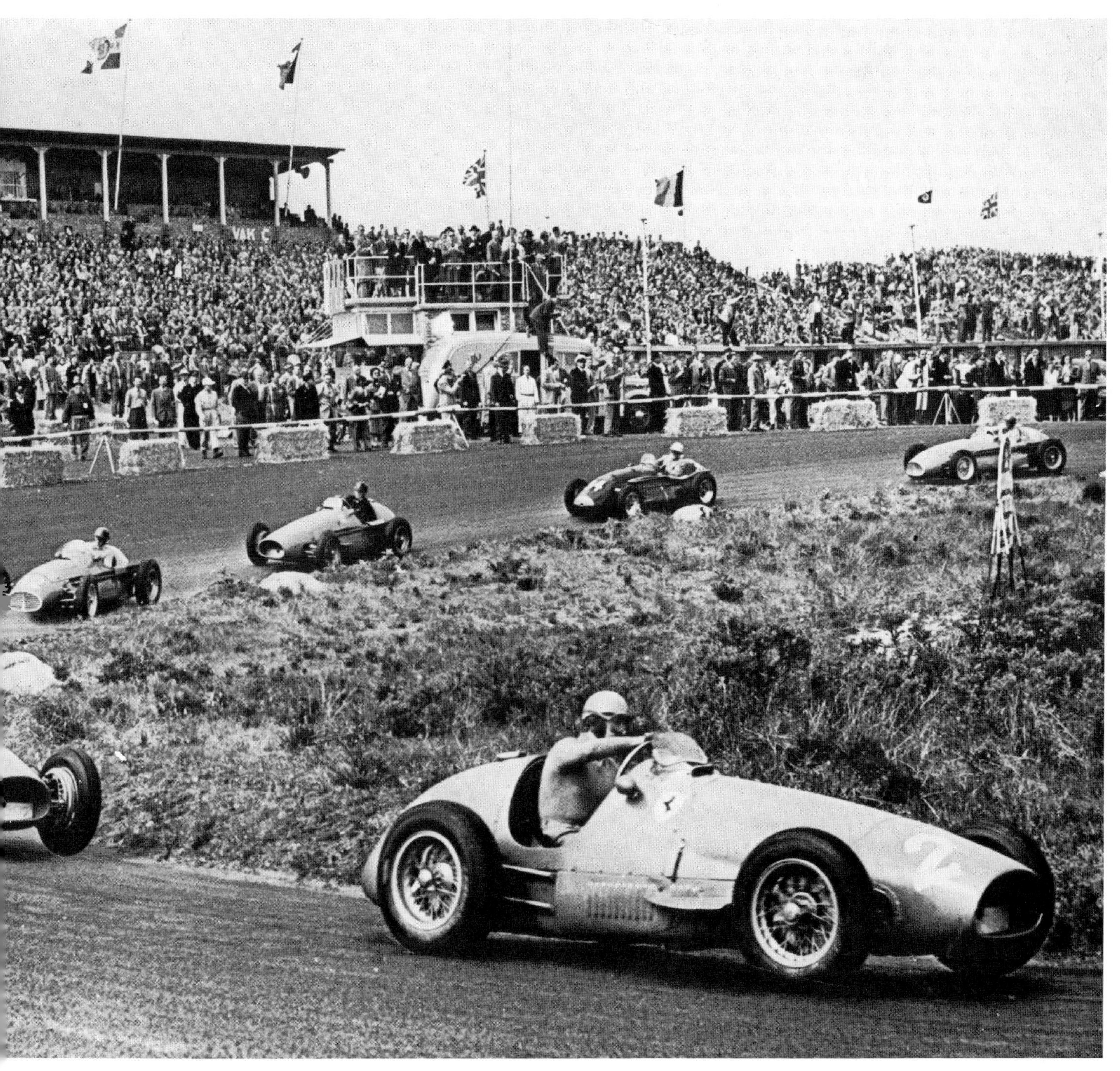

appearance there in 1950 with a Cadillac Special that the French called 'Le Monstre', taking eleventh place with Phil Walters. The following year he had returned with two Chrysler-engined sports cars of his own construction. Together with Bill Spear he drove one of them into fourth place in 1952, and in 1953 the heat was really on between the wealthy American driver-patron and the Coventry factory. For most of the twenty-four hours it was neck and neck until finally Tony Rolt and Duncan Hamilton's Jaguar took the flag ahead of their team-mates Moss and Walker at an average speed of 105.85mph (170.35kph) with Walters and Fitch's blue and white Cunningham in third place at 104.04mph (167.42kph), Briggs Cunningham himself coming seventh. Sadly, the coveted title eluded him, for in 1954 Bill Spear and Sherwood Johnson could only manage to bring their C-4R Cunningham home third behind Gonzalez and Trintignant's Ferrari and the Rolt-Hamilton D type, with Briggs and John Bennett behind them in fifth place. Still, for these privately built cars from Palm Beach, Florida, it was a noteworthy effort. When the factory D Types won again in 1955 (the year of the Levegh tragedy) and Ecurie Ecosse scored Jaguar's fourth victory in 1956 and went on to achieve a 1-2-3-4-6 procession in 1957, the great endurance race seemed once more to have become virtually a British benefit – especially as David Brown's Aston Martins were always nudging up behind, taking second place in 1955 and 1956, and finally pulling it off at an average of 112.5mph (181kph) in 1959.

While the Italians monopolized formula racing, British sports cars were sweeping the board. Moss twice won the Tourist Trophy at Dundrod in a Jaguar, and Collins and Griffiths drove an Aston Martin to victory there in 1953, with an MG clinching the production car award. On top of this Moss won the twelve hour sports car race at Rheims in a C Type Jaguar, and in 1954 Peter Whitehead and Ken Wharton headed a grand slam victory for the new D Types in the same French classic.

At which point Mercedes-Benz reappeared on the scene. Stuttgart had been bombed to bits during the war, and although production of bread-and-butter cars recommenced, Herr Neubauer bided his time in a sparsely furnished office recovering pre-war racers for the Mercedes Museum, and the great days of German glory seemed to have passed. Then the legendary 300 SL 'gull-wing' Coupé made its bow, notching up successes at Le Mans, Nürburgring, Berne, the Carrera Panamericana and not quite in the Mille Miglia. Finally in 1954, when the new 2.5 formula came into effect, the greatest of German manufacturers chose the senior race on the calendar to contest their first post-war *Grande Epreuve*, just as at twenty year intervals they had done in 1914 and 1934.

Rheims has an atmosphere entirely of its own. For one thing, it is the centre of the champagne industry. For another, the triangular five mile circuit is one of the fastest on the Continent, with two tight hairpins, a flat-out right hander after the pits and a sensational ski-schuss-like straight down the narrow Soissons road to Thillois, known as 'the best view in Europe'. What's more, the twelve hour sports car race preceding the Grand Prix begins at midnight: 'It is the only race I know that starts in the dark and is quite the most electrifying start I think I've ever taken part in, or ever seen,' Graham Hill declares in his autobiography, reckoning that it was run from start to finish like a two hour Grand Prix. In fact it was the equivalent of six Grand Prix on a high speed circuit where the engine goes full bore for a longer period than anywhere except Le Mans. One had 'an almighty thrash in the dark with speeds of up to 180mph on this very narrow road. One moment we would be bursting into the brightly lit pit area and then rushing out into the darkness.' Over the brow of the hill came the fast right hander, almost flat out in the dark. 'We were just lifting a fraction and the car was getting into a great hairy old drift . . . It was really an

The scene of the Levegh tragedy (above), one of the worst in the history of motor racing, at Le Mans in 1955. Levegh's 300SLR Mercedes hit an Austin Healey and veered off into the crowd opposite the pits, killing Levegh and over eighty people. Right: Mike Hawthorn (D Type Jaguar) leads Stirling Moss (Mercedes) through the Esses in the early stages of the ill-fated 24 Hours of Le Mans, 1955.

exciting fight and the motor racing par excellence. It was also pretty hair-raising.'

Graham Hill was writing about his drive in a Ferrari ten years later, but the description holds good for any of the series. After all, the D Types with their 2.53 : 1 back end could reach nearly 200mph (322kph) (they whipped past my 356 Porsche as if I were tied to a post). Spectators were up all night and Jaguar's marathon performance in the twelve hour curtain-raiser almost scooped the Grand Prix that followed. But for Mercedes, it would have done, too.

When their silver W196s were unveiled in the paddock they caused a sensation. The straight-eight fuel-injected engines were laid almost horizontally in space-frames which were clothed in all-enveloping bodies. They were to be raced by Fangio, Kling and Herrmann. For the Italian works teams, Gonzalez and Hawthorn had Type 553 Squalo Ferraris, Trintignant a 4 cylinder model, while Ascari, Villoresi and Marimon were mounted on 250F Maseratis. Five independent Maseratis, two Ferraris, four Gordinis and Macklin's HWM made up the field.

From the 100mph transporter with its 300SL engine to the almost military discipline of the mechanics (to see them form up under Neubauer's command and march off from a curbside café was an astonishing sight for the horseplaying English) the Mercedes team bristled with science and efficiency. And the maestro's genius was never more apparent than when, a bare ten minutes before the end of the second day of practice, after Kling and Ascari had both set up new lap records at fractionally over two minutes thirty seconds, Fangio almost lazily got into his car and in a single lap brought the time down to 2:29.4

In the race itself, the German mastery was complete. Ascari lost his transmission on the first lap; neither Gonzalez nor Hawthorn could match the pace of the silver cars and blew up within the first half hour. Mercedes were 1-2-3 and would have remained so had

Herrmann not trailed smoke down the Soissons straight and landed up in a cornfield on lap seventeen. Finally in a grandstand finish the two silver arrows streaked up from Thillois across the line wheel to wheel with Fangio, as team leader, a token nose ahead. A devastating performance, to be sure.

That autumn Stirling Moss joined the Mercedes team and adopted the same highly professional approach in the 1955 Mille Miglia. In one of the greatest pieces of motoring reportage of all time his navigator, Denis Jenkinson, told the story of this epic drive in *Motor Sport*. Run on normal public roads from Brescia to Rome and back, going down the Adriatic coast across the Abruzzi and returning over the old Cassia route through Siena, Florence and Bologna with a loop up to Piacenza, a distance of one thousand old Roman *miglia*, the race was such a specialized affair that to compete in it with any hope of success was a formidable challenge for anyone not actually living in Italy. (True, Caracciola had won in 1931 with an SSK, but since that loss of *bella figura*, Italian drivers had got a stranglehold grip on the race.) The only way to win, Moss decided, was by applying science.

The navigator was to act, in effect, as a second brain, indicating all along the route precisely what lay ahead, so that the driver, constantly fed with information, could keep at the maximum possible limit throughout the race. 'The things we concentrated on were places where we might break the car', explains Jenkinson, 'such as very bumpy railway crossings, sudden dips in the road, bad surfaces, tramlines and so on. Then we logged all the difficult corners, grading them as "saucy ones", "dodgy ones" and "very dangerous ones", having a hand sign to indicate each type.' Slippery surfaces and long straights which could be taken at full chat even if visibility was restricted were likewise noted. After three practice sessions, involving numerous full laps and two smashed cars, Jenkinson transcribed some seventeen pages of notes on to a special sheet of paper eighteen feet in length which was fitted on rollers into an alloy case with a Perspex window. Nothing was left to chance. Even the seats of the 300SLR were tailored to measure. 'We lived and breathed Mille Miglia day in and day out, leaving no idea untried,' explains Jenkinson.

This intense concentration on detail enabled Stirling Moss to achieve what must have been the supreme drive of his whole career. Rome was reached in only three and a half hours at an overall average of 107mph (172.2kph) (from Brescia to Pescara they had averaged 118mph, after which the mountain section caused the speed to drop). The only anxious moment was when, overshooting a corner at Pescara, they slammed into some straw bales, overtaking a Gordini in the process.

> We certainly were not wasting any seconds anywhere. Moss was driving absolutely magnificently, right on the limit of adhesion all the time, and more often than not over the limit, driving in that awe-inspiring narrow margin that you enter just before you have a crash if you have not the Moss skill . . . He was doing it deliberately, his extra special senses and reflexes allowing him to go that much closer to the absolute limit than the average racing driver and way beyond the possibilities of you and me.

Up the Cassia and over the twisting Radicofani heights (where the brakes grabbed and the car spun) Stirling put all he knew into it to beat the Ferrari challenge of Taruffi and Castellotti. On the winding road from Siena to Florence the strain began to tell, but nevertheless the Mercedes roared over the Ponte della Vittoria in Florence at 130mph (218kph) and broadside across the square to the control point. They were leading the race and Moss had set his heart on crossing the Apennines to Bologna in less than an hour. Over the twisty Futa and Raticosa passes they went in one long series of slides that to Jenkinson felt completely uncontrolled but to Moss were obviously intentional (one particular one

Pat Moss, above right, (Stirling's sister), became one of the best known women drivers. In 1955 she won the Ladies' Invitation Race at Goodwood, the only women's race ever to be held on that famous circuit. In 1959 she and her partner, Ann Wisdom, tied with Eric Carlsson (to whom Pat is now married) for first place in the Liège-Rome-Liège and the following year won it outright—the first time a female team had ever won a major international event.
Cut-away drawing (right) of the Mercedes-Benz 300 SLR engine. It had eight cylinders in line, and positively operated valves. In 1955 the company won both the International Cup for Formula 1 Manufacturers as well as the sports car championship, while Fangio won the drivers' world championship.

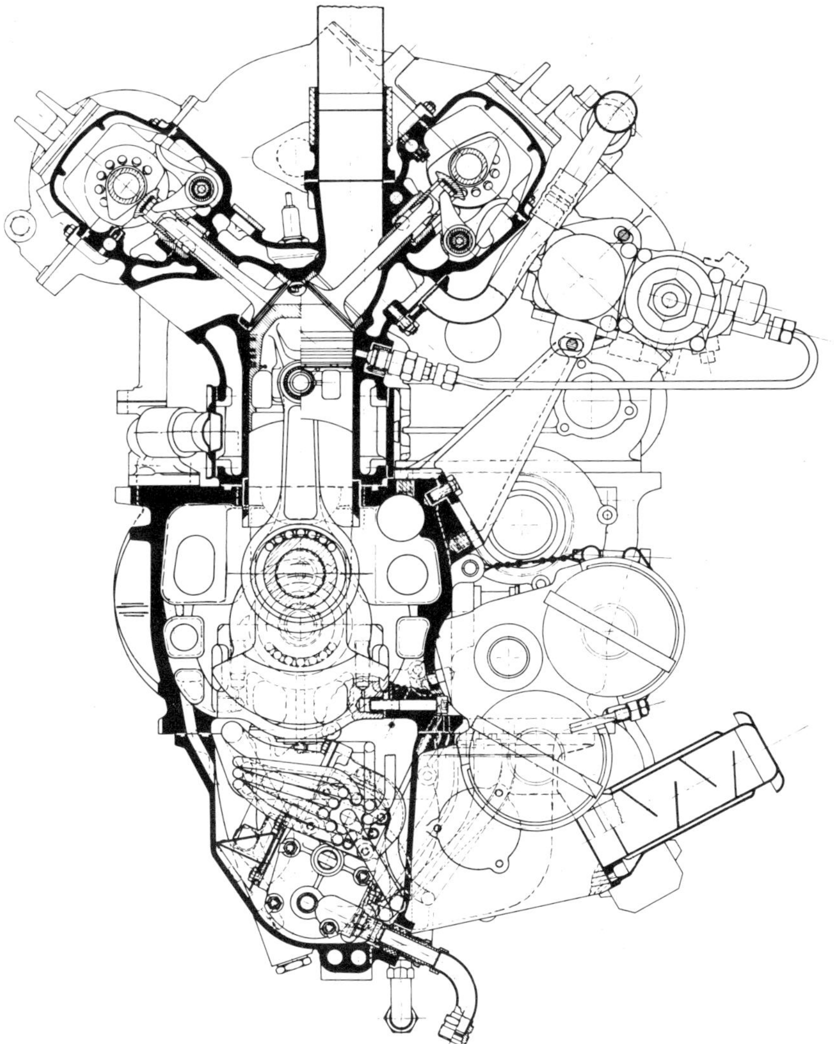

was not intentional, but luckily 'the stone parapet on the outside of the corner stepped back just in time, and caused us to make rude faces at each other') and plunged into Bologna at 150mph (240kph). They had crossed the mountains in an unbelievable one hour one minute, and were far ahead of previous records. The hard part was over, but now Moss set out to reach Brescia in a round ten hours, to make a race average of 100mph. Up the long straights through Modena, Reggio, Emilia and Parma (on the old Emilia, not the Autostrada del Sole) they went, cruising at high speed, cutting off only where Jenkinson indicated corners or bumpy hill-brows. Looking up, he recalls,

> I suddenly realized that we were overtaking an aeroplane, and then I knew I was living in the realms of fantasy, and when we caught and passed a second one my brain began to boggle at the sustained speed. They were flying at about 300 feet filming our progress . . . This really was pure speed, the car was going perfectly and reaching 7,600rpm in fifth gear in places, which was as honest a 170mph plus, as I'd care to argue about.

In one village, less than fifty miles from the finish, they had an enormous slide on some melted tar, but Moss calmly tweaked the wheel this way and that and caught the car just before it crashed into a concrete wall. The last corner into the finishing area at Brescia was taken broadside with the power full on and they crossed the finishing line at well over 100mph (160kph). When at the garage realization dawned that they had not only won but broken all records, each grinned happily at the other's black face and Stirling Moss chuckled: 'I'm so happy that we've proved that a Britisher can win the Mille Miglia, and that the legend "he who leads at Rome never leads at Brescia" is untrue.' In fact they had done more: they had put up an all-time record for the Mille Miglia that could never be bettered. For two years later the Marquis de Portage and Edward Nelson crashed their Ferrari into the crowd, killing themselves and eleven spectators, and the government, as after the Paris–Madrid in 1903, put an end to this last and most romantic of all road races.

In the meantime, only a couple of months after Moss's epic drive in the Mille Miglia, tragedy had struck at Le Mans. On his forty-second lap the gallant Pierre Levegh (who had led the 1952 race in his Talbot driving single handed until one and a quarter hours from the finish) came full bore into the grandstand area just as Hawthorn braked hard into the pits and Lance Macklin's Austin Healey swerved to avoid him. Levegh's 300SLR Mercedes hit the back of the Healey and literally rocketed off into the crowd, killing the driver and over eighty spectators. It was the worst disaster in the history of racing and had far reaching repercussions on the sport. The French Grand Prix was cancelled, no further races were held in France that year, and the Swiss government banned all racing in Switzerland.

The Tourist Trophy, which as a championship event had attracted a full international entry to the Dundrod circuit outside Belfast, was also the scene of disaster in September that year. Only minutes after the start, as the leaders went round on the second lap, seven cars (including a Porsche 550 Spyder entered by myself, and the luckless Macklin once again) were involved in a multiple pile-up at a fast but narrow spot known as the Deers Leap, in which Jim Mayers and Bill Smith were killed. Stirling Moss and John Fitch won on the 300SLR Mercedes, but the pall of smoke from the burning cars and a further fatal accident towards the end put a damper on the race and spelled the end of the Ulster circuit.

Despite all these setbacks, racing was almost back to normal in 1956, although Mercedes-Benz had withdrawn, leaving Fangio and Moss without the cars and the company they had served so well. Fangio moved over to Ferrari and Moss to Maserati. Peter Collins, who had blossomed almost suddenly as a leading GP driver, joined Mike Hawthorn at Ferrari, too. With the right equipment at their disposal, the British drivers were now challenging the rest. While Moss won the Monaco and Italian GPs, Collins won the Belgian and French, and Fangio the Argentine, British and German. Peter Collins in fact had the world title in his hands at Monza, but seeing Fangio abandoning in the pits he pulled voluntarily in and with an unparalleled sporting gesture, gave the Argentinian his car. Thus Fangio was able to clinch his fourth championship.

He had come a long way since the early pre-war days when he drove cut-down Ford and Chevrolet coupés in South American versions of the Mille Miglia. But by winning the International Gran Premio del Morte, a 5,900 mile (9,500km) chase across the pampas from Buenos Aires over the Andes to Lima, Peru, and back, he became Argentine National Champion; and after the war, at the suggestion of President Peron, he was sent to Europe by the Argentine Club with a new San Remo 4CLT/48 Maserati. In 1949, his first full European season, he chalked up victories at San Remo, Pau, Perpignan, Marseilles, Monza and Albi. At thirty-eight, 'El Cheuco' (the 'Bowlegged One') had arrived. Not surprisingly, he was signed up by Alfa Romeo and came second to Farina in the 1950 world championship. But the following year he clinched it with 31 points (out of a possible 36) to Alberto Ascari's 25.

When Alfas retired from racing Fangio was without a car. So in 1952 he drove for both BRM and Maserati. Also, he had his only serious accident. Arriving at Monza from the Ulster Trophy only two hours before the race began he was placed at the back of the grid, having had no time to practise. On the second lap, catching up with the leaders, he accelerated too early coming out of the 140mph Seraglio corner, and inverted his Maserati. 'At that moment', he recalls, 'I knew what it was like to die racing.' He was rushed to hospital with a broken neck.

For all this, he was back again on form a year later. Driving a Maserati, he won at

Fangio (above) winning the 1954 Belgian Grand Prix at Spa in a 250 F Maserati. Stirling Moss (right) in the winning Vanwall at the 1957 Italian Grand Prix. He also took the British Grand Prix the same year–the first time the event had been won by a British driver in a British car.

Monza and Modena and came second in the British, French and German GPs. He also took second place with an Alfa Romeo *Disco Volante* coupé in the Mille Miglia, negotiating the last stretches with only one wheel steering, and no brakes, of course!

In 1954 he headed the Mercedes team, leading the silver arrows to victory in France, Germany, Switzerland and Italy and notching up his second world championship. He repeated the performance in 1955 with Mercedes, in 1956 with the 2.5 Lancia-Ferrari, and in 1957 with the already aging Tipo 250F Maserati. At this point the forty-seven-year-old champion announced his retirement. Against drivers often young enough to be his sons he had won twenty-four Grand Prix and taken the world title five times. No other man in motor racing could match his record, nor indeed has quite done so since. (Even though Jim Clark and Jackie Stewart each subsequently beat Fangio's total of wins, they did so in an era when there were far more events; and on a percentage basis of races won and world championships notched up Fangio remains supremely on top.)

Above all, he seemed to stamp the quality of the whole era. 'The best classroom of all time was about two car lengths behind Juan Manuel Fangio,' thought Stirling Moss: 'I learned more there than I did anywhere else.' Froilan Gonzalez, the huge bear-like Argentinian who seemed to bulge out of any car, was often as fast as Fangio between 1951 and 1954, but he lacked the dazzling artistry of his friend, and after a bad crash during practice for the Tourist Trophy at Dundrod his appearances were limited. Alberto Ascari, with his blue shirt and blue linen helmet, was also a name to be conjured with. Graduating from pre-war motorcycling, he first appeared outside Italy when Dusio's Cisitalia staged a one-make event on Gezira Island in Cairo in 1947, along with Gianni Lurani, Brivio, Taruffi, Cortese and Chiron. By 1949, however, he was very much in the top league, notching up five victories in Europe as well as the Peron GP at Buenos Aires. In 1950 he scored nine victories for Ferrari, and in 1951, six. But once Alfa Romeo had retired he won just about everything in sight and carried off the world championship in both 1952 and 1953. Then in 1955, suddenly losing control of his D50 Lancia during the Monaco Grand Prix, he made a spectacular somersault, car and all, into the harbour waters. From this unexpected ducking he escaped with minor facial injuries, only to crash four days later at Monza – this time, unhappily, to his death.

By now, British drivers had reached the summit which they have maintained ever since, and Stirling Moss, more than all others, symbolized this dramatic renaissance. In fourteen years, from 1948 to 1962, he made his mark in just about every type of motor sport – hill-climbs, speed trials, Grand Prix, sports car races, rallies, sprints and even record attempts. Statistically speaking, he competed in an incredible total of 466 events, winning 194 outright and being placed in 290 – which means that he was in at the kill almost two out of every three times he appeared. For all this, the world championship eluded him, probably because he insisted on trying to win it in a British car. Yet had it not been for his accident at Goodwood in 1962 he would very likely have pocketed the title in the end. Enzo Ferrari, who rated him as the greatest driver ever, was ready to back him to the hilt. It was only patriotism that held Moss back. 'I think it would be anti-climatic, winning the World Championship on an Italian car after all these years,' he explained in his autobiography. Who knows, he was probably right. One thing is certain: for a whole generation he was Mr Motor Sport itself – as professional as they come, a master craftsman of genius, yet a romantic at heart for all that.

His friend and rival, Mike Hawthorn, Britain's first world champion, broke dramatically into the limelight in 1952 at the Goodwood Easter Meeting when he was second to Gonzalez' Thinwall Special in a Cooper-Bristol. Shortly after that he won a Coupe des Alpes in a works Sunbeam Talbot and drove for both BRM and Vandervell with such verve that Ferrari offered him a contract for 1953. Hawthorn responded by winning the French Grand Prix – the first Englishman to do so since Segrave had carried it off in 1923. He won Le Mans and Sebring in 1955 in the D Type Jaguar, but for most of his career he remained with Ferrari and in 1958, after triumphing in the French Grand Prix for the second time, he carried off the world title from Stirling Moss by a single point. But for the tall ash-blond new champion, whose easy-going manner and beer-drinking good humour masked a sensitive strain, there was a bitter side to all this. Of his fellow Ferrari drivers, Alberto Ascari, 'Fon' Portago, Eugenio Castelotti and Luigi Musso had all been killed – the latter when chasing him around the long Gueux curve at Rheims. When his great friend and team mate, the

Mike Hawthorn (above) briefly leads Stirling Moss's Vanwall at Monza during the 1958 Italian Grand Prix. Hawthorn became the first British World Champion that season, with Moss a close runner-up.

Giorgio Scarlatti (above) of Italy in a Cooper-Climax leads Stirling Moss, also in a Cooper, at Monza during the 1959 Italian Grand Prix, which Moss eventually won. Behind them, pressing hard, are the Ferraris of Dan Gurney (No 36) and Phil Hill (No 32).

ebullient Peter Collins, to whom he was wont to refer, in fractured French, as 'mon ami mate', crashed fatally in front of his eyes at Nürburgring, Mike had had enough. (Other intimate friends – Julien Crossley, Stuart Lewis-Evans and Don Beauman – had also just died in racing accidents.)

Peter Collins, who graduated from the rough and tumble world of Formula 3 to Grand Prix racing via HWM and Vandervell Thinwall Special, joined Ferrari in 1956 and almost overnight became a top rank name. The championship title would have been his in 1957 had he not voluntarily handed his car over to Fangio in the closing stages of the Italian Grand Prix. A press-on driver who achieved many memorable successes in sports car racing as well, he won the British Grand Prix at Silverstone in 1958 and would surely have matched both Moss and Hawthorn but for that fatal moment when, chasing Tony Brooks's leading Vanwall around Pflanzgarten, he attempted to pass and hit the bank.

These, then, were the old foxes and young tigers who – along with Phil Hill, Olivier Gendebien, Caroll Shelby, Harry Schell, Jean Behra, Ivor (The Driver) Bueb, Reg Parnell, Louis Rosier, Maurice Trintignant, Ken Wharton and so many other colourful figures – made up the scene and spirit of the fifties: those 'passionate' years, as Stirling Moss himself once called them, when the sport itself was at its romantic best.

The Age of Technology

Start of the 1,000 Kilometre sports car race (above) at Nürburgring in 1960 won by Stirling Moss and Dan Gurney in a 3 litre 'Birdcage' Maserati, so called because of the innumerable small-diameter tubes of the chassis. Driving a Cooper-Climax, Jack Brabham (right) takes the flag in the British Grand Prix at Aintree in 1959. He went on to win the world title that year with the rear-engined Cooper that spear-headed a new technological era.

TIMES WERE CHANGING, though. A new effervescence was sweeping through Britain (expressed culturally by the arrival of Pop Music and politically by the Campaign for Nuclear Disarmament) and this atmosphere of innovation, spreading as it did from the grass roots up, had a far reaching impact on motor sport too.

Back in 1955 the Coopers, father and son, had progressed from their 500cc 'blacksmith's jobs' to produce a rear-engined sports model powered by a Coventry Climax engine, which in its turn was developed (via Formula 2) into a light, whippy Formula 1 machine with a tremendous power-to-weight ratio and superb road holding. Jack Brabham drove the Type 60 Cooper with such gusto that he walked off with the world championship in both 1959 and 1960, becoming thereby the first Australian to hold the title. (Later, of course, he was to become the first racing driver to win the championship in a car of his own manufacture.)

So electrifying, indeed, was the Cooper revolution – which counterpointed the commercial success of the rear-engined Volkswagens and Porsches – that by 1961 Ferrari,

Lotus and BRM had all switched to driver in front of engine layout. When Jack Brabham first took his 'funny car' (as the old guard at Indianapolis mockingly dubbed it) to the Brickyard, A. J. Foyt thought the Cooper looked like 'a bunch of pipes lashed up with chicken wire'. But he soon changed his tune when Brabham qualified at 145mph (233kph) – only 2mph slower than the pole man. And, arguably, Cooper's design theories heralded a new technological era that changed the whole face of motor racing. Today's Formula 1 cars, no less than the humblest go-karts, find their genesis in the Cooper's basic logistics of driver and engine.

Nothing perhaps illustrated the new look in racing better than the grid for the 1960 French Grand Prix at Rheims, where no less than seventeen of the twenty starters were mounted on British machines, ten of them driving Coopers (along with three BRMs, three Lotus, three Ferraris and a Vanwall which made up the field). Seated in them, what's more, was a new generation of drivers who were henceforth to dominate the scene: Jack Brabham in pole position, Graham Hill from north London, the bearded Jo Bonnier from Stockholm, Dan Gurney from California, Bruce McLaren from New Zealand, and Jim Clark from Scotland. Of the old brigade only the veteran, Maurice Trintignant of France, remained in company of recently established names such as Phil Hill, Innes Ireland, Ron Flockart, 'Taffy' von Trips and Masten Gregory. (Stirling Moss had crashed at Spa and was temporarily out of action.) After little more than an hour's racing, as it turned out, each of the three Ferraris had stripped its final drive gear and Brabham led in a 1-2-3-4 Cooper procession with Lotus following 5-6-7. An astonishing performance, to be sure. After all, no British car had won the French Grand Prix since 1923. But from now onwards, thanks largely to the technical genius of Colin Chapman and the driving skill of Graham Hill, Jim Clark and later Jackie Stewart, the British were becoming a force to be reckoned with – as they have indeed remained ever since.

To some extent Lotus took over from their rivals, the Coopers. Colin Chapman had begun by producing 'do-it-yourself' specials in a stable at Hornsey in north London (just why they were called Lotus remains a cherished secret) before moving on to sports cars and his first formula single-seaters in 1956. As an aeronautical engineer, he had a knack of adopting unusual solutions – such as the use of fibre-glass for the chassis-cum-body of the Lotus Elite coupé – and his formula for success was to develop extremely light chassis and suspension systems to offset the modest power output of proprietary engines. Even if they tended to shed bits and pieces at embarrassing moments, the early Mark 6s and 8s made their presence felt in Club racing during the fifties (Peter Gammon, for instance, won fourteen out of seventeen events that he entered in 1954); but although Lotus subsequently recorded class wins at Le Mans and Nürburgring, their breakthrough really dated from the moment that, taking a leaf out of Cooper's book, Colin Chapman switched to the rear-engined layout.

The Mark 18 with its boxy multitubular space frame in which the driver reclined rather than sat (relying on low frontal area rather than streamlining for drag reduction) appeared in everything from Formula 1 to Formula Junior. In this new international 1,100cc class, which stemmed from Italy where the 500cc movement was beginning to wane (and eventually took over the title of Formula 3) the Lotus, using Ford-based engines modified by Cosworth, soon became the Junior to beat. Of the nineteen major races in 1960, for instance, Lotus won 13, Cooper 4 and Osca 2.

For 1961, anxious as ever about rising speeds, the governing body of motor sport decreed a $1\frac{1}{2}$ litre limit for Formula 1 – thereby (to the dismay of the British who dominated the $2\frac{1}{2}$ litre scene) once again promoting Formula 2 to Grand Prix status. While English manufacturers kicked against

Indomitable but accident-prone. Willy Mairesse of Belgium was badly injured in a high speed collision with Trevor Taylor's Lotus at Spa, but was back within weeks at the wheel of the new FI Ferrari (above) at Monza in September 1962. Maurice Trintignant (right), in a Cooper-Maserati, leads Phil Hill and Jo Bonnier round the station hairpin in the 1961 Monaco Grand Prix.

the FIA's decision to reduce capacity and even tried to set up an opposition 'Inter-Continental' 3 litre formula, Ferrari pressed on perfecting their rear-engined Formula 2 based design (in fact a new car, using the V6 Dino engine) and thus were ready for the season's racing – which the British weren't. As a result Phil Hill, Wolfgang von Trips, Richie Ginther, Olivier Gendebien and Giancarlo Baghetti swept the board in their Ferraris with something like a 30bhp advantage over the others – although Stirling Moss's victories at Monaco and Nürburgring when he outdrove the whole Ferrari team in a privately owned Lotus 18, did much to revive British spirits. Sadly, though, this Ferrari-dominated year ended in tragedy. The championship lay between Phil Hill and Wolfgang von Trips until, in the deciding Italian GP at Monza, Jim Clark's Lotus and von Trips's Ferrari collided as they entered the notorious *Curvetta*. Both cars spun and the Ferrari ploughed up a bank into the crowd-lined fence, killing von Trips and fourteen spectators. Neither driver was to blame: but the gloom was compounded by legal recriminations, and two years later, when Jim Clark won his well-deserved world title at Monza, he was hounded by the police with the threat of imprisonment. In Italy of all places, the local *Questura* had chosen to ignore that motor racing is a dangerous business.

Be this as it may, Phil Hill won at Monza in the Ferrari and thus became the first and only American to secure the world championship.

For the 1962 season both BRM and Coventry Climax had produced new V8 engines, and when the Lotus-Climax 25 with its aerodynamic monocoque construction first appeared at Zandvoort it created a sensation. Apart from all else, the driver was not just reclining, as if in a deckchair, but lying almost horizontal with a worm's-eye view of the track. No one could doubt that a new era of racing cars had arrived, and indeed the 1962 world championship developed into a neck to neck struggle between Graham Hill in the Type 56 BRM and Jim Clark in the Lotus 25.

For, sadly enough, Stirling Moss' racing career had been cut short by an inexplicable accident at Goodwood that Easter. Graham Hill, who saw it happen, remembers that swinging through Fordwater he spotted Moss in his mirror. 'As I was going into the right kink before St Mary's I was braking on the left of the road. Stirling suddenly flashed by me on the outside on the grass, out of control,' he recalls. 'He just went straight across the track, the car went over a bump, a flame shot out of the exhaust pipe and he didn't seem to be making any effort to correct . . . he just went head first into the bank. It was a terrifying sight.' Although Graham Hill suspected that something had gone wrong with the car, Moss himself admits that he has never understood the mistake that put him into retirement at the age of thirty-one.

Yet even as Britain lost its greatest hero, these two new stars were waiting in the wings, and their duel for the top title made spectacular sport. Hill won at Zandvoort, Nürburgring and Monza; Clark took the flag at Spa, Aintree and Watkins Glen. With each in the running, the championship was decided in South Africa a few days after Christmas.

On the East London circuit Jim Clark shot immediately into the lead and built up an impressive 27sec margin. 'I got in just behind him, but I was not able to challenge him, though I was driving as hard as I could', recalls Hill. Then, on lap 59 a crankcase bolt sheared. There was a puff of blue smoke from the Lotus and Graham Hill cruised in for the title. In so doing, he became the first Englishman to win the championship in a British car, and brought success to BRM after twelve years of frustration.

Moreover, the much voiced fears that 1.5 litre formula would be second league stuff were conclusively disproved. In the season's first race Graham Hill had lapped Zandvoort during practice at 1min 32.6sec, thereby equalling the previous lap record. For although the 'noddy cars' were some 90bhp down on their predecessors, developing about 180bhp, against 270bhp, their lightness and improved tires made them just about the fastest GP machines yet devised.

In 1963 the struggle continued. But this time, with his Lotus 25 converted to fuel injection and giving 200bhp, Jim Clark swept the board with victories in the Belgian, Dutch, French, British, Italian, Mexican and South African GPs. For the first time on record, a driver won seven world championship events. During the course of the season in fact he took first place in twelve of the twenty Formula 1 races. (As runner up for the title, Graham Hill scored only at Monaco and Watkins Glen.)

Through all this Clark even found time to challenge the American establishment at

Start of the 34th Italian Grand Prix at Monza in September 1963. It was won by Jim Clark (Lotus 25), who won six Grandes Epreuves that year, four of them consecutively, to secure the world championship (the first for both himself and Colin Chapman).

Indianapolis, turning up at the Brickyard with an aluminium version of the Ford Fairline engine in his Lotus. Although virtually world champion he had to take the rookie test. He responded by lapping at 146mph, provoking Parnelli Jones to an all-out effort to gain pole position. 'The last thing I was going to see happen was one of them goddam funny cars take the pole,' snorted the Californian favourite, who was driving a traditional Offenhauser-engined roadster built by A. J. Watson. Looking back on the race, Clark recalled that he was taken aback by the start. 'There was nothing but smoke, dust, and all these giant cars around me. It was unreal.' His main pre-occupation was how to pass them: 'It wasn't easy – they took up such an awful lot of road.' With 150 miles to go, it became a Goliath and David duel between Parnelli Jones in the lead and Clark 40sec behind. Driving like a tiger, Jim narrowed the gap until only 4sec separated them. 'There was smoke coming from his car,' he noted. 'I felt sure that he wouldn't finish the race.' Jones began to throw oil, making the track dangerous. The stewards got ready to black-flag him in. But with only ten laps to go, they were naturally reluctant to disqualify the favourite. Clark made no do-or-die attempt to pass him. 'I simply reckoned it was better to finish on the track in second place than to crash off the track completely,' he said afterwards.

Second place or not, it was an astonishing performance. Yet if 1963 was a high-water mark for both Jim Clark and Lotus, the following year involved intense competition for the world cup. Above all it saw the graduation of John Surtees from two wheels to four. Seven times motorcycle champion (four in the 500cc and three in the 350cc class) 'Big

John' now scooped up the Grand Prix title in the new V12 Ferrari. Right up to the last championship race on the tight twisty Mexican circuit the issue was in doubt. Hill led on points but various combinations and permutations enabled both Surtees and Clark to be still in the running. As it turned out, Graham Hill lost time in the pits after being clouted by Bandini while, in a Hollywood-style finish, Jim Clark's Lotus ran out of oil on the last lap of all and Surtees slipped through for the title.

After all these excitements, 1965 once again saw Jim Clark top of his form, winning six Grand Prix in the Lotus 33 and clinching his second world title. For the first time since 1906 there were no French drivers in the French Grand Prix, but a young Scot named Jackie Stewart made his appearance in the BRM and won the Italian GP at Monza.

And then, in 1966, came some far reaching developments. For one thing, a new Formula was introduced, doubling the previous limitation. Fast as the 1½ litre cars had been, some of the new big sports cars were now lapping the circuits even quicker, which was obviously bad for the Grand Prix image. For another, Coventry Climax, who had powered the machinery that had won four championship titles and forty Grand Prix since 1958, announced that they would not be producing engines for the new 3 litre formula.

Needless to say, this put most constructors in a quandary. Only Ferrari, BRM and Porsche (who had withdrawn from Formula 1 in 1963 anyway) built every major part of their formula cars. The others, producing 'kit cars' that used proprietary power units and gearboxes, now found themselves without a suitable engine.

Resourceful as ever, Colin Chapman persuaded Ford of Britain to sponsor Cosworth Engineering, as they had done in the past, to develop a Ford-based Grand Prix engine for Lotus. Jack Brabham, on the other hand, beat the problem by resorting to Repco in Australia for a lightweight V8 based on the Oldsmobile F85 block. Additionally, two other leading drivers also turned constructor. Bruce McLaren's M2B had an unusual stressed skin fuselage made of aluminium bonded to balsa wood and was powered by a destroked version of the Ford 'Indianapolis' V8 and on occasions an Italian Serenissima (ATS) V8. Dan Gurney's AAR Eagle was more prominent at Indianapolis than in Formula 1 (but nevertheless, by winning at Spa in 1967, achieved the distinction of being the first American car and driver to notch up a Grand Prix victory since Jimmy Murphy won the French GP at Le Mans in 1921). Another newcomer was the exciting 3 litre V12 engined Honda 273 that arrived in time for the 1966 Italian Grand Prix. And Matra was already showing its paces in Formula 2.

A side effect of reducing Formula 1 to 1.5 litres in the early sixties was in fact to give an extra impetus to Formula 2 for drivers wanting to complete their racing programmes. Lotus and Brabham, for instance, ran parallel works teams with Jim Clark and Graham Hill driving in both. So long as Brabham had a monopoly of the technically advanced Honda engine, Denny Hulme was able to beat just about everything in sight – until that is the SCA Cosworth engine became generally available (rather in the same way as March's sole use of the BMW engine in 1973 enabled Jean Pierre Jarrier to walk away with the Formula 2 championship that year). And when Honda aspired to break into GP racing they started with Formula 2, if only as a technical exercise. Matra, too, were particularly competitive from the moment that this aeronautical and missile engineering firm entered the motoring field in 1964 (through the acquisition of René Bonnet's remarkably successful small car operation) and opened a competition department under Claude le Guezec at Villacoublay.

During 1965 five single-seaters were built there which were the genesis of the aluminium-bodied MS5. In both Formula 3 and Formula 2 the characteristic square-cut Matras, using Cosworth engines, became the pace-setters. Tyrrell's drivers gained five victories and

For 1966-7 a 3 litre V12 Maserati engine was fitted by Cooper for the new Formula I. Under the crash helmet is ex-champion on both two and four wheels, John Surtees, who won the 1966 Mexican GP with one of these Cooper-Maseratis.

Jacky Ickx won the first Formula 2 championship, which became more and more dominated by the French cars and drivers, J. P. Beltoise winning the championship in the works MS7 in 1968 and Johnny Servoz-Gavin in 1969.

The start of the European Formula 2 championship in 1967 along with the increase to a 1.6 limit, turned Formula 2 into the area in which Grade B drivers became the key men since only they were eligible even if graded Formula 1 drivers were participating. It became, in fact, the arena in which young drivers could match their skills against acknowledged stars in machines that were hardly less potent (a 1975 Formula 2 car costs approximately £65,000 against £100,000 for a Formula 1). Jacky Ickx, Jean Pierre Beltoise, Clay Regazzoni, Ronnie Peterson and Patrick Depailler all entered Grand Prix racing with a European Formula 2 champion title to their credit.

Indianapolis

JIM CLARK may have been content to take second place at Indianapolis with his 'funny car' in 1963 and to hang the 'Rookie of the Year' plaque alongside the world championship trophies in the sitting room of his Berwickshire farmhouse, but both he and Colin Chapman had their sights firmly trained on the richest and most famous race in the United States. They returned to the Brickyard the following year, only to be eliminated by tire trouble which collapsed the rear suspension of the Lotus when it was in the lead and enabled A. J. Foyt to take the flag at the wheel of a splendid if traditional front-engined Sheraton-Offenhauser roadster. But on his third attempt in 1965 Jim Clark drove the Lotus-Ford 38 with such icy verve that, lapping at an incredible 155mph (249kph), he was far enough ahead of the opposition to be able to pit twice without ever losing his advantage. Not only was he the first foreign driver to have won the '500' since Dario Resta did so for Peugeot in 1916, but he was also the first to have achieved a speed of over 150mph.

This epochal victory marked a full circle back to the days of nearly half a century earlier when Peugeot, Delage and Mercedes had triumphed on the historic Indiana battlefield. For European domination of the

Line-up for the start of the '500' in 1923 (above), when single-seaters already predominated. Tommy Milton won the race in a Miller Special. Milton, who was born without sight in one eye, started racing on dirt tracks around 1914 and managed to conceal his defect by memorizing standard eye charts until the 1920s. By that time he was established as a first class driver and was allowed to continue.

Start of the 1974 '500' (above), won by Johnny Rutherford in a British-built McLaren. This was the second time McLarens have been successful in this unique American race.

'500' had been terminated in 1920 by Gaston Chevrolet on a Monroe-Frontenac (which admittedly was powered by a Peugeot-inspired engine), and since that moment European and American racing had gone their own ways – the one to road events and the other to the oval track. In the States, engineers like Harry Miller and the Duesenberg brothers had concentrated their energies on how to travel ever faster round a geometrical strip to such good effect that (apart from Wilbur Shaw's two victories on a Maserati in 1939 and 1940) Indianapolis had become an exclusively American domain in which first the Duesenbergs and Millers and subsequently the Offenhauser-engined specials had it all their own way.

Among the great names at the Brickyard in the early twenties were Tommy Milton, who, although blind in one eye, won at the wheel of Louis Chevrolet's new twin ohc straight-eight Frontenac in 1921 and again in 1923 on an HCS Miller special at an average of 90.95mph (146.37kph); Jimmy Murphy, his protégé, who, having purchased the Duesenberg with which he had triumphed in the French Grand Prix and fitted it with a Miller engine, clinched the honours in 1922 at an average of 94.48mph (151.85kph); and Lora Corum the Duesenberg engineer, who with

Joe Boyer, a wealthy Detroit amateur, drove a blown Dusie to victory in 1924 at a record-breaking average of 98.23mph (158.01kph). This was the first time that a supercharged car had won the '500' and the friendly rivalry between the Duesenberg brothers and Harry Armenius Miller reached its peak as the 100mph target approached. Both, after all, were producing the most famous American racing cars of their era. Seven of the next nine cars behind Jimmy Murphy in 1922 had been Duesenbergs, but in 1923 the Millers swept the board, taking six out of the first seven places; and despite the Dusie victory in 1924 the majority of the year's honours went to Millers. Memorial Day 1925 was therefore something of a confrontation at the Brickyard.

Indeed four Duesenbergs found themselves opposed by no less than sixteen Millers out of a total field of twenty-two (the two others were a special T Model Ford-Frontenac, and a Fiat GP machine). A surprise among the Millers was a new front-wheel drive model driven by a young Kansan named Dave Lewis. The Duesenberg challenge was led by a yellow machine that its driver, Peter de Paolo (a nephew of Ralph de Palma), irreverently referred to as the 'Banana Wagon'. With it he swept into the lead and remained there for the first fifty laps, averaging 105mph (162kph), until he was forced to pit with his hands badly blistered by steering-wheel judder from the brick surface. While he was having them bandaged a relief driver took over, and when De Paolo rejoined the race the Banana Wagon was back in fourth position with Lewis in the lead. Ten laps later he had moved up to second position and gradually whittled down the Miller's lead from 43 to 17sec. By now Lewis was tiring after four hours' wrestling with the heavy front-drive steering and all too late he let his relief driver take over. Peter de Paolo brought the Banana Wagon home a comfortable 54sec ahead, at an average of 101.13mph (162.75kph). It was Duesenberg's finest hour, and Peter de Paolo's record remained unbroken until 1932. Yet even if Duesenberg won more races in 1925, Miller came back to the fore in 1926 with a splendid low-line single-seater tailored for the new 95.1 cubic inches (1,499cc) restriction, including intercoolers to chill the supercharge mixture, in which Frank Lockhart won the '500' as a rookie. Duesenbergs responded with an offset chassis to meet the centrifugal pressures of the left hand curves, and George Sonders, also making his first appearance, gave the gallant Dusies their last Indianapolis victory after both Lockhart and De Paolo had retired with engine troubles. From this moment onwards Miller-engined cars in one guise or another dominated the Brickyard until 1939.

It should not be overlooked, to be sure, that the entry list at Indianapolis had been shrinking steadily since World War I, mainly because manufacturers of stock automobiles were faced with the fact that they could not compete successfully with the specialized products of Louis Chevrolet, Harry Miller and the Duesenberg brothers. Indeed almost all of the manufacturers discontinued their factory racing teams and during the ten year period beginning in 1920 there was a full field of thirty-three starters on only two occasions.

On top of this deteriorating situation, what is more, when Eddie Rickenbacker, the celebrated war ace, bought the Speedway in 1927, he soon found himself faced with the problems of the Depression. A front-wheel drive Miller cost 15,000 dollars, or considerably more than a Rolls-Royce, and since that kind of money was no longer readily available, Rickenbacker tried to keep racing alive by introducing what was known as the 'Junk Formula', raising the capacity limit to 366 cubic inches (or 6 litres) and banning superchargers in the hope of cutting the cost of racing and getting the big passenger car manufacturers back into the act with modified production engines. Many cars powered by improved stock units did in fact find their way to the grid, but notwithstanding the factory support they enjoyed none of them

Mechanics and pit crews watch (above) as contestants speed by during the 1928 500 Miles, won by 23 year old Louis Meyer in a Miller. Meyer was the first driver to win the '500' three times: in 1927, 1928 and, much later, in 1936 at an average speed of 109.07mph (175.53kph), a new race record.

Tommy Milton (right), with Barney Oldfield and Louis Chevrolet, winner of the '500' in 1921 with an 8 cylinder engine Frontenac, designed by Chevrolet.

finished better than third in all the series. Distressed on the other hand by the turn of events, Harry Miller sold out; but Leo Goossen and Fred Offenhauser remained with the firm and turned one of its marine units into a 4.2 litre twin-cam, 16 valve 'Four' that in due course became the most successful racing engine ever seen at Indianapolis – the famous 'Offie' that powered most of the winning cars right up into the sixties. In fact, the only break in the string of Offenhauser successes was when the formula was brought into line with international regulations in 1938 and Wilbur Shaw (who had won in 1937 on an Offie-engined Gilmore at an average of 113.58mph (182.79kph) and finished second behind Floyd Roberts the following year) persuaded his sponsor, Mike Boyle, to buy a 3 litre 8CTF Maserati with which he took the flag both in 1939 and 1940, and became, incidentally, the only man who had won twice in a row. Then in 1946 George Robson led the field home in a 6 cylinder Thorne Engineering special. But apart from these three occasions, Offenhauser-engined cars triumphed year after year at Indianapolis until Jim Clark's win in 1965.

All the same there were some technical advances during this long period. Harry Miller reappeared on the scene in 1938 with the remarkable Miller Gulf special whose 2,950cc 6 cylinder engine, inclined at 45 degrees, was not only rear-mounted but also drove all four wheels through a four-speed gearbox. Although to some extent inspired by the Auto Unions it was nevertheless prophetic of what was to be the shape of things two decades later. Leo Goossen likewise came up during the war years with the highly advanced Novi V8 (featuring four gear-driven overhead cams, a centrifugal blower, and credited with 600bhp) that had a long career at Indianapolis but somehow was always too temperamental for outright success. More unusual still was the Pat Clancy special with its six wheels, and the front-and-rear powered Twin Coach, in which the driver sat astride the superchargers between two Miller engines. But these were exceptions, and the general post-war pattern was that of the conventional Kurtis roadster powered by an Offenhauser engine. Frank Kurtis, a Californian midget specialist, produced fifty-eight Indianapolis cars in all, including five outright winners, as well as Freddy Agabashian's Cummings Diesel. Disguised though they may have been under exotic trade names (such as 'Wynn Friction Proof', 'Belond Exhaust' and 'Blue Crown Spark Plug') these specials consisted of a conventional tubular chassis frame, rigid differential-less axles, a front-mounted Offenhauser engine (increasingly fuel-injected) and a handsome roadster body, with everything somewhat offset for the left-hand Indy corners.

For all this, speeds grew steadily, even if revolutionary development didn't. Bill Holland won at 120mph (193kph) in 1949; five years later Bill Vukovitch passed the 130mph mark, and in 1962 Roger Ward lifted the race average to 140.29mph (225.77kph). Even so they were still behind Lang's winning speed of 162.62mph (261.71kph) in the 1937 Avusrennen, although (to make the comparison fair) when leading American drivers were invited to compete, Indy-style, on the newly completed banked track at Monza in 1957. Tony Bettenhausen qualified with his Nova at no less than 177mph (285kph) (and then blew up), whereas Jim Rathmann won the Monza '500' the following year at 166.72mph (268.31kph) in the 'Leader Card Special'.

Prize money also increased. When Anton Hulman Jr bought the Speedway from Rickenbacker after World War II (ahead of speculators who wanted to take it over for real estate development, thus saving the Brickyard from a similar fate to Brooklands) the purse was just under 100,000 dollars. Twenty-five years later, in 1970, it was over a million dollars. Hulman, to whom hats should be lifted, decreed that all profits should be used to improve facilities and increase prize money. The track was resurfaced, the pit area rebuilt, the grandstands extended to hold 230,000 reserved seats, and free parking space

1965 winner: Jim Clark (above, in the Lotus-Ford) was first non-American to take the famous '500' since 1914. This was Clark's third attempt at the '500'; the previous year he had finished second.
A. J. Foyt's Coyote-Ford (right) that won in 1967. Foyt won the '500' three times as well as being the only driver ever to take the national championship five times.

for 25,000 vehicles was provided. Understandably the '500' became one of racing's most glittering events.

Yet for all its glamour, the Brickyard remained curiously isolated from the mainstream of international sport, even though (in an effort to bring European and American racing nearcr together) the '500' was named as one of the qualifying rounds in the Drivers' Championship between 1950 and 1960. Ascari, who entered a 375 Ferrari in 1952, and went on to take the world title that year, soon discovered that although the Americans might be out of the picture in road racing, they had oval track racing completely sewn up. Other European-style drivers, including Fangio himself, who tried their hands at Indianapolis during the fifties got left behind like him. There was, in truth, something incestuous about the oval strip. 'The old-style Indy driver . . . was baptized on tight, short, paved ovals where he rapidly learned that a mistake would bounce him off the wall and into the path of the oncoming pack,' explains Charles Fox. 'Only if he could endure this apprenticeship and avoid Valhalla would he come to confirmation at the Speedway.'

For Jim Clark, no less than Jack Brabham – who had taken a Cooper to Indianapolis in 1961 – it was an act of faith to have challenged such an entrenched establishment with their fragile 'funny cars'. Among the big roadsters the Australian's little Cooper looked like a toy, but it beat them round the turns and finished in ninth position. The diehards may have been surprised, but only Mickey Thompson got the message sufficiently to have a car built along the Cooper lines with a Buick V8 engine. It turned out to be fast, but still no match for the roadsters.

The obvious superiority of the lightweight rear-engined machines only became apparent with Jim Clark's performance in 1963. The big, pearly roadsters hung on for another season but already in 1964 a third of the field and seven out of ten of the fastest qualifiers were rear-engined. The revolution was consummated by Jim Clark who led from start

53
8

Dramatic pile-up a mere 100yd from the start of the 1966 500 Miles race. Sixteen cars were involved, but although some spectators were slightly hurt by flying debris and eleven cars were eliminated, there were no serious injuries.

to finish in 1965 with Parnelli Jones in another Lotus just behind him, and to compound the total rout of the old-style Indy cars, Graham Hill drove a Lola to victory the following year as a 'rookie' – the first to do so since Frank Lockhart in 1926. 'Gentlemen,' said one owner sadly, as reporters inspected his fleet of front-engined roadsters, 'you are looking at a million dollars worth of junk!'

The great Indy drivers of the sixties – such as Bobby and Al Unser, A. J. Foyt, Parnelli Jones and Mario Andretti – all converted to rear-engined cars and pushed the speeds up to new highs. Mario Andretti drove his turbo-charged Ford STP to a fresh race record of 156.87mph (252.46kph) in 1969. Peter Revson qualified for the pole in 1971 with a speed of over 178mph and Al Unser (who had won in 1970, too) pushed the race average up by a further mile per hour. All this had a decisive effect not only at Indianapolis but throughout the whole of the American racing scene. For, since the slim, lightweight 'funny cars' were not suitable for the rutted, dust-choked, small-town dirt tracks which had been the breeding ground for so many American drivers, it meant that the new generation had to concentrate, as in Europe, on road racing, which in itself has opened up intriguing possibilities for the future of the sport.

Land Speed Records: towards the Sound Barrier [from 1945]

IN AUGUST 1947 John Cobb took the Railton back to Bonneville with the hope of topping the 400mph mark – which in fact he did on one of the two runs, even if the mean was 394.2mph (634.4kph). Even so, he had increased his previous LSR by nearly 25mph. Cobb himself was killed on Loch Ness in his jet-engined craft 'Crusader' in 1952, but his record, so tantalizingly near to the magical figure, remained unbroken for seventeen years. The post-war world, it seemed, was no longer interested in such things.

Apparently. And yet the lull was deceptive. For as the dragster cult got under way in the fifties some odd-looking devices made their appearance at the Bonneville National Speed trials each autumn, and men like Craig Breedlove, Art Arfons and Mickey Thompson put up electrifying performances in the most unlikely machinery. Each year the hot-rodders pushed their speeds up further, until some of them were accelerating up to 250mph or more in the side by side runs. In the process, they made mincemeat of most of the existing class records. Mickey Thompson, for instance, established no less than 485 national and international records during his twenty-year career. But none of them had a crack at the absolute record. None of them, that is, until Donald Campbell came along.

He already held the record on water, and his ambition (like his father) was to secure the double crown. Backed by BP, Rubery Owen, Dunlop and a number of other British firms, the new Bluebird with its Bristol-Siddeley Proteus gas-turbine engine driving all four

Rocket propulsion of a car was first tried by the German, Fritz von Opel (above), with two cars designed by Max Valier, called Rak 1 and Rak 2. Von Opel here demonstrates the latter car in 1928 at the Avus track outside Berlin, exceeding 125mph (201.17kph). America's famous Bonneville salt flats in the State of Utah have been used for countless speed record attempts ever since the mid-1930s, by small cars as well as land speed record monsters. Goldie Gardner's famous Gardner-MG special (right) set new 1500cc world class figures on the Bonneville salt at speeds up to 189.5mph (304.96kph) in 1952.

wheels had been built for the attempt quite regardless of cost. But the news of this massive British onslaught on the world title galvanized a number of local aspirants into action at last. When Donald Campbell and his team of some eighty helpers arrived at Bonneville in August 1960, they found a momentous gathering of American contenders lined up with the same intention.

First out on the sands was Athol Graham's aero-engined 'City of Salt Lake', which veered suddenly off course, somersaulted several times and ended up a pile of scrap, killing the unfortunate driver on the spot. After this dispiriting start Dr Nathan Ostich had a go with his cylindrical-shaped 'Flying Caduceus', which was powered by the turbo-jet engine from a Boeing bomber, but the steering failed and he had to withdraw. Next came Mickey Thompson's ingenious 'Challenger 1' which was motivated by four rebuilt and supercharged Pontiac engines arranged in pairs, one lot driving the front wheels and the other the rear, while the driver conducted operations from the overhang behind (a bumpy pursuit, to be sure, since the car had no springs). Thompson put in one or two preliminary runs, and then wooshed through the measured mile at 406.6mph (654.36kph). But unfortunately a drive-shaft broke on the return leg, and he had to be satisfied with having made the fastest-ever one-way run – which, for a backyard special, was a remarkable performance to say the least.

Less impressive, by contrast, was Art Arfons' aero-engined 'Green Monster' which put in a trial run at 257mph and then, plagued with teething troubles, prudently withdrew. Finally it was Bluebird's turn to show its paces.

Donald Campbell made a few probe runs, increasing his speed each time, and then gave Bluebird full power. At around 350mph the car began to slew. It rolled, bounded into the air, shedding two wheels, and finally skidded to a sickening stop. Miraculously enough, Campbell escaped with a broken skull and a pierced eardrum, but the million-pound car

France's nationalized car concern, Regie Renault, built a special turbine-powered car (above) called 'L'Etoile Filante' (Shooting Star) which established a world turbine-powered record in 1956, attaining 242mph (389kph) on the famous salt flats of Bonneville. L'Etoile Filante (left) at speed on the salt; it was powered by a Turbomeca unit installed behind the driver.

was a write-off.

Undaunted, nevertheless, by this terrifying accident, Campbell persuaded his sponsors to rebuild Bluebird. But for the next attempt he decided against returning to Bonneville and chose instead the deserted salt bed of Lake Eyre in Australia. The story of his frustrations there – mainly on account of the weather – would fill a book. (As indeed it did: *Bluebird and the Dead Lake*, by John Pearson.) 'Nothing, not one blind, bloody thing has gone right since I first saw the place four years ago,' is how Donald Campbell summed it all up.

To add to his trials came the news that an American dragster had done over 400mph at Bonneville in a jet-powered three-wheeler. Craig Breedlove's 'Spirit of America' certainly looked more like a wingless fighter aircraft than a car, but it was through the mile in 9sec on its first run and hit 428.37mph (688.39kph) on the way back, to give a mean of 407.45mph (655.73kph).

Even if, academically speaking, Spirit of America took the motorcycle record rather than the LSR, since it did not have four wheels of which two at least were driven. the fact was that at dawn on 5 August 1963 Craig Breedlove had driven quicker on land than anyone before. Thus when Donald Campbell finally covered the measured mile at an identical speed of 403.1mph (648.73kph) both ways under appalling weather conditions at Lake Eyre on 17 July 1964 to set up a new land speed record and become, officially, the fastest man on earth, there were people in the States who didn't think he was. And were going to show it, too.

Indeed within 100 days poor Campbell (who was by then successfully attempting his sixth water speed record at Perth) saw his hard-won LSR eclipsed four times, and the absolute record pushed up by an incredible 130mph.

Ever since the first enthusiast had gone out to show that he could conduct his self-propelled vehicle quicker than the next horseless carriage, the urge to be the fastest on wheels had provoked many confrontations, but none more spectacular than what took place at Bonneville in October 1964. First of all, Tom Green, who had been cruising up and down the salt flats for a week in Walt Arfons' 'Wingfoot Express' without jolting any stop-watches, finally fitted a new 10,000hp Westinghouse J46 triple-jet engine into the car and galvanized the bored timekeepers by covering the mile at 406.5mph (654.2kph) and then blasting back at 420.07mph (676.04kph) to set up a new record.

Three days later, on 5 October, Art Arfons reappeared with the Green Monster (rather inappropriately named, since it was actually painted red, white and blue, though being virtually a 17,500hp General Electric J79 engine on wheels it was certainly a monstrous device) and after an outward run of 396.3mph (637.78kph) came back at a sizzling 479mph (771kph), which wiped the smile off his brother's face (they were not, it is said, on the best of terms anyway) by pushing the record up to 434.02mph (698.49kph).

It was probably not too much to the liking of Craig Breedlove either. Anyway, on 13 October he brought out his rebuilt Spirit of America, and almost disdainfully did the return trip at a mean of 468.72mph (754.33kph). And then, when all concerned were mulling this over, he went out again, just forty-eight hours later, and repeated the performance at a staggering 526.28mph mean (846.96kph), ending up, rather incongruously by nose-diving into a brine lake several miles off course when the drag parachute failed and the brakes burned out.

A 25 per cent increase on Donald Campbell's speed (to say nothing of John Cobb's record which had stood for so long) would have seemed enough for one season. But lo and behold, out came Art Arfons twelve days later with the Green Monster and rocketed to and fro at 536.71mph (863.75kph). To set the seal, what is more, on a stupendous year that had seen five new LSRs and the speed pushed up by 142.5mph, the FIA in Paris agreed to recognize records established by cars without driven wheels, henceforth to be designated as 'specials' (as distinct from 'automobiles'). So while Donald Campbell's Bluebird remained officially the fastest automobile in the world, Art Arfons held the international record for special vehicles with the Green Monster.

The year 1965 had its share of excitement, too. Three contenders turned up in the autumn for what was now becoming an annual record-breaking festival. Bobby Tatroe was at the wheel of an entirely new rocket-impelled, delta-shaped 'Wingfoot Express', but the gremlins were still present and its best showing was 476.6mph (654.36kph). Which was kids' stuff by now. More promising was Craig Breedlove's latest version of the Spirit of America. Christened Sonic 1, but generally known as the 'Coca-Cola Bottle' because of its waisted fibre-glass body, it now had four wheels (in deference to the FIA) and was powered by a J79 turbo-jet engine. On its first outing Sonic 1 became skittish at around 600mph and nearly landed up in the brine lake again, but after new nose fins had been fitted Craig Breedlove had little difficulty in lifting the record to 555.48mph (893.96kph). Two days later, in a rather endearing gesture, he handed Sonic 1 over to his wife Lee, who sailed through the timing traps at a mean speed of 308.56mph (496.58kph) to become the fastest woman on wheels.

Art Arfons cheered with the rest at this spirited his-and-hers performance. But no sooner had his allotted time come along (he had booked the sands for 7 November) than the Green Monster was out and almost before anyone realized what was happening had covered the measured mile both ways at a new high of 576.55mph (927.87kph) – though not without incident. For just after crossing the line on his return trip, the right hand rear tire burst at a velocity of around 600mph, ripping away one of the automatic parachute releases, and for a heart-stopping moment the car swung off course, hit a marker, and the driver's cockpit filled with smoke. But still travelling at something like nine miles a minute, Arfons broke the windshield to get some visibility and managed, working the remaining parachute by hand, to bring the crippled monster to a halt.

The next move was obviously up to Breedlove. But in the meantime an astonishing golden apparition appeared on the sands, looking like an elongated Dutch panatella cigar. This elegant, knee-high newcomer had four stock fuel-injected Chrysler 'hemi' engines in a row, and the driver sat, dragster style, behind almost thirty feet of glistening hood and only an inch or two off the ground. 'Goldenrod' had been built by hot-rodders Bill and Bob Summers of Ontario, California, to challenge Bluebird's record in the 'automobile' class.

The row of engines inevitably caused problems, and the weather was breaking, too. Bob Summers twice clocked over 400mph, but on each occasion some trouble cropped up to prevent the return run. Finally on 13 November, with rain drizzling down, Goldenrod made it. Without actually getting into top gear, Bob Summers reached 417mph on the outward run and a mean of 409.28mph (658.67kph), thus dethroning Donald Campbell by almost exactly ten kilometres per hour, or just over six miles per hour.

America now held both land speed records (to say nothing of the fastest woman!) but the battle of the behemoths continued. Craig Breedlove had two objectives. The one was to regain his title from Art Arfons; the other to exceed 600mph. On 15 November he achieved both, covering the measured mile at 593mph one way and 608mph the other to close the season with an exuberant mean of 600.6mph (966.57kph).

This record stood for five years. Art Arfons brought an improved Green Monster back to Bonneville in 1966 in the hope of beating it, but instead survived the fastest accident in history when a front wheel collapsed at over 600mph and the great machine cart-wheeled over and over, scattering wreckage around a four mile area. But by now Apollo II had reached the moon and in-

Four years' hard labour preceded Donald Campbell's final, but qualified, success with the Proteus turbine-powered Bluebird (above), so named in memory of his father's cars. After repeated setbacks, Donald broke the land speed record for wheel-driven cars at 403.1mph (648.72kph), in July 1964, on Lake Eyre, Australia. By then the unrestricted speed record stood at 407.45mph (655.73kph).

evitably the idea cropped up of beating the jet-setters with a liquid-fuel rocket-powered car. Dick Keller, who had worked at the American Institute of Gas Technology, Ray Dausman, and a dragster exponent named Peter Farnsworth formed Reaction Dynamics Inc, and backed to the tune of half a million dollars by the National Gas Industry built what looked like a horizontal missile, but in fact came within the FIA's definition of a 'ground effect vehicle'.

Art Arfons (right) and his 17,500hp jet-engined Green Monster, with which he broke the land speed record three times in 1964-65 at Bonneville. He left it at 576.553mph (927.87kph) in November 1965, but lost it eight days later to Craig Breedlove, who broke the 600mph barrier with a figure of 600.601mph (966.57kph) in his Spirit of America, Sonic 1.

Known as 'Blue Flame' and powered by a rocket engine similar to those used in the American Space programme (giving a thrust of 21,000lb, and propelled by a mixture of liquefied natural gas and hydrogen peroxide) this awesome firework on wheels made its appearance at Bonneville in September 1970. A number of unexpected troubles occurred: for instance, the fiery blast from the tail set fire to the parachutes. But finally, on his twenty-sixth run Gary Gabelich, who had hitherto made his name as a dragster and a test astronaut, thundered it through the measured mile of salt in 5.829sec one way and 5.737sec back again, lifting the absolute speed record to 622.41mph (1001.63kph) for the mile and 630.388 for the flying kilometre.

The Sound Barrier was now within measurable distance. And this, indeed, was the next objective.

The Megadollar Sport

JUST AS RACING sharpens the breed, so competition successes do much to burnish the image. When Maurice Gatsonides won the 1953 Monte Carlo Rally in a Ford Zephyr people chuckled happily all around England. 'If it's good enough to win the Monte, it's good enough for me,' they intoned, little knowing that 'Gatso' had spent weeks reconnoitering the special test area in the hills behind Nice, so that it was as much a triumph of navigation as of performance. But the point had not been lost on Fords, who gave increasing support to private entrants and even flirted with racing themselves. Through their dealer organization, they competed in the Carrera Panamericana with notable success, and were equally active in the NASCAR stock car races in the

Graham Hill (top) won his second world championship in 1968, greatly boosting Lotus morale, which was sagging badly following Jim Clark's tragic death at Hockenheim. Another master driver in wet (and in the dry!) was Jackie Stewart (above), here at work in very damp conditions while winning the 1968 Dutch GP at Zandvoort with the Ford-engined Matra. Jim Clark (right), one of the greatest racing drivers of all time, winning his twenty-fifth and last Grand Prix, the South African, at Kyalami in 1968 with his Lotus-Ford.

States (in the Grand National Division Ford and Mercury won 19 out of 56 events in 1956 and 27 out of 53 in 1957). Ford equipment, moreover, featured in much of the machinery seen around the club circuits and in the early days of drag racing. Although in 1957 the American manufacturers agreed among themselves to abstain from racing, they continued to be involved behind the scenes, and in 1962 Henry Ford II, whose grandfather had launched the company's competition career, repudiated the agreement and embarked on a major motor sport programme that took in stock, drag, track and sports car racing as well as international rallies. To break into the top echelons of the game, what is more, they decided to buy up Ferrari.

As it happened, the Commendatore (who for years had been threatening to retire) seemed prepared to do a deal. For ten billion lire (or approximately eighteen million dollars), he told the Americans the Maranello factory would be theirs and its cars would become Ford-Ferraris.

Upon which, high-powered teams of accountants and management experts zeroed from Detroit, and after a few weeks came up with a counter-offer of something like ten million dollars. But in the meantime Enzo Ferrari had been having second thoughts. For one thing, there was an outcry in Italy against the sell-out of what was regarded as a national symbol. For another, as an individualist dedicated to the cult of speed and the development of machinery to its highest pitch regardless of cost, the Commendatore had found himself needled by the corporate mentality that required a cost-analysis on every washer in the plant. Seen at close quarters, Ford's computerized bureaucracy was more than he could bear. The essential conflict between the renaissance artist-engineer and a great corporation geared to mass-production broke through. When Ford's top brass arrived to sign the contract, he unceremoniously showed them the door.

Understandably miffed, they determined to beat Ferrari at his own game and on his home ground. Cost what it might, a Ford was going to win the 24 Hours of Le Mans. The scene was thus set for the most extravagant and intriguing battle in motoring history: between individual flair and space-age technology.

The corporation's virtually limitless resources were mobilized to produce the fastest and most reliable sports car ever known. Recalling that Eric Broadley had just introduced an exciting monocoque coupé powered by a centrally located Ford V8 engine (which was just what the Ford engineers had in mind) they whisked the whole project off to the new Ford Advanced Vehicles plant at Slough to form a test-bed for the GT40 – so called because it was only forty inches high. Fitted with a 4.2 litre aluminium version of the engine that Jim Clark had used at Indianapolis mounted centrally in a strong monocoque hull with gull-wing doors above unusually wide sills incorporating petrol tanks on both sides, the first prototypes proved that they were capable of 200mph but so light in the tail as to be virtually undriveable at that speed. And, apart from roadholding, that there were problems with the gearbox and braking as well.

On the GT40's first appearance at Nürburgring, Bruce McLaren and Phil Hill had to retire after only a third of the race had been run. Two weeks later Hill set up a new lap record at Le Mans, but the three GT40s were soon out and Ferraris swept the board. At Rheims, it was the same story. In three races not a single one of the cars managed to finish, and Ferraris had the field to themselves.

After this fiasco the Ford technical muscle really got to work. While production continued at Slough, Carroll Shelby (who had won Le Mans in 1959 on an Aston Martin and whose Cobras were proving their paces) was put in charge of development at Dearborn, where every aspect of the design and each part of the cars were computer programmed. Both the 4,736cc Cobra version of the Fairlane V8 and the 7 litre Galaxie engine (which had been tuned up for stock car racing)

A great driver/manufacturer, infinitely mourned after his fatal crash while testing at Goodwood in June 1970, was Bruce McLaren (above), the young New Zealander who came to Britain in 1958, raced Coopers until 1965, and then launched his own make, the McLaren, with immense success.

The flagman (right), scarcely betrays the intense excitement of the last seconds of the Italian Grand Prix at Monza, 1969, with Jackie Stewart in Matra-Ford No 20 forcing ahead of Jochen Rindt's Lotus-Ford No 4 to win by half a length.

were used in substitution for the original 4.2 litre unit, and a ZF replaced the Colotti gearbox. To handle the additional power new transaxles were built, and to cope with the problem of braking (at Mulsanne, for instance, the now overheavy cars would have to decelerate from over 200mph to under 40mph in 7sec) heavily ventilated 3/4in thick discs were devised.

The first hint of success came at Daytona, where Ken Miles and Ruby Lloyd won the 2,000km Continental, and the McLaren/Miles GT40 took second place at Sebring behind a Chaparral. But once again Ford's assault on the classic European events ended in discomfiture. Not one of the six GT40s finished at Le Mans. All retired with engine or transmission failures. Nor was there much consolation in the knowledge that the works Ferraris had also failed, since Jochen Rindt and Masten Gregory took the flag in their privately entered Ferrari ahead of two other similar cars to give Maranello a 1-2-3 victory. Once again it was game, set and match to the Commendatore.

But Ford had no intention of giving up the struggle. On the contrary, they were 'out for bear', as a top executive put it. Development continued at a high pitch throughout the winter and spring, and after further successes at both Daytona and Sebring no less than eight of the big Mark 2s and five GT40s lined up to challenge the Ferraris again at Le Mans in 1966. Yet as it happens, Maranello was ill-equipped to face such an armada. There had been a strike at the factory and their driver, John Surtees, had walked out after a management row on the eve of the race. All the same, Dan Gurney's Ford and Scarfiotti's Ferrari were leading neck and neck after six hours of racing when the heavens opened and a torrential downpour flooded the track. Two of the back-markers came to grief in the esses, blocking the way, and Scarfiotti crashed into them, wrecking his car. When at 3am Pedro Rodriguez' Ferrari also dropped out, it was clear that Fords had the race in their pocket at last. This time it was the three surviving Fords (all Mark 2s) that finished triumphantly 1-2-3.

Flying high (left): by the start of 1969 the aerofoil principle, of imparting downward pressure to improve roadholding, was being exploited to the full by designers, who prescribed huge wings, strut-mounted high above the wheels. This South African GP scene at Kyalami, with Jackie Oliver's BRM leading Hulme's McLaren, typifies the scene. The late François Cevert (above), selected by famous talent-spotter Ken Tyrrell to be No 2 to Jackie Stewart in the Tyrrell-Ford team in 1970. He won the lucrative United States Grand Prix in 1971, but sadly lost his life practising for the same race two seasons later.
Monaco Grand Prix, 1969 (right): Denny Hulme's McLaren-Ford, in its distinctive orange, taking the 'Gasworks' hairpin, slowest corner on the world's most famous 'round-the-houses' GP circuit. Hulme finished sixth on this occasion.

To prove that this reversal of form was no fluke, Dearborn sent its team back to Le Mans in 1967 with up-dated Mark 4s that had an aluminium honeycomb hull construction and a 7 litre engine producing 500bhp at only 5,000 revs. Ferrari fielded the P4, a 4 litre V12 giving 450bhp at 8,000rpm. Now it was the Fords that ran into trouble in the small hours of the morning, when the left front disc of Mario Andretti's Mark 4 suddenly locked on the esses. The car spun and was clouted in quick succession by his team mates Roger McCluskey and Jo Slessor. Luckily no one was injured, but it left only the Gurney/Foyt Ford in contention, making it a straight contest between them and Scarfiotti. Speeding up the pace, the two cars covered lap after lap in fifteen seconds less than the previous year's times. Gradually, though, Detroit's huge investment in the Mark 4 began to tell. Its lead over the Ferrari increased until it finally romped home, having

SHELL
Shell
SHELL
SHELL

Tragic end to what should have been a triumphant season for Jochen Rindt (right) came during practice for the 1970 Italian Grand Prix at Monza, when his Lotus-Ford suddenly careered out of control into a guard rail. Rindt was killed instantly. Having already won five GPs that season, he was pronounced the 1970 World Champion posthumously.

Fire is one of the greatest hazards in motor racing. At Brands Hatch in October 1971 the great Swiss driver, Joseph Siffert (left), lost his life when his BRM crashed at nearly 150mph and caught fire. The rest of the runners were brought to a standstill while rescuers tackled the blazing BRM in a useless effort to retrieve the driver. On lap 1 of the 1970 Spanish Grand Prix at Jarama (above), the Ferrari of Jacky Ickx and the BRM of Jackie Oliver collided. Amazingly both Oliver and Ickx escaped comparatively unhurt.

covered over 3,200 miles (5,150km) at an average of 135mph (217kph).

The Ford Motor Company had achieved its objective. But to do so it had spent something like fifteen million dollars – rather more, indeed, than the price they had offered for the whole Ferrari factory (and about 250 times what it had cost Bentley Motors for their five wins between 1924 and 1930). The point had been proved that given a big enough investment it is possible to win at Le Mans – or get to the moon, for that matter.

Ford's megadollar involvement emphasized the degree to which automobile racing was becoming big business. For by now motor sport was booming throughout the globe as never before. True, Grand Prix had been held in Australia since 1928 (when Arthur Waite won in a 747cc Austin Seven) and New Zealand's first international meeting had been run at Ardmore in 1954; but they had tended, if only for geographical reasons, to remain local affairs. It was not until 1964 that the Tasman Series of international races brought world class motor racing to Australia and New Zealand. Similarly, the South African GP became a championship event in 1962, first at East London and, from 1967 onwards, on the Kyalami circuit outside Johannesburg. Austria's Zeltweg course (superseded in 1969 by the Osterreichring); Belgium's circuit of Zolder; Japan's Suzuka International and Fuji Speedways; Canada's Speedway Park circuit at Edmonton, St Jovite near Montreal and Mosport Park on the shores of Lake Ontario; Sears Point at San Francisco, Road Atlanta at Gainesville, Ga. (to say nothing of the already well-established Road America circuit at Elkhart Lake, Wisconsin and Riverside International Raceway east of Los Angeles in the shadow of the San Bernardino mountain); along with the Autodromo de la Ciudad at Mexico City, the Lourenço Marques circuit and Rhodesia's Kumalo circuit, Keimola and Hämeenliuna in Finland and others around the world all testified to the globular popularity that racing had now achieved. In the United States, for instance, it had already become a highly popular spectator sport – second only to baseball in attendance figures.

Naturally enough, the impact of this on the media and above all on television did not pass unnoticed by Madison Avenue. Sponsorship had been a feature of Indianapolis for years and the roadsters of the fifties were blazoned with decals. Yet in the great European classics national colours were *de rigueur* (like wearing white at Wimbledon) until Colin Chapman thumbed his nose at tradition in 1966 and turned the Formula 1 Lotus into a 200mph ambassador for Player's Gold Leaf cigarettes. The other followed suit, and within three years even BRM appeared in the livery of Yardley's After-Shave. They had very little choice. With costs soaring, the subsidies from oil companies and component manufacturers were simply not sufficient.

Luckily, perhaps, Eurovision and coast-to-

Ford

Jackie Stewart (left), Scotland's greatest driver since the ever-lamented Jim Clark, hit the racing scene with a bang in 1964, when he won eleven out of thirteen Formula 3 races, driving a Cooper with Ken Tyrrell as manager. He won his first Formula 1 Grand Prix for BRM at Monza in 1965, and eight years and twenty-six more victories later announced his retirement. He was World Champion three times, in 1969, 1971 and 1973, and remains very active in the GP scene as an ardent safety campaigner. Old Master from down under, Jack Brabham (above), contested world championship events from 1957 to 1970, when he retired from racing after winning the championship title three times, in 1959, 1960 and 1966. Here we see the famous 'Black Jack' scoring his last Grand Prix victory of all, that of South Africa in 1970, held at Kyalami, near Johannesburg; he was driving his own Ford-powered BT33 monocoque Brabham. One of Britain's high hopes for 1975, James Hunt (right), once known as 'the Shunt' for his crashing propensity, won the International Trophy race at Silverstone early in 1974, driving Lord Hesketh's new Hesketh-Ford in impeccable style.

coast exposure of the top events at peak viewing time tempted the marketing giants to allocate substantial budgets to their new protégés. Previously, constructors of racers had in the main been large concerns such as Alfa Romeo, Mercedes, Jaguar and Ferrari who built their cars from the ground up. But the new wave of specialized assemblers – the 'kit car' brigade using Ford Cosworth engines, Hewland gearboxes along with bought-in wheels, suspension, steering and other major components and building only a handful of machines a year – could never have survived without the sponsorship of advertisers. To run a couple of cars in the Formula 1 championship required a budget of some £250,000 ($600,000) a year. The Grand Prix circus as a whole spent something like three million pounds each season, only half of which was covered by starting and prize money. The balance had to be made up by sponsors.

Obviously the big money was primarily interested in the top box-office draws – such as Formula 1, the Can-Am series and Le Mans – all of which moved quickly from the realms of sport into that of show-business. And since most of the cars, using identical equipment, were distinguished only by the idiosyncrasies of design, steering geometry, weight distribution and aerodynamic profile, it meant, more than ever before, that races were won by the skill and courage of the drivers. Not surprisingly, these modern gladiators became 'superstars', holding the centre of the stage in their white flameproof overalls, most of them with a business manager, a tax-free pad, a 'mod' hair-do and a private aircraft to hop from circuit to circuit.

Gone were the romantic days of the inter-city races, of blinding over the Alps, of Moss in the Mille Miglia. Speeds were increasing every year and competition was so tight that a couple of seconds meant the difference between pole position and barely qualifying on an autodrome like Monza. There was no room now for an amateur, devil-may-care approach. Nor indeed for cat-and-mouse tactics. 'Never forget,' Sammy Davis had once said, 'that you have an appointment with a man with a chequered flag at the end. You can be late for it if you like, but if you don't keep that appointment you might just as well not have started.' Now speed was all-important, and Formula 1 races were sometimes even decided in practice. 'Grand Prix are won from the starter's flag,' said Clay Regazzoni recently. 'The time is over when a driver could start at the back and win the race. Today whoever has pole position and gets off well is likely to stay in front if his car holds up.' Driving on the limit in a machine no more than seven times their own weight, it is not surprising that the protagonists insisted on greater track safety, making their point felt through a union known as the Grand Prix Drivers' Association that was headed by Jo Bonnier of Sweden. For in this most dangerous of all professions, the toll was alarming. Of the thirty-two drivers who had won Grand Prix races in the first twenty years of the championship, eight had been killed against eleven who had retired and thirteen who still raced. And these were just the champions: there had been so many other fatalities. Their preoccupation about the elimination of all possible risks was absolutely understandable. 'I'm not paid to risk my life,' Jackie Stewart once pointed out. 'I'm paid to drive a racing car as fast as I can. And to live to drive another day.'

More rewarding, perhaps, than its assault on Le Mans (and certainly less expensive) was Ford of England's sponsorship of the Cosworth engine. As it happens, these units were not ready until the middle of 1967, and although Ferrari produced a 60 degree V12 (known as the 312, and derived from the 3.3 litre sports car engine reduced in capacity to 2,978cc to qualify for the new Formula) 1966 turned out to be a Brabham year. With his Australian Repco engine in the back of a workmanlike chassis frame evolved by Ron Taurenac from the original GP Brabham, Jack Brabham won the French, British, Dutch and German Grand Prix to take the drivers' championship for the third time, and the manufacturers' championship as well – which gave him the distinction of being the first racing driver to win the title in a car of his own make. In 1967, moreover, he took second place in the world championship, behind his New Zealand team mate Denny Hulme who won the title in the final round at Mexico City.

Yet once the impressive Cosworth DFV engine appeared in the back of Jim Clark's Lotus (looking, thought Graham Hill, like a piece of modern sculpture) it was obvious that this beautifully designed engine was going to call the tune. During the latter part of the year Clark won four Grand Prix (including Watkins Glen, which in sheer advertising terms justified Ford's investment, even if it didn't give sufficient points to take the title) and on form all the pointers were that 1968 would be another Clark and Lotus year. But after winning the South African GP to chalk up his 25th Grand Prix victory, Jim Clark crashed inexplicably in a minor Formula 2 race at Hockenheim and was killed on the spot. The whole of the racing world was stunned by this tragedy which left the championship wide open. It developed, in fact, into a contest between Graham Hill, who had moved over to Lotus, Denny Hulme in the McLaren-Ford, and Jackie Stewart in the new Matra.

Starting with a little monocoque Formula 3 and an equally successful Formula 2 car, the French aeronautical and missile firm of Engins Matra SA had been backed by a loan of six million new francs, by General de Gaulle's government, to build an all-French Formula 1 machine (along with a sports-prototype to win at Le Mans). Since time was needed to develop the engine, Matra concluded an agreement with Ken Tyrrell, who had helped them gain a foothold in Formula 2 racing, to run a Grand Prix team under his own auspices using a Matra chassis with a Cosworth engine. Jackie Stewart was persuaded to drive for them.

As things turned out, it was neck and neck until Mexico, where Stewart's Matra and Hulme's McLaren both ran into trouble, leaving Graham Hill to win the needle

Peter Revson of the United States gave everyone a shock when he won the 1973 British Grand Prix at Silverstone in masterly style, driving a Yardley-sponsored McLaren-Ford. A wealthy man, he had laid a £100 bet at 14 to 1 on his own victory, just for fun!

Overpage: Brazilian 'Bomb' Emerson Fittipaldi, winning the 1972 British GP at Brands Hatch with his John Player Special Lotus-Ford. With four other victories that season, he became World Champion with 61 points to the 45 of runner-up Jackie Stewart. Fittipaldi was champion again in 1974, this time driving for McLaren.

match and the 1968 championship in the Lotus-Ford. But in 1969 Jackie Stewart really came into his own with the Matra-Ford, winning the South African, Spanish, Dutch, British and Italian Grand Prix to secure his first world title. Jochen Rindt of Austria and Jacky Ickx of Belgium were the runners-up behind him.

In Grand Prix, as elsewhere, there are vintage years and 1970 turned out to be both exciting and tragic. Among other things it saw the astonishing appearance of an entirely new marque called March (an anagram, as it happens, of the owners' initials) that gate-crashed glamorously into the Grand Prix scene not only with their own works team but also untried Formula 1 machines that they had seemingly conjured out of thin air and sold to customers such as Ken Tyrrell and Andy Granatelli of STP.

Logically, of course, Jackie Stewart should have gone on driving Matras for Tyrrell. But the French factory now had a tie-up with Chrysler and in any case had decided to press on with their own V12 engine; with the result that since Stewart felt that the only power unit for him was the Cosworth-Ford V8, and no other Cosworth-engined Formula 1 car was available, he and Tyrrell felt obliged to opt for the new marque. Before a single car had been built, in fact, the reigning world champion and several other top drivers (such as Chris Amon, Ronnie Peterson, Jo Siffert and Mario Andretti) were committed to March. Perhaps it was all really too good to be true. After an early success by Stewart at Madrid and a 1–2 victory at Silverstone, March failed to live up to its precocious expectations and ended the season behind Lotus and Ferrari. Jochen Rindt, on the other hand, won at Monaco with the Lotus-Ford 49C and went on to take the Dutch, French, British and German GPs in the revolutionary new Lotus-Ford 72 before crashing fatally at the Parabolica during practice at Monza. But no one could touch him on points and thus, sadly enough, he became the first posthumous world champion.

If Ken Tyrrell had kept his team going this season with the March, he nevertheless had a surprise in store for 1971. Behind closed doors in his timber mill in a Surrey wood a new GP car had been put together that was destined to win the world championship at its first attempt. There was nothing very revolutionary, to be sure, about its design. But unlike many of its rivals, it was sturdy. And, of course, the new Tyrrell was powered by the Ford Cosworth DFV. What it did have, also, was a curious elevated airscoop intended, as the designer Derek Gardner put it, to 'remove the froth from the beer' and allow the engine to breathe better. Before long all the other GP cars were wearing similar periscope-like devices behind the driver's head.

Starting from the second row of the grid behind the Ferraris of Ickx and Regazzoni and Chris Amon's V12 Matra, Jackie Stewart got into the lead in the Spanish Grand Prix and pulled off Tyrrell's first victory. A fortnight later at Silverstone his throttle stuck open on the first corner and Stewart plunged straight for the television cameras, involving several million viewers, if only vicariously, in a spectacular shunt. But this was not a championship race and the following week, after hectic surgery to the car, Jackie Stewart won at Monte Carlo, establishing a new lap record. At the French GP on the new Paul Ricard track, he led from start to finish with his team mate François Cevert in second position, and followed this

John

up with a similar performance in the German Grand Prix at Nürburgring. By the time he had won the British Grand Prix at Silverstone as well, Stewart already had the title in his pocket, so that even a broken stub-axle in Austria and engine trouble at Monza made no difference to the result.

In Canada, however, Stewart chalked up his sixth win of the season, and although at Watkins Glen he lost the lead when his tires overheated, which put him back to fifth position, François Cevert nevertheless carried off the honours for Tyrrell, who had every reason for celebration. Even if Jackie Stewart's total of six victories was one short of Jim Clark's record of seven in 1963, his domination of the circuits had been really more conclusive. And while Ronnie Peterson had finished second in the championship in the Ford-engined March, François Cevert had convincingly taken third place with his Tyrrell.

On form, therefore, it looked as if the Tyrrell triumph would continue in 1972. Stewart started the season well by winning at Buenos Aires, but error crept in both at South Africa and at Madrid, by which time Stewart was bedevilled with a bleeding stomach ulcer that kept him out of racing for a full six weeks. Despite a splendid comeback on the twisting Clermont-Ferrand circuit, where he won the French Grand Prix, it was too late. Emerson Fittipaldi, driving the Lotus (now known as the John Player Special), had reached the peak of his form and went on to win the championship.

At twenty-three he was the youngest driver to have become world champion in what is, surprisingly enough, not entirely a young man's sport. Both Farina and Fangio were in their forties when they first took the title; Jack Brabham and Graham Hill were both nudging that age when each recaptured it for the last time. A racing driver often reaches the peak of his form when over thirty. Yet it was just at this point, when only thirty-four, that Jackie Stewart, the super-star, decided to retire. 'Motor racing can be the world's most exhilarating sport, but it can also be the most cruel,' he explained. Bruce McLaren, the soundest of drivers, had been killed in June 1970 while testing a car of his own make at Goodwood. Two weeks later Piers Courage had died in a gory accident during the Dutch Grand Prix. Jochen Rindt had lost his life that September during practice at Monza. On Stewart's birthday (11 June) in 1972 Jo Bonnier, who had campaigned so long for greater safety measures, was killed at Le Mans. 'One by one I watched close friends die on the race track, yet each time I slipped back into the cockpit, away from the harsh glare of the awkward truth,' Stewart confessed. 'Then I saw the strain on Helen and the boys, and I made my decision.' On 5 April 1973 Jackie Stewart told Fords and Tyrrell that he would retire after the US Grand Prix in October, which would have been his hundredth event in world championship racing. By a tragic twist of fate, he never drove that hundredth race. Because of François Cevert's death in practice, the Tyrrells were withdrawn from Watkins Glen. But already by Monza Jackie Stewart had won the title for the third time. In nine seasons of racing, he had scored 360 championship points, representing 27 victories in 99 Grand Prix.

His retirement left the field open in 1974. Ferrari made a determined comeback and by the end of the European season Clay Regazzoni (with the German GP to his credit) and the South African Jody Scheckter (who won in Sweden and in England) were leading on points ahead of Fittipaldi (the winner in Brazil and in Belgium) and Niki Lauda (who had won in Spain and Holland). Some distance behind the leaders, despite their respective victories (the one in South Africa and Austria, the other in Monaco, France and Italy) were Carlos Reutemann and Ronnie Peterson. In all there were seven drivers in five different marques, none of whom had scored twice on the trot (which showed how close the competition had become).

The issue was decided in America. Driving brilliantly in the Canadian GP at Mosport

Jody Scheckter, the young South African who joined the Tyrrell team on Jackie Stewart's retirement, leads the pack in the 1974 Swedish Grand Prix at Anderstorp.

He led from start to finish to score his first outright GP victory.

Park, Fittipaldi drew level with Regazzoni and each moved on to Watkins Glen with 52 points (and Scheckter on 45). But, as it turned out, the great battle of the Glen came to nought. Regazzoni was sidelined quite early with tire problems, Scheckter retired at half distance, and the TV commentators were already hailing Emerson Fittipaldi as the new world champion before he cruised his Brabham into fourth place behind Reutemann, Pace, and Hunt. Of all the championships since the series began, this had been the most open, and the line up on the grid at Monza of twenty drivers from no less than twelve countries testified beyond doubt to the strength and international character of the sport today.

Lotus chief, Colin Chapman, has the habit of throwing his cap into the air or under the wheels when one of his cars takes the chequered flag, as seen above, with Jacky Ickx winning the 1974 Race of Champions in the wet at Brands Hatch.

Old timer with unsurpassed experience in today's Grand Prix world is the ever-popular Londoner, Graham Hill (left), World Champion in 1962 with a BRM, and in 1968 with a Lotus. The year 1974, when he raced an Embassy-Lola, marked his sixteenth season in Formula 1.

'The Old Bear': Denny Hulme (right) came from New Zealand in 1960, rising via Formula Junior and Formula 2 to Grand Prix status by 1965. Driving for Jack Brabham, he became World Champion in 1967, joined McLarens in 1968, and became Can Am Champion twice, in 1968 and 1970.

The Scene Today

Getting the power to the road—the essence of dragster racing, with big V-8 motor and even bigger tires. It is on split seconds used up in getting off the mark that records are lost or won in this exacting sport.

Britain's hardiest annual in motoring events is the London to Brighton Veteran Run (right) held on the first Sunday of November each year to commemorate the emancipation of motoring from crippling laws in 1896. This scene from the 1953 Run features a de Dion-Bouton and a Gillet-Forest, both of 1902 vintage, crossing Westminster Bridge with Big Ben in the background.

WHILE EUROPE REMAINS the heartbeat of activities and Grand Prix is still the top draw, the centre of gravity is nevertheless shifting. Since 1966 the Canadian-American Challenge Cup, which blossomed into being at St Jovite in the hills behind Montreal, has become not only the richest but also the fastest of all contests. Sponsored by such firms as Johnson's Wax (under the active eye of Stirling Moss as racing director) and Andy Granatelli's STP, the Can-Am series attracts the top talent from Europe and the States with an average starting field of twenty-eight cars, an attendance of 400,000, and a purse of nearly a million dollars. If for nearly half a century the American public's interest has been solidly focused on Indianapolis and the dirt or board tracks, there has now been a dramatic revival of sports car racing on road circuits spearheaded by enthusiasts looking for something fresh. The difference is that whereas in Europe such machines are subdivided into classes and hedged by regulations, in the Can-Am Series almost no holds are barred. The cars are two-seater racers with full-width bodies and ever more powerful engines that make them, in many cases, faster than the Formula 1 machinery.

Intriguingly enough, they are mostly Anglo-American hybrids, built by specialist British firms such as Lola, McLaren and Brabham around the powerful 7 litre Chevrolet V8 engine. Indeed with the exception of Jim Hall's astonishing Chaparral (featuring automatic transmission and an elevated aerofoil immediately copied by the Formula 1 cars) that won at Monterey in 1966, and Tony Dean's Porsche 908 that took the honours at Road Atlanta in 1970, all the Can-Am series in the first five years were carried off either by Eric Broadley's Lolas, with six victories to their credit, or more impressively still by the McLaren M6As and M8As that registered a remarkable total of thirty-one wins and lifted Bruce McLaren into the millionaire class. Or certainly should have done. For with its wide 15in tires, its 600bhp Lucas fuel-injected Chevrolet 427 engine mated to a five-speed Hewland transaxle, and its 12in. ventilated Girling discs that could decelerate the 1,300lb car by 100mph (160kph) in 3sec, the M8A was a masterpiece. Sadly enough it

O 464
P100

All three pictures show drag, or hot car racing in Great Britain. Drag racing started in the United States in an effort to channel the activities of street racers, who were chasing one another along the public highways. The course is a straight quarter mile (440yd or 402m) and cars accelerate to over 200mph (322kph) in 7sec—tires scream, smoke billows out, and the driver's weight is doubled as he is forced back into his special seat.

was when testing its successor, the M8D (nicknamed the 'Batmobile' because of the two high fins and aerofoil at the back) that McLaren was killed at Goodwood on 2 June 1970.

For all this, what much of the American public loves most is sheer, unadulterated squirt – which to six million *aficionados* means dragging. This is in fact an acceleration contest between two matched cars at a time over a quarter of a mile from a standing start, and many are the weird and wonderful devices that have appeared since Hot Rodders first started 'channelling' production cars back in the thirties. 'Long before flashing lights, din, brilliant colours and violence ushered in the psychedelic age of the mid-60s, drag fans were relishing similar assaults on their senses,' explains Al Bochroch. 'Within 15 seconds they experience blinding lights, shocks of sound from 1,000hp engines, the shriek of enormous tires fighting for traction, orange engine flames and enough smoke momentarily to hide the cars; then two streaks of colour and a quarter of a mile away popping parachutes looking like twin blossoms.' Some 4,000 events on 200 strips contested, unbelievably enough, by nearly half a million participants who notch up speeds of anything up to 260mph have turned dragging into the most contemporary of American sports.

From coast to coast, too, are hundreds of tracks that hold weekly stock car races, and NASCAR (the National Association for Stock Car Auto Racing) holds some fifty Grand Nationals of between 150 and 300 miles on steeply banked oval tracks. On the 2.7 mile long Talladega Tri-oval, opened in 1969, lap speeds of 200mph (322kph) are regularly recorded as drivers take the 33 degree banked turns at 210mph and reach 220mph down the straights. To achieve such speeds production cars have been transformed into highly sophisticated machinery, often at enormous cost, and in marked contrast to the European scene where stock cars are cut down to a minimum, and as often as

The racing of restored vintage sports and racing cars is highly popular in Britain. Leaping like a spring lamb during a Prescott hill-climb in 1960, is a 1923 Brescia Bugatti (above) driven by Hamish Moffatt.

Speeds of over 200mph are attained by modified 'stock' saloon cars in NASCAR races on the Daytona Speedway in Florida, USA. This tense nose-to-tail scene (left) was shot in 1973.

Biff, bang, crash, wallop . . . Stock car racing (above) at Brands Hatch, with Derek Green and James Gannon on the outside, mixing it well and truly during a heat for the 'Race of Stars' Trophy in 1966.

not the object of the exercise is to eliminate opposition by smashing into rival cars or driving them off the track – anything, in fact, to give the paying public a thrill.

Autocross, a form of cross-country hill-climb with cars competing in pairs against the stop-watch, and the rather lengthier rally-cross in which four cars at a time race each other over the equivalent of a special test section in a normal rally, both now enjoy a considerable vogue in England and are beginning to catch on in other places where mud, sweat and cheers are considered good fun. In contrast, the great days of hill-climbs and international rallies seem to be over, in Europe at least. Admittedly the Mountain Championship was revived in 1957, for sports cars up to 2 litres, with classes for touring and GT machines, and by 1969 the FIA European Hill Climb Championship consisted of sprints up Montseny, Mont Ventoux, Cesena-Sestrière, Trento-Bondone, Schauinsland, Mont Dore, and Sierre-Montana-Crans. But although both Ferrari and Porsche have continued to back and dominate the series, often putting up spectacular performances, and Shelsley Walsh still attracts an enthusiastic following, hill-climbs no longer make such great waves in the sport as they did.

Inevitably, too, congested roads and escalating costs have had a depressing effect on the classic European rallies. Already by 1963 the Alpine Rally was so professionally orientated that its special, almost lyrical, character had been lost and it had devolved (one tended to feel) into a dangerous blind through holiday traffic. In fact from 1964 onwards its route was confined to the remoter areas of the French Alps that hitherto had been the province of the Evian–Mont Blanc, and by 1970 it was cancelled altogether because of the hazards of tourist-filled roads. Similarly in 1961 the Liège–Rome–Liège had to be re-routed from Italy into Yugoslavia and Bulgaria, becoming the Liège–Sofia–Liège in the process, and four years later was transformed into a marathon round the Nürburgring, thus ceasing to be a road event any more. Even if the Acropolis Rally continues

TDH404

Go-Karting (above), which began in the mid-1950s, has become a very popular, and cheap, motor sport. The East African Safari (left and top) recaptures the adventurous spirit of the early European rallies. The 1966 winners were Shankland and Rothwell in a Peugeot 404 (left).

in Greece, and the Monte Carlo Rally is still held each January, Europe has become too small for the international trials, which have been replaced by such events as the East Africa Safari, run through sparsely inhabited country where the hazards are more likely to be floods and big game.

At lunch one day in 1968 Sir Max Aitken, Jocelyn Stevens and Keith Schellenberg hit on the idea of running a long-distance rally from London to Sydney through Europe, Asia and Australia. Sponsored by the *Daily Express* and the Sydney *Daily Telegraph*, the marathon attracted almost 100 starters (Keith Schellenberg's 1930 8 litre Bentley among them) who left London late in November, drove through Turkey, Afghanistan, and India, and were shipped from Bombay to Perth. Some fifty-seven cars managed to finish the 10,000 mile (16,000km) jaunt in a blaze of publicity, a works-entered Hillman Hunter being declared the winner after the Citroen DS21 and the Ford Taunus 20 which had led across Australia were both involved in accidents just before the finish.

Shortly afterwards ninety-six cars – most of them works entries – left Wembley Stadium for an even longer marathon of 17,000 miles (28,500km) from London to Mexico City. This took them (in a somewhat roundabout way) first down to Sofia and back to Lisbon to catch the boat to Rio de Janeiro, thence south to Montevideo, Buenos Aires, San Antonio, Santiago, and up the western coast

Plenty of dust and mud are encountered in the great East African Safari Rally (above). This is the 1972 winner, Hannu Mikkola, trailing an impressive dust-cloud as he blasts across

a Kenyan landscape. Think of crossing this at night! Above right, one of the many hazards encountered during the London to Mexico World Cup rally of 1970.

of South America via Lima, Cuenca, Cali and Cristobal. By Montevideo the field had already been reduced by half and twenty-five cars eventually reached Mexico headed by the Mikkola-Palm Ford Escort with four other similar models in third, fifth, sixth and eighth places, and Triumph 2500 P1s notching in second and fourth (a Citroen DS21 was seventh). 'It's been the toughest event I ever took part in,' conceded Hannu Mikkola at the end of it all. 'But I wouldn't hesitate to do it again.' Here, indeed, may lie the future of international rallying on the grand scale, while nearer-home enthusiasts will presumably continue to paint competition numbers on their workaday transport, ready to challenge whatever the local rally organizer can dream up for a week-end's sport.

For, whether it is Grand Prix, Formula 5000, the Monte Carlo Rally, or a Bugatti Owners' Club meeting, the lure of speed and competition is as central to human nature as when the first pioneer motorists challenged each other with the taunt that 'anything your car can do, mine can do better'.

Nostalgia there may be for the good old days when cars were cars and not projectiles advertising someone's cigarettes that could not otherwise get television exposure. There is something grotesque, to be sure, at the thought that the British Grand Prix should now be named after a brand of tobacco. But without sponsorship, racing would be in a bad way, and over commercialized though it may have become, at least the sport isn't dead. The drivers are as good if not better than ever, and (ugly accretions and all) today's cars are fabulously fast. Even the most blasé must surely be stirred by the tearing, rattling, throaty roar of a Cosworth engine or the higher, rasping pitch of a 12 cylinder Ferrari, and the stupendous sight of the pack streaking down, like road-borne jet fighters, to the Parabolica at Monza. In a nuclear age, such machinery is absolutely in tune with the times.

Who would have guessed, moreover, during the energy crisis in the winter of 1973, when the Monte Carlo Rally was cancelled and pessimists forecast an end to all racing, that the new season would see a greater boom than ever before? Hitherto, the average Formula 1 field had been fifteen cars. Yet in the Italian Grand Prix last year no less than thirty-eight cars fought for a place on the grid, and four new American teams, along with contenders from Japan and Hong Kong, are swelling the ranks in 1975.

In eighty years of history, so much has changed. Yet, come to think of it, there is so much that hasn't.

Glossary

Glossary of Terms and Abbreviations

AAA American Automobile Association
ACF Automobile Club de France
AIACR Association Internationale des Automobile Clubs Reconnus
In 1947 this became the
FIA Fédération Internationale de l'Automobile
LSR Land Speed Record
RAC Royal Automobile Club
bhp brake horsepower
ohc overhead camshaft
ohv overhead valves

We have used the American terms 'windshield' and 'hood' throughout, rather than the British 'windscreen' and 'bonnet'.

Results

European Formula 2 Championship

1967 Jacky Ickx *Matra*
1968 Jean-Pierre Beltoise *Matra*
1969 Johnny Servoise-Gavin *Matra*
1970 Clay Regazzoni *Techno-FVA*
1971 Ronnie Peterson *March*
1972 Mike Hailwood *Surtees*
1973 J. P. Jarier *March BMW*
1974 Patrick Depailler *March BMW*

Grand Prix: Britain 1926–1974

1926 Senéchal and Wagner *Delage*
1927 Benoist *Delage*
no race until
1949 de Graffenried *Maserati*
1950 Farina *Alfa Romeo*
1951 Gonzales *Ferrari*
1952 Ascari *Ferrari*
1953 Ascari *Ferrari*
1954 Gonzales *Ferrari*
1955 Moss *Mercedes-Benz*
1956 Fangio *Lancia-Ferrari*
1957 Brooks and Moss *Vanwall*
1958 Collins *Ferrari*
1959 Brabham *Cooper*
1960 Brabham *Cooper*
1961 von Trips *Ferrari*
1962 Clark *Lotus*
1963 Clark *Lotus*
1964 Clark *Lotus*
1965 Clark *Lotus*
1966 Brabham *Brabham*
1967 Clark *Lotus*
1968 Siffert *Lotus*
1969 Stewart *Matra*
1970 Rindt *Lotus*
1971 Stewart *Tyrrell*
1972 Fittipaldi *John Player Special*
1973 Revson *McLaren-Ford*
1974 Scheckter *Tyrrell-Ford*

Grand Prix: France 1906–1974

1906 Szisz *Renault*
1907 Nazzaro *F.I.A.T.*
1908 Lautenschlager *Mercedes*
no race until
1912 Boillot *Peugeot*
1913 Boillot *Peugeot*
1914 Lautenschlager *Mercedes*
no race until
1921 Murphy *Duesenberg*
1922 Nazzaro *Fiat*
1923 Segrave *Sunbeam*
1924 Campari *Alfa Romeo*
1925 Benoist and Divo *Delage*
1926 Goux *Bugatti*
1927 Benoist *Delage*
1928 Williams *Bugatti*
1929 Williams *Bugatti*
1930 Etancelin *Bugatti*
1931 Chiron and Varzi *Bugatti*
1932 Nuvolari *Alfa Romeo*
1933 Campari *Maserati*
1934 Chiron *Alfa Romeo*
1935 Caracciola *Mercedes-Benz*
1936 Wimille and Sommer *Bugatti*
1937 Chiron *Talbot*
1938 von Brauchitsch *Mercedes-Benz*
1939 Müller *Auto Union*
no race until
1947 Chiron *Talbot*
1948 Wimille *Alfa Romeo*
1949 Pozzi *Delahaye*
1950 Fangio *Alfa Romeo*
1951 Fangio and Fagioli *Alfa Romeo*
1952 Ascari *Ferrari*
1953 Hawthorn *Ferrari*
1954 Fangio *Mercedes-Benz*
1955 no race
1956 Collins *Ferrari*
1957 Fangio *Maserati*
1958 Hawthorn *Ferrari*
1959 Brooks *Ferrari*
1960 Brabham *Cooper*
1961 Baghetti *Ferrari*
1962 Gurney *Porsche*
1963 Gurney *Porsche*
1964 Gurney *Brabham*
1965 Clark *Lotus*
1966 Brabham *Brabham*
1967 Brabham *Brabham*
1968 Ickx *Ferrari*
1969 Stewart *Matra*
1970 Rindt *Lotus*
1971 Stewart *Tyrrell*
1972 Stewart *Tyrrell*
1973 Peterson *John Player Special*
1974 Peterson *John Player Special*

Grand Prix: Germany 1926–1974

1926 Caracciola *Mercedes-Benz*
1927 Merz *Mercedes-Benz*
1928 Caracciola and Werner *Mercedes-Benz*
1929 Williams *Bugatti*
1930 no race
1931 Caracciola *Mercedes-Benz*
1932 Caracciola *Mercedes-Benz*
1933 no race
1934 Stuck *Auto Union*

1935 Nuvolari *Alfa Romeo*
1936 Rosemeyer *Auto Union*
1937 Caracciola *Mercedes-Benz*
1938 Seaman *Mercedes-Benz*
1939 Caracciola *Mercedes-Benz*
no race until
1950 Ascari *Ferrari*
1951 Ascari *Ferrari*
1952 Ascari *Ferrari*
1953 Farina *Ferrari*
1954 Fangio *Mercedes-Benz*
1955 no race
1956 Fangio *Ferrari*
1957 Fangio *Maserati*
1958 McLaren *Cooper*
1959 Brooks *Ferrari*
1960 Brooks *Ferrari*
1961 Moss *Lotus*
1962 G. Hill *BRM*
1963 Surtees *Ferrari*
1964 Surtees *Ferrari*
1965 Clark *Lotus*
1966 Brabham *Brabham*
1967 Hulme *Brabham*
1968 Stewart *Matra*
1969 Ickx *Brabham*
1970 Rindt *Lotus*
1971 Stewart *Tyrrell*
1972 Ickx *Ferrari*
1973 Stewart *Tyrrell-Ford*
1974 Regazzoni *Ferrari*

Grand Prix: Italy 1921–1974

1921 Goux *Ballot*
1922 Bordino *Fiat*
1923 Salamano *Fiat*
1924 Ascari *Alfa Romeo*
1925 Brilli-Peri *Alfa Romeo*
1926 'Sabipa' *Bugatti*
1927 Benoist *Delage*
1928 Chiron *Bugatti*
no race until
1931 Campari and Nuvolari *Alfa Romeo*
1932 Campari and Nuvolari *Alfa Romeo*
1933 Fagioli *Alfa Romeo*
1934 Caracciola and Fagioli *Mercedes-Benz*
1935 Stuck *Auto Union*
1936 Rosemeyer *Auto Union*
1937 Caracciola *Mercedes-Benz*
1938 Nuvolari *Auto Union*
no race until
1947 Trossi *Alfa Romeo*
1948 Wimille *Alfa Romeo*
1949 Ascari *Ferrari*
1950 Farina *Alfa Romeo*
1951 Ascari *Ferrari*
1952 Ascari *Ferrari*
1953 Fangio *Maserati*
1954 Fangio *Mercedes-Benz*
1955 Fangio *Mercedes-Benz*
1956 Moss *Maserati*
1957 Moss *Vanwall*
1958 Brooks *Vanwall*
1959 Brooks *Vanwall*
1960 P. Hill *Ferrari*
1961 P. Hill *Ferrari*
1962 G. Hill *BRM*
1963 Clark *Lotus*
1964 Surtees *Ferrari*
1965 Stewart *BRM*
1966 Scarfiotti *Ferrari*
1967 Surtees *Honda*
1968 Hulme *McLaren*
1969 Stewart *Matra*
1970 Regazzoni *Ferrari*
1971 Gethin *BRM*
1972 Fittipaldi *John Player Special*
1973 Peterson *John Player Special*
1974 Peterson *John Player Special*

Grand Prix: United States of America 1959–1974

1959 McLaren *Cooper*
1960 Moss *Lotus*
1961 Ireland *Lotus*
1962 Clark *Lotus*
1963 G. Hill *BRM*
1964 G. Hill *BRM*
1965 G. Hill *BRM*
1966 Clark *Lotus*
1967 Clark *Lotus*
1968 Stewart *Matra*
1969 Rindt *Lotus*
1970 Fittipaldi *Lotus*
1971 Cevert *Tyrrell*
1972 Stewart *Tyrrell*
1973 Peterson *John Player Special*
1974 Fittipaldi *John Player Special*

Indianapolis '500' 1911–1974

1911 R. Harroun and C. Patschke *Marmon*
1912 J. Dawson and D. Herr *National*
1913 J. Goux *Peugeot*
1914 R. Thomas *Delage*
1915 R. de Palma *Mercedes*
1916 D. Resta *Peugeot*
1919 H. Wilcox *Peugeot*
1920 G. Chevrolet *Monroe-Frontenac*
1921 T. Milton *Frontenac*
1922 J. Murphy *Duesenberg-Miller*
1923 T. Milton and H. Wilcox *Miller*

1924 L. Corum and J. Boyer *Duesenberg*
1925 P. de Paolo and N. K. Batten *Duesenberg*
1926 F. Lockhart *Miller*
1927 G. Souders *Duesenberg*
1928 L. Meyer *Miller*
1929 R. Keech *Miller*
1930 W. Arnold *Miller*
1931 L. Schneider *Miller*
1932 F. Frame *Miller*
1933 L. Meyer *Miller*
1934 B. Cummings *Miller*
1935 K. Petillo *Miller*
1936 L. Meyer *Miller*
1937 W. Shaw *Gilmore-Offenhauser*
1938 F. Roberts *Miller*
1939 W. Shaw *Maserati*
1940 W. Shaw *Maserati*
1941 F. Davis and M. Rose *Noc-Out Hose Clamp Spl*
1946 G. Robson *Thorne*
1947 M. Rose *Blue Crown Spl*
1948 M. Rose *Blue Crown Spl*
1949 W. Holland *Blue Crown Spl*
1950 J. Parsons *Wynn Friction Proof Spl*
1951 L. Wallard *Belanger Spl*
1952 T. Ruttman *Agajanian Spl*
1953 W. Vukovitch *Fuel Injection Spl*
1954 W. Vukovitch *Fuel Injection Spl*
1955 B. Sweikert *John Zink Spl*
1956 P. Flaherty *John Zink Spl*
1957 S. Hanks *Belond Exhaust Spl*
1958 J. Bryan *Belond Exhaust Spl*
1959 R. Ward *Leader Card Spl*
1960 J. Rathmann *K. Paul Spl*
1961 A. J. Foyt *Bowes Seal Fast Spl*
1962 R. Ward *Leader Card Spl*
1963 A. P. Jones *Agajanian Spl*
1964 A. J. Foyt *Sheraton-Offenhauser*
1965 J. Clark *Lotus-Ford*
1966 G. Hill *Lola-Ford*
1967 A. J. Foyt *Coyote-Ford*
1968 R. Unser *Eagle-Offenhauser*
1969 M. Andretti *Hawk-Ford*
1970 A. Unser *Colt-Ford*
1971 A. Unser *Colt-Ford*
1972 M. Donahue *McLaren*
1973 G. Johncock *Eagle*
1974 J. Rutherford *McLaren*

International Cup for Formula 1 Manufacturers 1950–1974

1950 Alfa Romeo
1951 Alfa Romeo
1952 Ferrari
1953 Ferrari
1954 Mercedes-Benz
1955 Mercedes-Benz
1956 Lancia-Ferrari
1957 Maserati
1958 Vanwall
1959 Cooper
1960 Cooper
1961 Ferrari
1962 BRM
1963 Lotus-Ford
1964 Ferrari
1965 Lotus-Ford
1966 Brabham-Repco
1967 Brabham-Repco
1968 Lotus-Ford
1969 Matra-Ford
1970 Lotus-Ford
1971 Tyrrell
1972 John Player Special
1973 John Player Special
1974 Matra-Simca

The Grand Prix World Champions 1950–1974

1950 Giuseppe Farina *Alfa Romeo* Italy
1951 Juan Manuel Fangio *Alfa Romeo* Argentine/Italy
1952 Alberto Ascari *Ferrari* Italy
1953 Alberto Ascari *Ferrari* Italy
1954 Juan Manuel Fangio *Maserati and Mercedes-Benz* Argentine/Italy/Germany
1955 Juan Manuel Fangio *Mercedes-Benz* Argentine/Germany
1956 Juan Manuel Fangio *Ferrari* Argentine/Italy
1957 Juan Manuel Fangio *Maserati* Argentine/Italy
1958 Mike Hawthorn *Ferrari* GB/Italy
1959 Jack Brabham *Cooper-Climax* Australia/GB
1960 Jack Brabham *Cooper-Climax* Australia/GB
1961 Phil Hill *Ferrari* USA/Italy
1962 Graham Hill *BRM* GB
1963 Jim Clark *Lotus-Climax* GB
1964 John Surtees *Ferrari* GB/Italy
1965 Jim Clark *Lotus-Climax* GB
1966 Jack Brabham *Repco-Brabham* Australia/GB (Australian engine)
1967 Denny Hulme *Repco-Brabham* New Zealand/GB (Australian engine)
1968 Graham Hill *Lotus-Ford* GB
1969 Jackie Stewart *Matra-Ford* GB/France-GB
1970 Jochen Rindt *Lotus-Ford* Austria/GB
1971 Jackie Stewart *Tyrrell-Ford* GB
1972 Emerson Fittipaldi *Lotus-Ford* Brazil/GB
1973 Jackie Stewart *Tyrrell-Ford* GB
1974 Emerson Fittipaldi *John Player Special* Brazil/GB

Le Mans 24 Hour Race 1923–1974

1923 A. Lagache and R. Leonard *Chenard-Walcker*
1924 J. Duff and F. C. Clement *Bentley*
1925 H. de Courcelles and A. Rossignol *Lorraine-Dietrich*
1926 R. Bloch and A. Rossignol *Lorraine-Dietrich*
1927 J. D. Benjafield and S. C. H. Davis *Bentley*
1928 W. Barnato and B. Rubin *Bentley*
1929 W. Barnato and H. R. S Birkin *Bentley*
1930 W. Barnato and G. Kidson *Bentley*
1931 Earl Howe and H. R. S. Birkin *Alfa Romeo*
1932 R. Sommer and L. Chinetti *Alfa Romeo*
1933 R. Sommer and T. Nuvolari *Alfa Romeo*
1934 L. Chinetti and P. Etancelin *Alfa Romeo*
1935 J. S. Hindmarsh and L. Fontes *Lagonda*
1937 J. P. Wimille and R. Benoist *Bugatti*
1938 E. Chaboud and J. Tremoulet *Delahaye*
1939 J. P. Wimille and P. Veyron *Bugatti*
1949 L. Chinetti and Lord Selsdon *Ferrari*
1950 L. and C. Rosier *Talbot*
1951 P. D. Walker and P. N. Whitehead *Jaguar*
1952 H. Lang and F. Riess *Mercedes-Benz*
1953 A. P. R. Rolt and J. D. Hamilton *Jaguar*
1954 J. F. Gonzalez and M. Trintignant *Ferrari*
1955 J. M. Hawthorn and I. Bueb *Jaguar*
1956 R. Flockhart and N. Sanderson *Jaguar*
1957 R. Flockhart and I. Bueb *Jaguar*
1958 P. Hill and O. Gendebien *Ferrari*
1959 R. Salvadori and C. Shelby *Aston Martin*
1960 P. Frere and O. Gendebien *Ferrari*
1962 P. Hill and O. Gendebien *Ferrari*
1963 L. Scarfiotti and L. Bandini *Ferrari*
1964 J. Guichet and N. Vacarella *Ferrari*
1965 M. Gregory and J. Rindt *Ferrari*
1966 B. McLaren and C. Amon *Ford*
1967 A. J. Foyt and D. Gurney *Ford*
1968 P. Rodriguez and L. Bianchi *Ford*
1969 J. Ickx and J. Oliver *Ford*
1970 R. Attwood and H. Herrmann *Porsche*
1971 H. Marko and G. van Lennep *Porsche*
1972 H. Pescarolo and G. Hill *Matra-Simca*
1973 H. Pescarolo and G. Larrousse *Matra-Simca*
1974 H. Pescarolo and G. Larrousse *Matra-Simca*

Mille Miglia 1927–1957

1927 Minoia and Morandi *OM*
1928 Campari and Ramponi *Alfa Romeo*
1929 Campari and Ramponi *Alfa Romeo*
1930 Nuvolari and Guidotti *Alfa Romeo*
1931 Caracciola and Sebastian *Mercedes-Benz*
1932 Borzacchini and Bignami *Alfa Romeo*
1933 Nuvolari and Compagnoni *Alfa Romeo*
1934 Varzi and Bignami *Alfa Romeo*
1935 Pintacuda and della Stufa *Alfa Romeo*
1936 Brivio and Ongaro *Alfa Romeo*
1937 Pintacuda and Mambelli *Alfa Romeo*
1938 Biondetti and Stefani *Alfa Romeo*
1940 von Hanstein and Baumer *BMW*
1947 Biondetti and Romano *Alfa Romeo*
1948 Biondetti and Navoni *Ferrari*
1949 Biondetti and Salani *Ferrari*
1950 Marzotto and Crosara *Ferrari*
1951 Villoresi and Cassani *Ferrari*
1952 Bracco and Rolfo *Ferrari*
1953 Marzotto and Crosara *Ferrari*
1954 Ascari *Lancia*
1955 Moss and Jenkinson *Mercedes-Benz*
1956 Castelotti *Ferrari*
1957 Taruffi *Ferrari*

Monte Carlo Rally 1911–1974

1911 Rougier (Paris) *Turcat-Méry*
1912 Beutler (Berlin) *Berliet*
1924 Ledure (Glasgow) *Bignan*
1925 Repusseau (Tunis) *Renault*
1926 Bruce (John o' Groats) *AC*
1927 Lefebvre-Despaux (Königsberg) *Amilcar*
1928 Bignan (Bucharest) *Fiat*
1929 Van Eijk (Stockholm) *Graham-Paige*
1930 Petit (Jassy) *La Licorne*
1931 Healey (Stavanger) *Invicta*
1932 Vasselle (Umea) *Hotchkiss*
1933 Vasselle (Tallinn) *Hotchkiss*
1934 Gas (Athens) *Hotchkiss*
1935 La Haye (Stavanger) *Renault*
1936 Zamfirescu (Athens) *Ford*
1937 Le Begue (Stavanger) *Delahaye*
1938 Bakker Schut (Athens) *Ford*
1939 Paul/Trevoux (Athens) *Delahaye/Hotchkiss*
1949 Trevoux (Lisbon) *Hotchkiss*
1950 Becquart (Lisbon) *Hotchkiss*
1951 Trevoux (Lisbon) *Delahaye*
1952 Allard (Glasgow) *Allard*
1953 Gatsonides (Monte Carlo) *Ford*
1954 Chiron (Monte Carlo) *Lancia*
1955 Malling (Oslo) *Sunbeam*
1956 Adams (Glasgow) *Jaguar*
1958 Monraisse (Lisbon) *Renault*
1959 Coltelloni (Paris) *Citroën*
1960 Schock (Warsaw) *Mercedes-Benz*

1961 Martin (Monte Carlo) *Panhard*
1962 Carlsson (Oslo) *Saab*
1963 Carlsson (Stockholm) *Saab*
1964 Hopkirk (Minsk) *Mini Cooper*
1965 Makinen (Stockholm) *Mini Cooper*
1966 Toivonen (Oslo) *Citroën*
1967 Aaltonen (Monte Carlo) *Mini Cooper*
1968 Elford (Warsaw) *Porsche*
1969 Waldegaard (Warsaw) *Porsche*
1970 Waldegaard (Oslo) *Porsche*
1971 O. Andersson (Marrakesh) *Alpine-Renault*
1972 S. Munari (Almeria) *Lancia-Fulvia*
1973 J. C. Andruet (Monte Carlo) *Alpine-Renault*
1974 no race
1975 S. Munari (Agadir) *Lancia-Statos*

RAC International Rally 1951–74

1951* Appleyard *Jaguar*
1952* Imhof *Cadillac-Allard*
1953 Appleyard *Jaguar*
1954 Wallwork *Triumph*
1955 Ray *Standard*
1956 Lyndon Sims *Aston Martin*
1957 no rally
1958 Harper *Sunbeam Rapier*
1959 Burgess *Ford*
1960 Carlsson *Saab*
1961 Carlsson *Saab*
1962 Carlsson *Saab*
1963 Trana *Volvo*
1964 Trana *Volvo*
1965 Aaltonen *Mini Cooper*
1966 Soderstrom *Ford*
1967 no rally
1968 Lampinen *Saab*
1969 Kallstrom *Lancia*
1970 Kallstrom *Lancia*
1971 Blomqvist *Saab*
1972 Clark *Ford*
1973 Makinen *Ford Escort*
1974 Makinen *Ford Escort*

**no overall classification*

RAC Tourist Trophy 1905–1974

Isle of Man
1905 J. S. Napier *Arrol-Johnston*
1906 C. S. Rolls *Rolls-Royce*
1907 E. Courtis *Rover*
1908 W. Watson *Hutton*
1914 K. Lee Guinness *Sunbeam*
1922 J. Chassagne *Sunbeam*

Ards
1928 K. Don *Lea-Francis*
1929 R. Caracciola *Mercedes-Benz*
1930 T. Nuvolari *Alfa Romeo*
1931 N. Black *MG*
1932 T. Nuvolari *MG*
1934 C. J. P. Dodson *MG*
1935 F. W. Dixon *Riley*
1936 F. W. Dixon and C. J. P. Dodson *Riley*

Donington Park
1937 G. Comotti *Darracq*
1938 L. Gerard *Delage*

Dundrod
1950 S. Moss *Jaguar*
1951 S. Moss *Jaguar*
1953 P. Collins and P. C. Griffiths *Aston Martin*
1954 P. Armagnac and G. Loreau *DB*
1955 S. Moss and J. Fitch *Mercedes-Benz*

Goodwood
1958 S. Moss and C. A. S. Brooks *Aston Martin*
1959 S. Moss, C. Shelby and J. Fairman *Aston Martin*
1960 S. Moss *Ferrari*
1961 S. Moss *Ferrari*
1962 I. Ireland *Ferrari*
1963 G. Hill *Ferrari*
1964 G. Hill *Ferrari*

Oulton Park
1965 D. Hulme *Brabham*
1966 D. Hulme *Lola*
1967 A. de Adamich *Alfa Romeo*
1968 D. Hulme *Lola*
1969 T. Taylor *Lola*

Silverstone
1970 B. Muir *Chevrolet*
1971 no race
1972 J. Mass and D. Glemser *Ford Capri*
1973 H. Erth and D. Bell *BMW*
1974 S. Graham *Chevrolet Camaro*

Targa Florio 1906–1974

'Great' Madonie
1906 A. Cagno *Itala*
1907 F. Nazzaro *Fiat*
1908 F. Trucco *Isotta-Fraschini*
1909 R. Ciuppa *SPA*
1910 F. Cariolato *Franco*
1911 E. Ceirano *SCAT*

Tour of Sicily
1912 C. Snipe *SCAT*
1913 F. Nazzaro *Nazzaro*
1914 E. Ceirano *SCAT*

'Medium' Madonie
1919 A. Boillot *Peugeot*
1920 G. Meregalli *Nazzaro*
1921 G. Masetti *Fiat*
1922 G. Masetti *Mercedes*
1923 U. Sivocci *Alfa Romeo*
1924 C. Werner *Mercedes*
1925 M. Costantini *Bugatti*
1926 M. Costantini *Bugatti*
1927 E. Materassi *Bugatti*
1928 A. Divo *Bugatti*
1929 A. Divo *Bugatti*
1930 A. Varzi *Alfa Romeo*

'Great' Madonie
1931 T. Nuvolari *Alfa Romeo*

'Short' Madonie
1932 T. Nuvolari *Alfa Romeo*
1933 A. Brivio *Alfa Romeo*
1934 A. Varzi *Alfa Romeo*
1935 A. Brivio *Alfa Romeo*
1936 C. Magistri *Lancia*

Palermo
1937 F. Severi *Maserati*
1938 G. Rocco *Maserati*
1939 L. Villoresi *Maserati*
1940 L. Villoresi *Maserati*

Tour of Sicily
1948 C. Biondetti and Troubetskoy *Ferrari*
1949 C. Biondetti and Benedetti *Ferrari*
1950 M. and F. Bornigia *Alfa Romeo*

'Short' Madonie
1951 F. Cortese *Frazer Nash*
1952 F. Bonetto *Lancia*
1953 U. Maglioli *Lancia*
1954 P. Taruffi *Lancia*
1955 S. Moss and P. Collins *Mercedes-Benz*
1956 U. Maglioli and H. von Hanstein *Porsche*
1958 L. Musso and O. Gendebien *Ferrari*
1959 E. Barth and W. Seidel *Porsche*
1960 J. Bonnier and H. Herrmann *Porsche*
1961 W. von Trips and O. Gendebien *Ferrari*
1962 W. Mairesse, R. Rodriguez and O. Gendebien *Ferrari*
1963 J. Bonnier and C. M. Abate *Porsche*
1964 A. Pucci and C. Davis *Porsche*
1965 N. Vaccarella and L. Bandini *Ferrari*
1966 W. Mairesse and H. Muller *Porsche*
1967 P. Hawkins and R. Stommelen *Porsche*
1968 V. Elford and U. Maglioli *Porsche*
1969 G. Mitter and U. Schütze *Porsche*
1970 J. Siffert and B. Redman *Porsche*
1971 N. Vaccarella and T. Hezemans *Alfa Romeo*
1972 W. Mairesse and H. Muller *Porsche*
1973 G. van Lennep and J. C. Andruet *Porsche Carrera*
1974 no race

Early Races 1895–1906

	DATE	NAME OF RACE	DRIVER	CAR
1895	11–13 June	Paris–Bordeaux–Paris	Levassor	Panhard
1896	24 September, 3 October	Paris–Marseilles–Paris	Mavade	Panhard
1897	29–31 January	Marseilles–Nice	Marquis de Chasseloup-Laubat	De Dion
	24 July	Paris–Dieppe	Jamin	Bollée
	14 August	Paris–Trouville	Jamin	Bollée
1898	March	Marseilles–Nice	Charron	Panhard
	1 May	Course de Périgueux	Leys	Panhard
	10 and 11 May	Paris–Bordeaux	R. de Knyff	Panhard
	7–12 July	Paris–Amsterdam–Paris	Charron	Panhard
	20 August	Bordeaux–Biarritz	Loysel	Bollée
	20 October	St Germain–Vernon–St Germain	Levegh	Mors
1899	26 January	Paris–Rouen–Paris	Girardot	Panhard
	21 March	Nice–Castellane–Nice	Lemaitre	Peugeot
	5 April	Pau–Bayonne–Pau	Lemaitre	Peugeot
	24 May	Paris–Bordeaux	Charron	Panhard
	4 July	Spa–Bastogne–Spa	R. de Knyff	Panhard
	16–24 July	Tour de France	R. de Knyff	Panhard
	30 July	Paris–St Malo	Antony	Mors
	27 August	Paris–Trouville	Antony	Mors
	1 September	Paris–Ostend	{ Girardot Levegh	{ Panhard Mors
	17 September	Paris–Boulogne	Girardot	Panhard
	1 October	Bordeaux–Biarritz	Levegh	Mors
1900	25 February	Circuit du Sud-Ouest	R. de Knyff	Panhard
	26 March	Nice–Marseilles	R. de Knyff	Panhard
	3 and 4 June	Bordeaux–Périgueux–Bordeaux	Levegh	Mors
	14 June	Paris–Lyons (Gordon-Bennett Cup)	Charron	Panhard
	25, 27, 28 July	Paris–Toulouse–Paris	Levegh	Mors
1901	17 February	Grand Prix de Pau	M. Farman	Panhard
	25 March	Nice–Salon–Nice	Werner	Mercedes
	29 May	Paris–Bordeaux including	Fournier	Mors
	29 May	Gordon-Bennett Cup	Girardot	Panhard
	27–29 June	Paris–Berlin	Fournier	Mors
1902	22 and 23 May	Circuit du Nord	M. Farman	Panhard
	26–29 June	Paris–Vienna including	M. Renault	Renault
	26–28 June	Paris–Innsbruck (Gordon-Bennett Cup)	Edge	Napier
	31 July	Circuit des Ardennes	Jarrott	Panhard
1903	24 May	Paris–Madrid (Bordeaux)	Gabriel	Mors
	22 June	Circuit des Ardennes	Baron de Crawhez	Panhard
	2 July	Gordon-Bennett Cup	Jenatzy	Mercedes
1904	20 May	French Gordon-Bennett Eliminating Trials	Théry	Richard-Brasier
	17 June	Gordon-Bennett Cup (Germany)	Théry	Richard-Brasier
	25 July	Circuit des Ardennes	Heath	Panhard
	4 September	Florio Cup	Lancia	Fiat
	8 October	Vanderbilt Cup	Heath	Panhard
1905	30 May	English Gordon-Bennett Eliminating Trials	Earp	Napier
	16 June	French Gordon-Bennett Eliminating Trials	Théry	Richard-Brasier
	5 July	Gordon-Bennett Cup (France)	Théry	Richard-Brasier

1905	7 August	Circuit des Ardennes	Hémery	Darracq
	10 September	Florio Cup	Raggio	Itala
	23 September	Vanderbilt Cup Eliminating Trials	Dingley	Pope-Toledo
	14 October	Vanderbilt Cup	Hémery	Darracq
1906	12 February	Cuban Race	Demogeot	Darracq
	26 and 27 June	Grand Prix	Szisz	Renault
	13 August	Circuit des Ardennes	Duray	De Dietrich
	6 October	Vanderbilt Cup	Wagner	Darracq

Record-Breaking Speeds

	DATE	VEHICLE	DRIVER	SITE	mph	kph
1898	18 December	Jeantaud	Chasseloup-Laubat	Achères	39.24	63.16
1899	17 January	Jenatzy	Jenatzy	Achères	41.42	66.66
	17 January	Jeantaud	Chasseloup-Laubat	Achères	43.69	70.31
	27 January	Jenatzy	Jenatzy	Achères	49.92	80.34
	4 March	Jeantaud	Chasseloup-Laubat	Achères	57.60	92.70
	29 April	Jenatzy	Jenatzy	Achères	65.79	105.88
1902	13 April	Serpollet	Serpollet	Nice	75.06	120.80
	5 August	Mors	Vanderbilt	Ablis	76.08	122.44
	5 November	Mors	Fournier	Dourdan	76.60	123.27
	17 November	Mors	Augières	Dourdan	77.13	124.13
1903	17 July	Gobron-Brillié	Duray	Ostend	83.47	134.33
	5 November	Gobron-Brillié	Duray	Dourdan	84.73	136.36
1904	*12 January	Ford	Ford	Lake St Clair	91.37	147.05
	27 January	Mercedes	Vanderbilt	Daytona	92.30	148.54
	31 March	Gobron-Brillié	Rigolly	Nice	94.78	152.53
	25 May	Mercedes	de Caters	Ostend	97.25	156.50
	21 July	Gobron-Brillié	Rigolly	Ostend	103.55	166.65
	13 November	Darracq	Baras	Ostend	104.52	168.21
1905	*25 January	Napier	Macdonald	Daytona	104.65	168.42
	30 December	Darracq	Hémery	Arles-Salon	109.65	176.46
1906	23 January	Stanley	Marriott	Daytona	121.58	195.65
1909	8 November	Benz	Hémery	Brooklands	125.95	202.70
1910	*16 March	Benz	Oldfield	Daytona	131.27	211.27
1911	*23 April	Benz	Burman	Daytona	141.37	227.51
1914	24 January	Benz	Hornsted	Brooklands	124.10 (two ways)	199.72
1919	*17 February	Packard	de Palma	Daytona	149.87	241.19
1920	*27 April	Duesenberg	Milton	Daytona	156.03	251.11
1922	17 May	Sunbeam	Guinness	Brooklands	133.75	215.25
1924	6 July	Delage	R. Thomas	Arpajon	143.31	230.63
	12 July	Fiat	Eldridge	Arpajon	146.01	235.00
	25 September	Sunbeam	Campbell	Pendine	146.16	235.22
1925	21 July	Sunbeam	Campbell	Pendine	150.76	242.63
1926	16 March	Sunbeam	Segrave	Southport	152.33	245.15
	27 April	Babs	Thomas	Pendine	169.30	272.46
	28 April	Babs	Thomas	Pendine	171.02	275.23
1927	4 February	Bluebird	Campbell	Pendine	179.88	289.40
	29 March	Sunbeam	Segrave	Daytona	203.79	327.97
1928	19 February	Bluebird	Campbell	Daytona	206.96	333.07
	22 April	Triplex	Keech	Daytona	207.55	334.02
1929	11 March	Golden Arrow	Segrave	Daytona	231.45	372.47

1931	5 February	Bluebird	Campbell	Daytona	246.09	396.04
1932	24 February	Bluebird	Campbell	Daytona	253.97	408.72
1933	22 February	Bluebird	Campbell	Daytona	272.46	438.41
1935	7 March	Bluebird	Campbell	Daytona	276.82	445.50
	3 September	Bluebird	Campbell	Bonneville	301.13	484.62
1937	19 November	Thunderbolt	Eyston	Bonneville	312.00	502.12
1938	27 August	Thunderbolt	Eyston	Bonneville	345.50	556.00
	15 September	Railton	Cobb	Bonneville	350.20	563.59
	16 September	Thunderbolt	Eyston	Bonneville	357.50	575.34
1939	23 August	Railton	Cobb	Bonneville	369.70	594.99
1947	16 September	Railton	Cobb	Bonneville	394.20	634.40
1963	*5 August	Spirit of America	Breedlove	Bonneville	407.45 (three-wheeler)	655.73
1964	17 July	Bluebird	D. Campbell	Lake Eyre	403.10 (wheel-driven)	648.73
	2 October	Wingfoot Express	Green	Bonneville	413.20	664.98
	5 October	Green Monster	Arfons	Bonneville	434.02	698.49
	13 October	Spirit of America	Breedlove	Bonneville	468.72 (three-wheeler)	754.33
	15 October	Spirit of America	Breedlove	Bonneville	526.28 (three-wheeler)	846.96
	27 October	Green Monster	Arfons	Bonneville	536.71	863.75
1965	2 November	Spirit of America (Sonic 1)	Breedlove	Bonneville	555.48	893.96
	7 November	Green Monster	Arfons	Bonneville	576.55	927.87
	13 November	Goldenrod	Summers	Bonneville	409.28 ('automobile' class)	658.67
	15 November	Spirit of America (Sonic 1)	Breedlove	Bonneville	600.60	966.57
1970	23 October	The Blue Flame	Gabelich	Bonneville	622.41	1001.78

* not recognized by European authority

Tracks and Closed Road Circuits

ANDERSTORP

In 1973 Sweden's first world championship Grand Prix race was held on the Anderstorp track. The 2.5 mile (4.02km) circuit is built on reclaimed swamp land with a long main straight that doubles as a landing strip for planes, and a series of constant radius corners. The race was won by Denny Hulme in a McLaren, by a margin of four seconds from Sweden's Ronnie Peterson.

Anderstorp was already being used for Formula 2 and 5000 events before it graduated to Formula 1 in 1973. Above, we see salvage men attempt to turn the wreck upright after Welsh driver Derrick William's fatal accident in July 1970.

BRANDS HATCH

Brands Hatch started as a grass motorcycle track and had developed by 1950 into the cradle of 500cc Formula 3 racing. Extended in 1960 for Grand Prix use with a lap length of 2.65 miles (4.27km) it has become one of the most popular—and tricky—of British circuits.

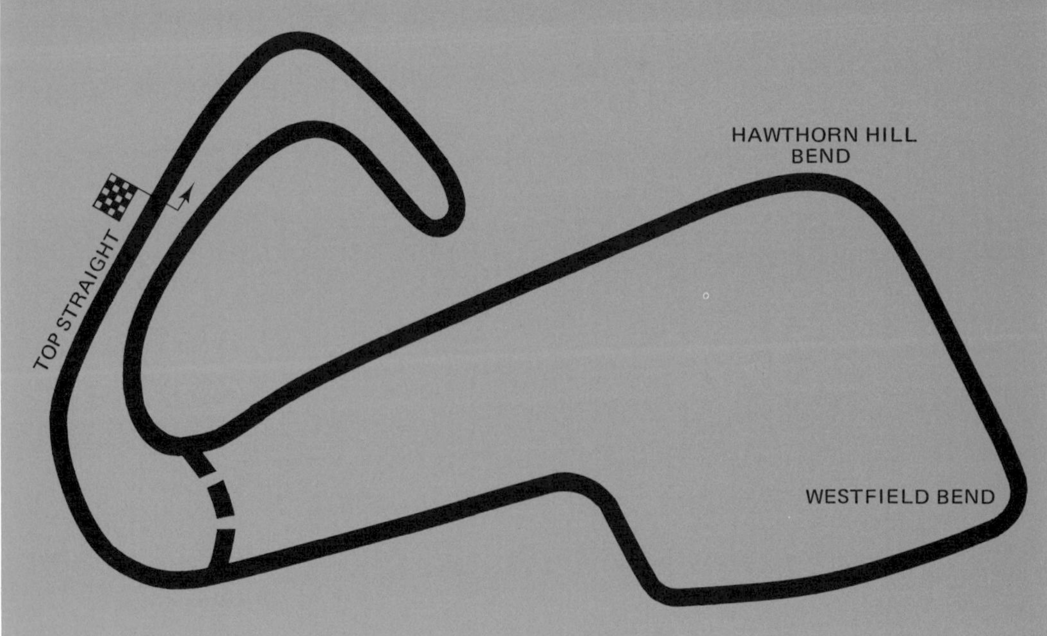

Brands Hatch, 1973. Ronnie Peterson (John Player Lotus Special) during the Race of Champions (below), sponsored by the Daily Mail. The race is held annually at Brands Hatch, always in the spring. In that year's race, the Grand Prix cars dropped out of the event, which was won by Peter Gethin in a Formula 5000 Chevron.

Brooklands, late 1930. All four wheels in the air as Chris Staniland (above), famous Brooklands record-breaker and test pilot for the Fairey Aviation Company, attacks the Brooklands 3 litre class lap record in October 1938 with his Alfa Romeo-based Multi-Union. Staniland beat the 10 mile record at 133.69mph (215.15kph), the 5 mile record at 131.32mph (211.33kph) and the Brooklands class lap record at 141.45mph (227.64kph).

Brooklands as it was in its last years (below), between 1937 and 1939, showing the high speed outer circuit and the road circuit laid within it. There seems very little hope of the track ever being re-opened, though for those with a nostalgic turn of mind the shape of the course and the bankings can still plainly be made out today.

BROOKLANDS

Built by H. F. Locke-King on his estate at Weybridge, Surrey, the pear-shaped circuit with its two high-speed bankings was opened on 6 July 1907. As the first real car race-track in the world, Brooklands became the legendary epicentre of British motor sport. Sadly, it fell victim to war production and was bought by Vickers Armstrong for £330,000 after World War II. The outer circuit record was established by John Cobb in a Napier- Railton at 143.4mph (230.7kph).

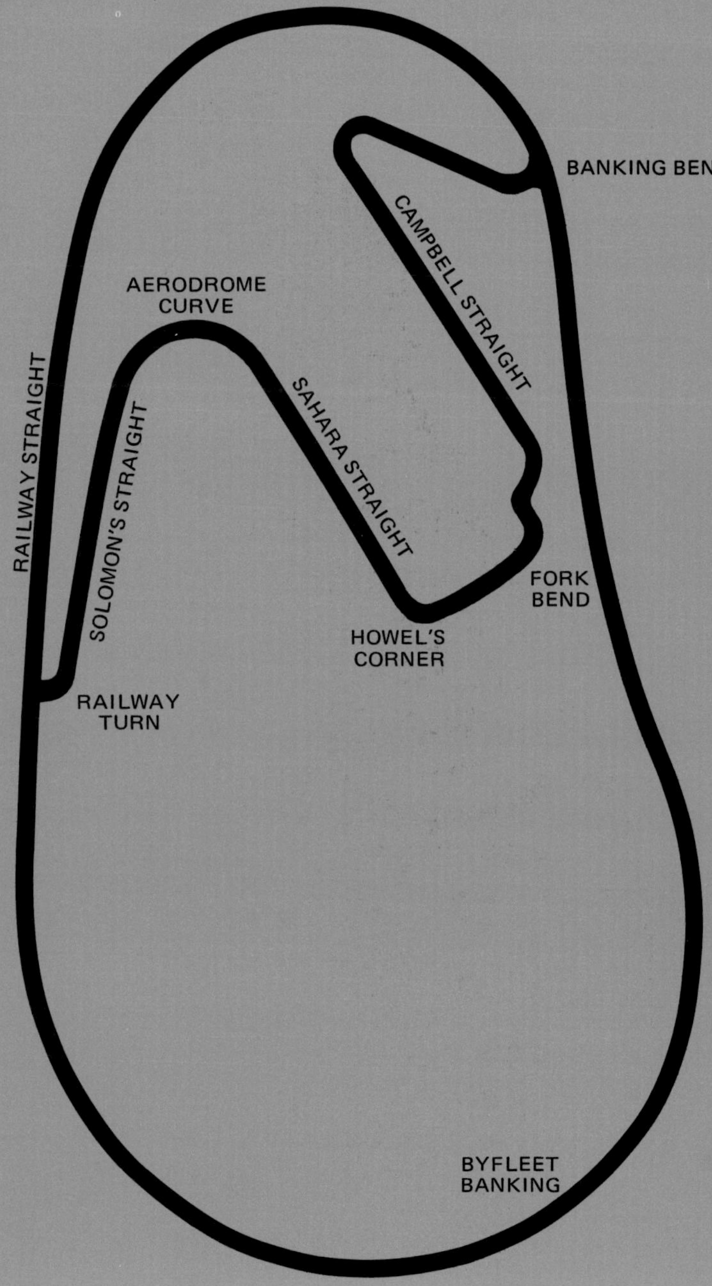

CLERMONT–FERRAND

Opened in July 1958, this beautiful but difficult circuit in the hills of Auvergne has 57 corners (including 3 hairpins) with a height drop of some 600ft (180m), all in just 5 miles (8.05km) lap length. It hosted the French Grand Prix for the first time in 1965.

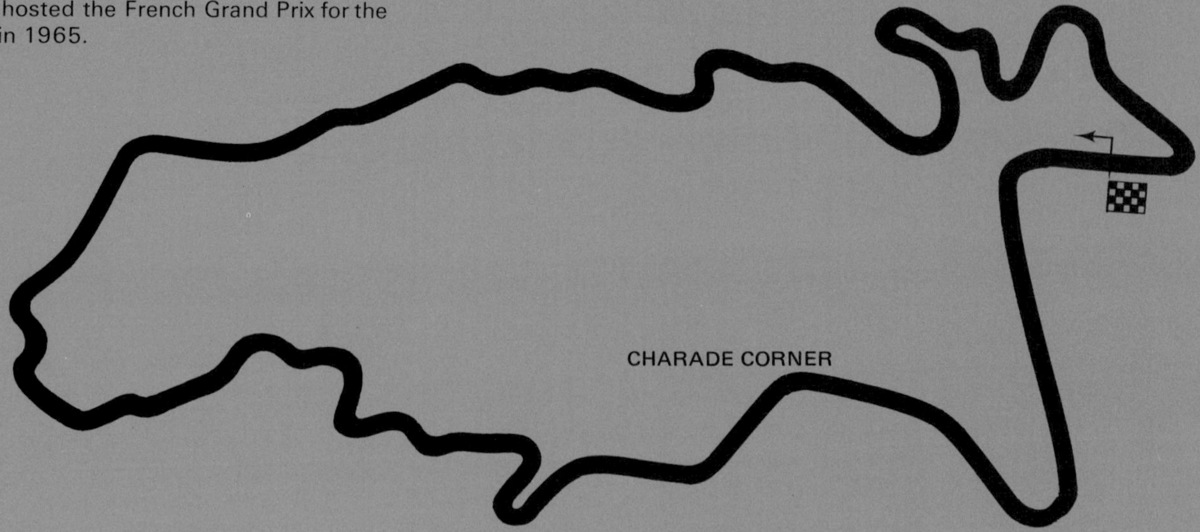

CHARADE CORNER

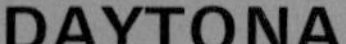

DAYTONA

This 3.81 mile (6.13km) circuit was opened in 1959 as the headquarters of American stock car racing, and became the site of the Daytona Continental in 1962. Every February the Daytona '500' is the high spot in a crowded programme of sports car and stock car racing.

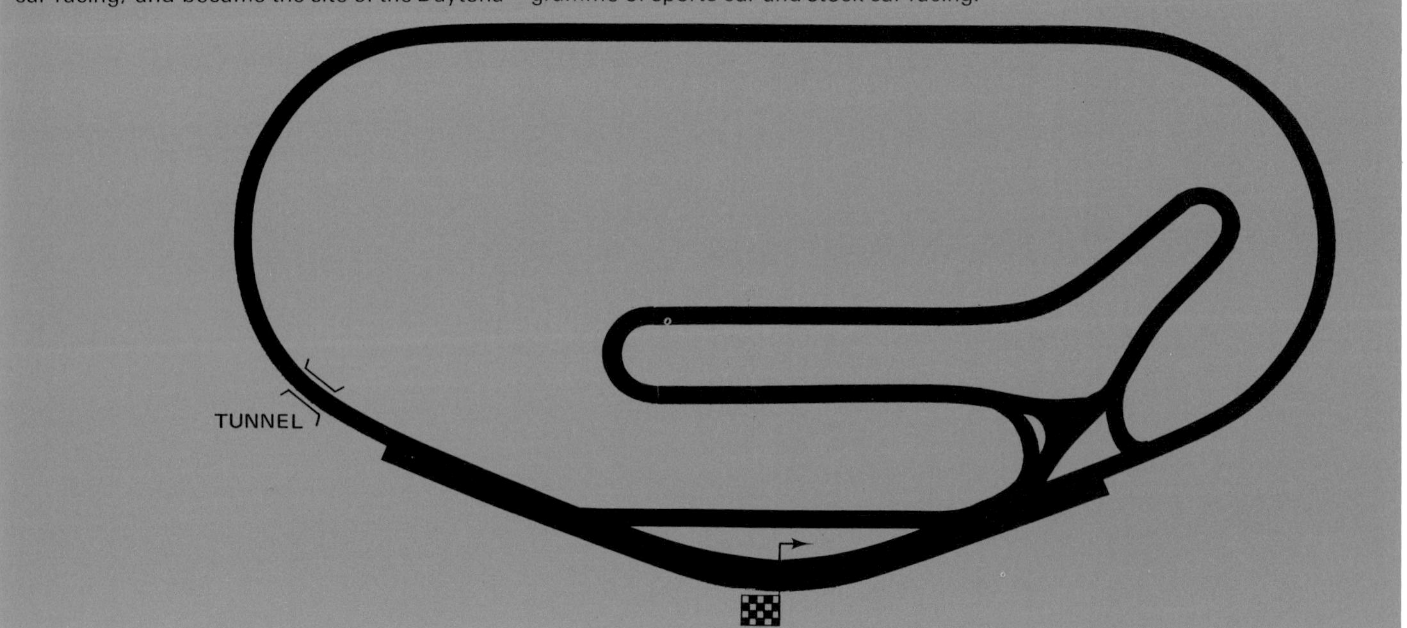

Richard Seaman (above), Britain's top driver, became the first Englishman to join the famous Mercedes-Benz Grand Prix team. He is seen at the start of the Donington Grand Prix, 1937, where his countrymen's high hopes of victory were dashed after his collision with another car.

DONINGTON PARK

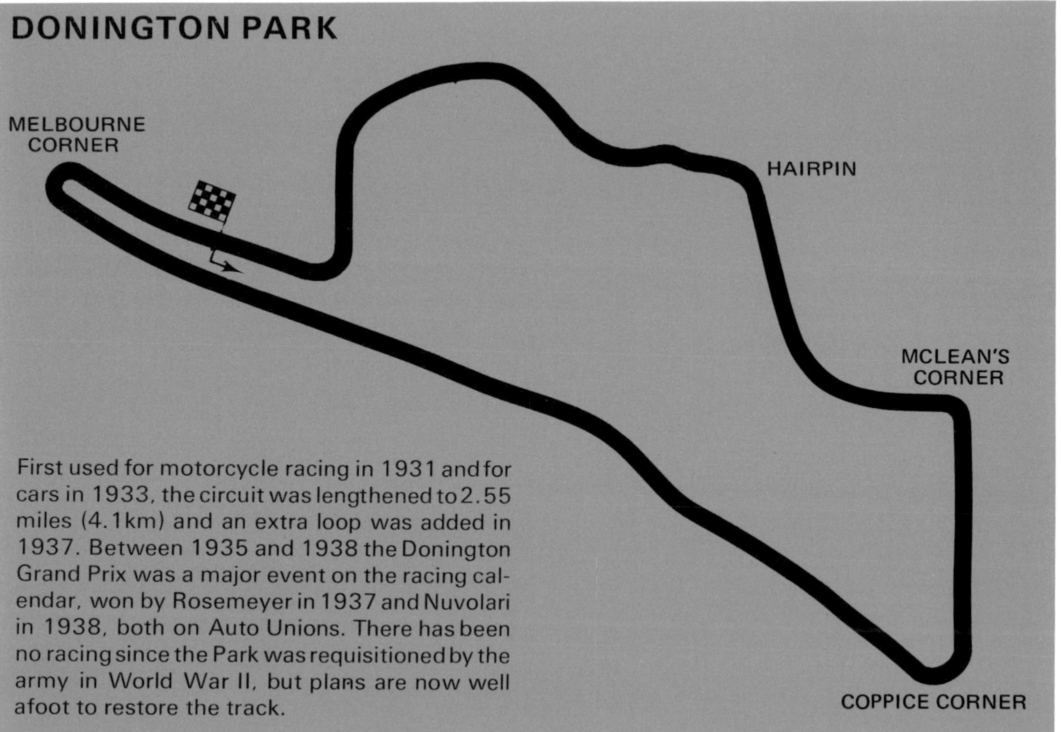

First used for motorcycle racing in 1931 and for cars in 1933, the circuit was lengthened to 2.55 miles (4.1km) and an extra loop was added in 1937. Between 1935 and 1938 the Donington Grand Prix was a major event on the racing calendar, won by Rosemeyer in 1937 and Nuvolari in 1938, both on Auto Unions. There has been no racing since the Park was requisitioned by the army in World War II, but plans are now well afoot to restore the track.

Daytona, 1973. Spectacular start of the Daytona 6 Hours Race for production cars (below), held annually under NASCAR rules over one of the world's fastest tracks. Lap speeds approach 200mph (322kph).

Typical heart-stopping incident during the same race. Happily, accidents frequently look worse than they are, as safety measures are very stringent, cars being well re-inforced internally and drivers firmly harnessed.

FUJI INTERNATIONAL

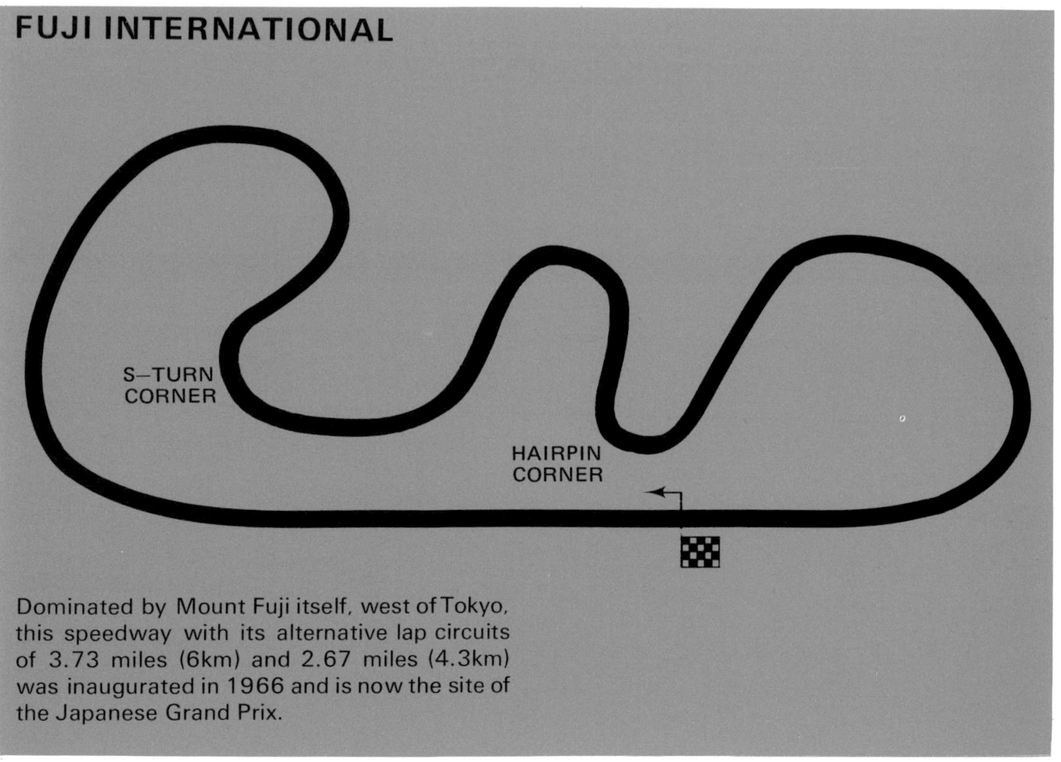

Dominated by Mount Fuji itself, west of Tokyo, this speedway with its alternative lap circuits of 3.73 miles (6km) and 2.67 miles (4.3km) was inaugurated in 1966 and is now the site of the Japanese Grand Prix.

GOODWOOD

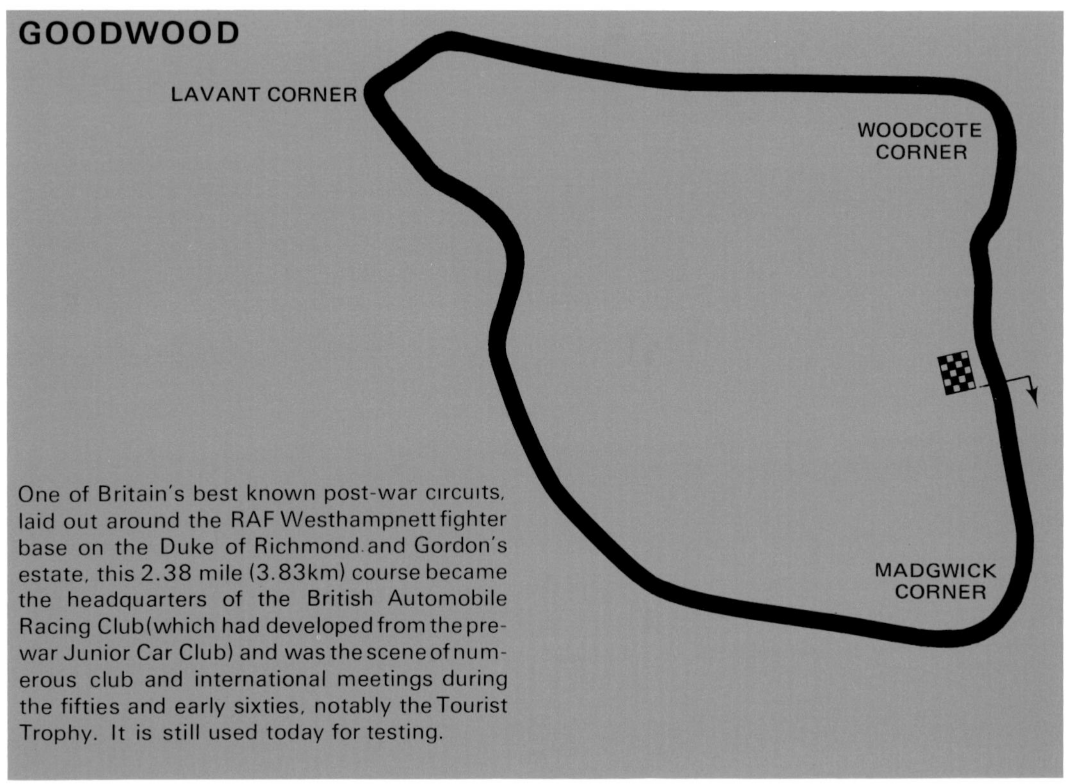

One of Britain's best known post-war circuits, laid out around the RAF Westhampnett fighter base on the Duke of Richmond and Gordon's estate, this 2.38 mile (3.83km) course became the headquarters of the British Automobile Racing Club (which had developed from the pre-war Junior Car Club) and was the scene of numerous club and international meetings during the fifties and early sixties, notably the Tourist Trophy. It is still used today for testing.

Goodwood, 1952. The picturesque circuit in Sussex was popular for all classes of racing from Formula 1 down to club level. Competition was always keen, and above is a typical harmless spin-out by an XK 120 Jaguar while in pursuit of a similar car. The wattle fencing was an occasional casualty.

HOCKENHEIM

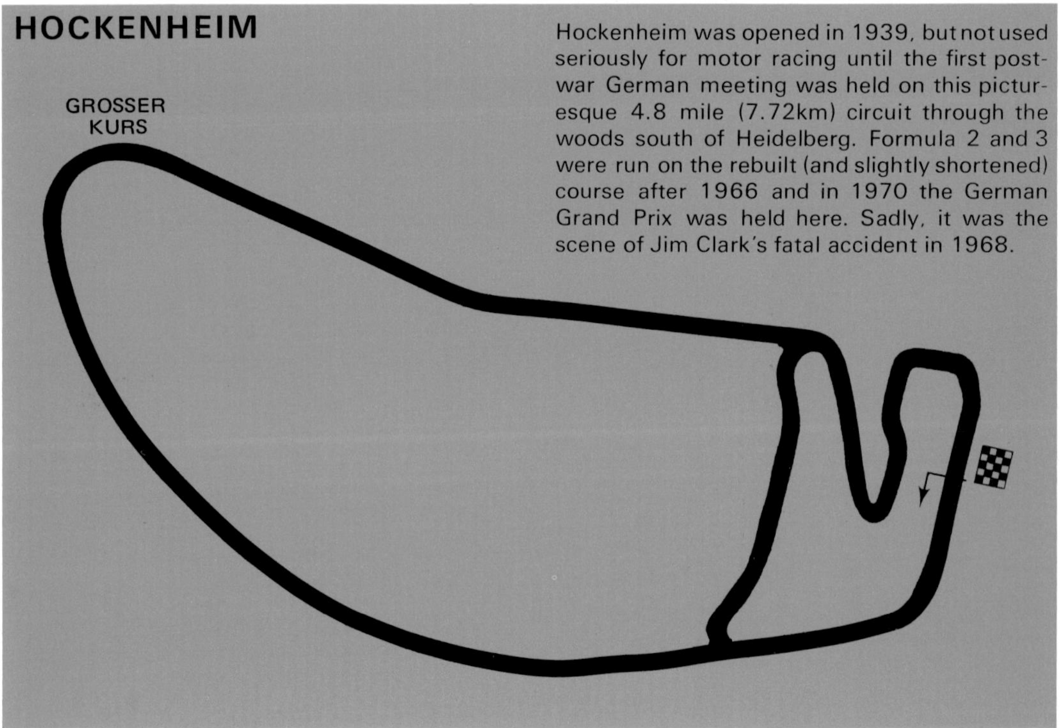

Hockenheim was opened in 1939, but not used seriously for motor racing until the first post-war German meeting was held on this picturesque 4.8 mile (7.72km) circuit through the woods south of Heidelberg. Formula 2 and 3 were run on the rebuilt (and slightly shortened) course after 1966 and in 1970 the German Grand Prix was held here. Sadly, it was the scene of Jim Clark's fatal accident in 1968.

Aerial view of Indianapolis (below), the world's most famous high-speed race track with its four left-hand banked corners. Originally it was paved with bricks but these have long since been re-surfaced, just a narrow band of bricks being retained for the sake of tradition.

INDIANAPOLIS

Central point of American racing and the oldest race track in the world that has operated continuously since its inauguration in 1909, the rectangular 2.5 mile (4km) 'Brickyard' is a world of its own and the famous '500' race on Memorial Day carries the highest prize money in the business.

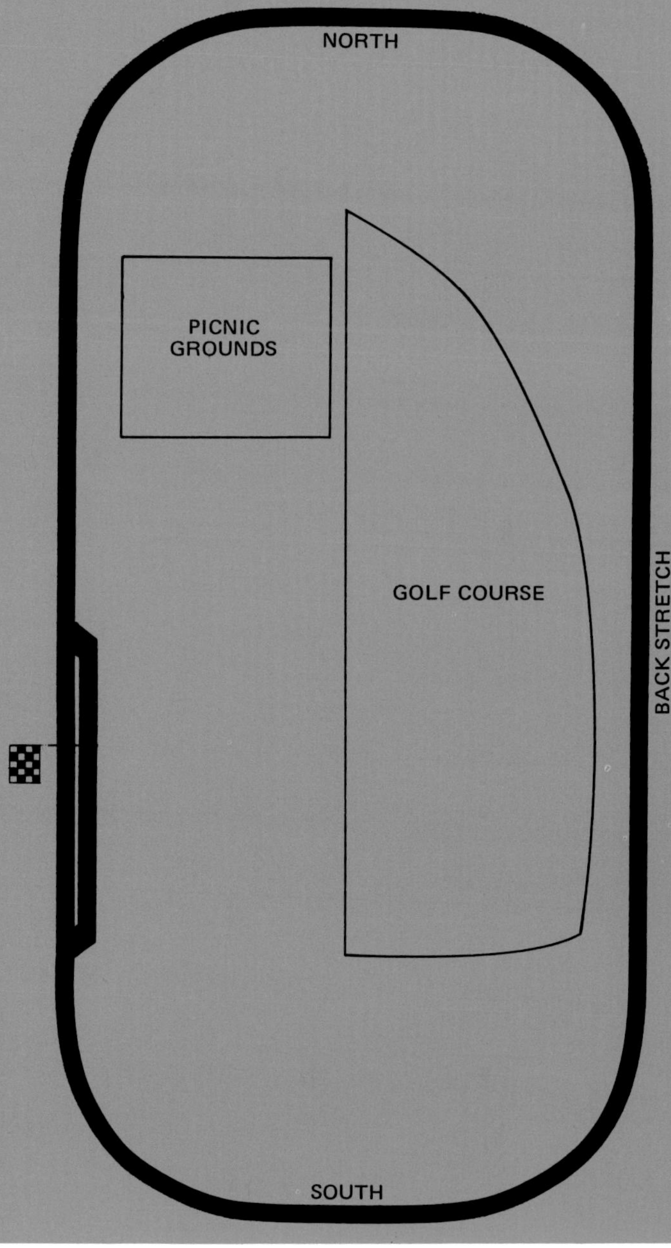

NORTH

PICNIC GROUNDS

GOLF COURSE

BACK STRETCH

SOUTH

Indianapolis, 1915. Ralph DePalma wins the '500' (below) with one of the famous 1914 4.5 litre GP Mercedes. This was the only time DePalma, who took part in ten Indianapolis 500s, actually won the race, but he still holds the record for leading more laps in this famous classic than any other driver.

JARAMA

Situated in the hills north of Madrid, this circuit, opened in 1967, packs a dozen corners and a half mile straight into a length of only just over 2 miles (3.4km). Since 1970 it has been the site of the Spanish Grand Prix.

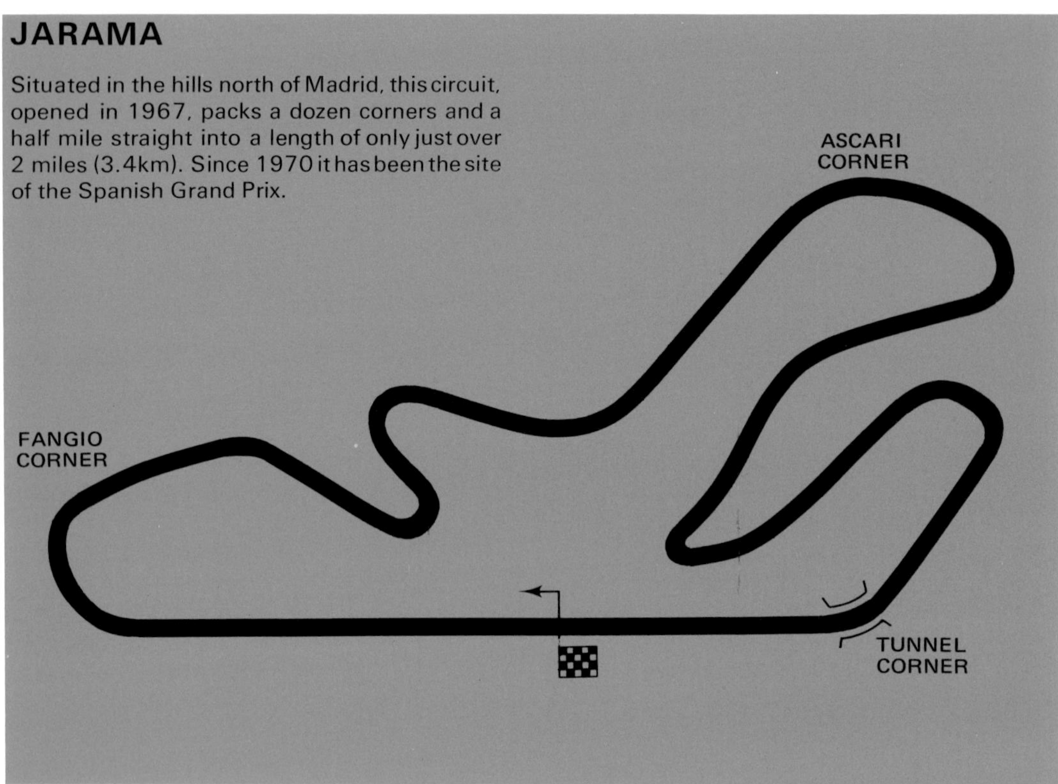

Jarama, 1970. Jackie Ickx (Ferrari) and Jacky Oliver (BRM) crash during the first lap of the Spanish Grand Prix (above) and burst into flames. Neither driver was badly hurt, though inefficient fire-fighting facilities prolonged the blaze needlessly. The race was won by the third Jackie (Stewart) in a March-Ford.

Le Mans, 1964. A general view of the 24 Hour Race (above) – the winners were Jean Guichet and Nino Vaccarella in a Ferrari. This was the year when Ford made their initial Le Mans challenge with the GT40s, designed to take the race away from Ferrari. It took them three years to achieve their objective, in 1966. They then hammered home their victory with four successive Le Mans wins.

KYALAMI

Johannesburg's 2.5 mile (4km) circuit replaced the East London track as the site of the South African Grand Prix in 1967. Situated at an altitude of 5,000ft (1,524m), it also hosts the well known nine hour sports car races.

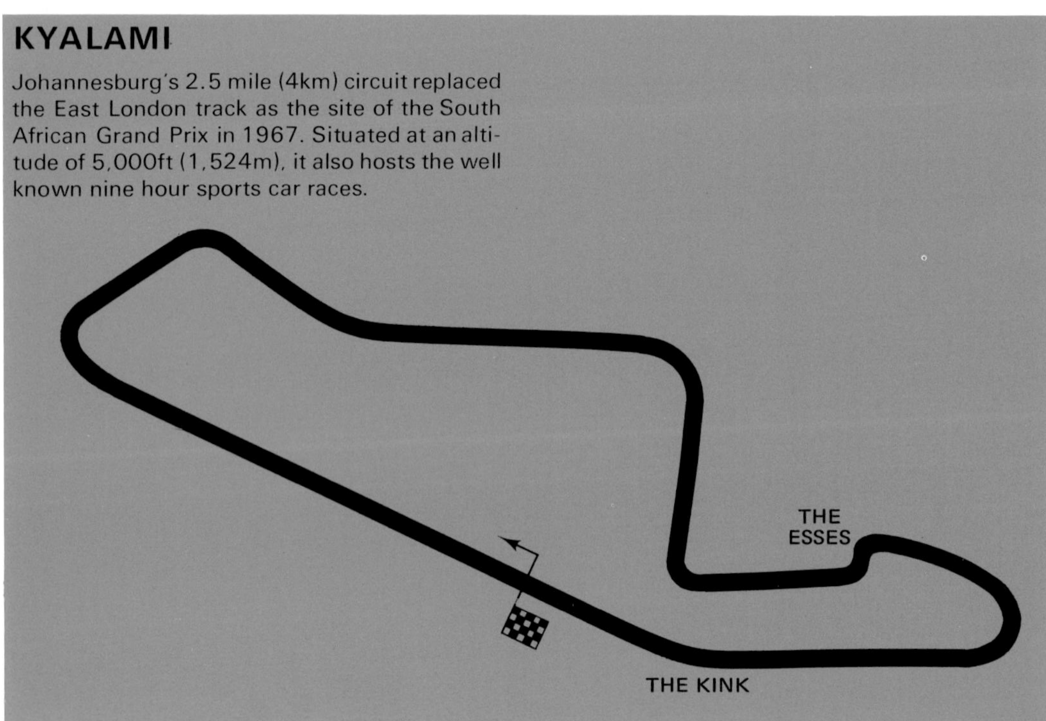

Monaco, 1956. Heavy traffic at the gas-works hairpin (below), immediately after the start of the Grand Prix. Stirling Moss is in the No 28 Maserati taking the lead which he retained to the end. Harry Schell (Vanwall) is No 16, while Castellotti and Fangio are on the inside in Ferraris.

LE MANS

Although races have been held on the Sarthe track since 1906, the new circuit was devised on the outskirts of Le Mans in 1920 and subsequently modified to its present length of 8.6 miles (13.5km) in 1933. The 24 Hours of Le Mans is the most famous of all sports car races.

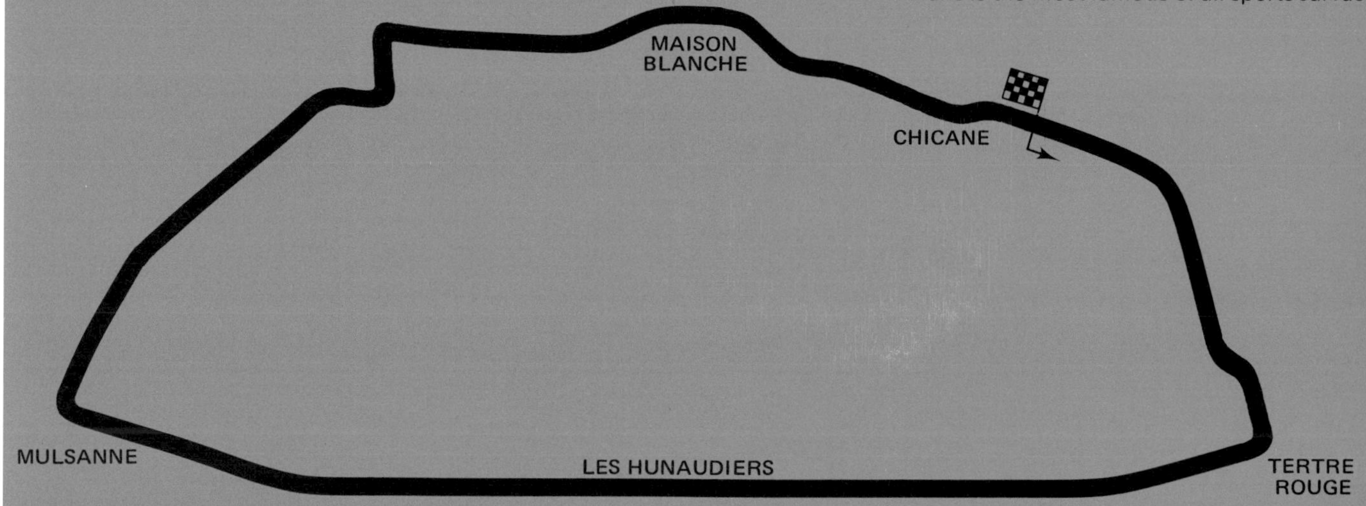

MAISON BLANCHE
CHICANE
MULSANNE
LES HUNAUDIERS
TERTRE ROUGE

MONACO

Conceived in 1929 as a unique race which could be run entirely on Monégasque soil, the Monaco Grand Prix wound sinuously through the streets of Monte Carlo. It quickly developed into the most glamourous and long-lived of all the round-the-houses circuits, and also one of the most gruelling for car and driver.

MIRABEAU
TOBACCO CORNER
CHICANE
GASWORKS HAIRPIN

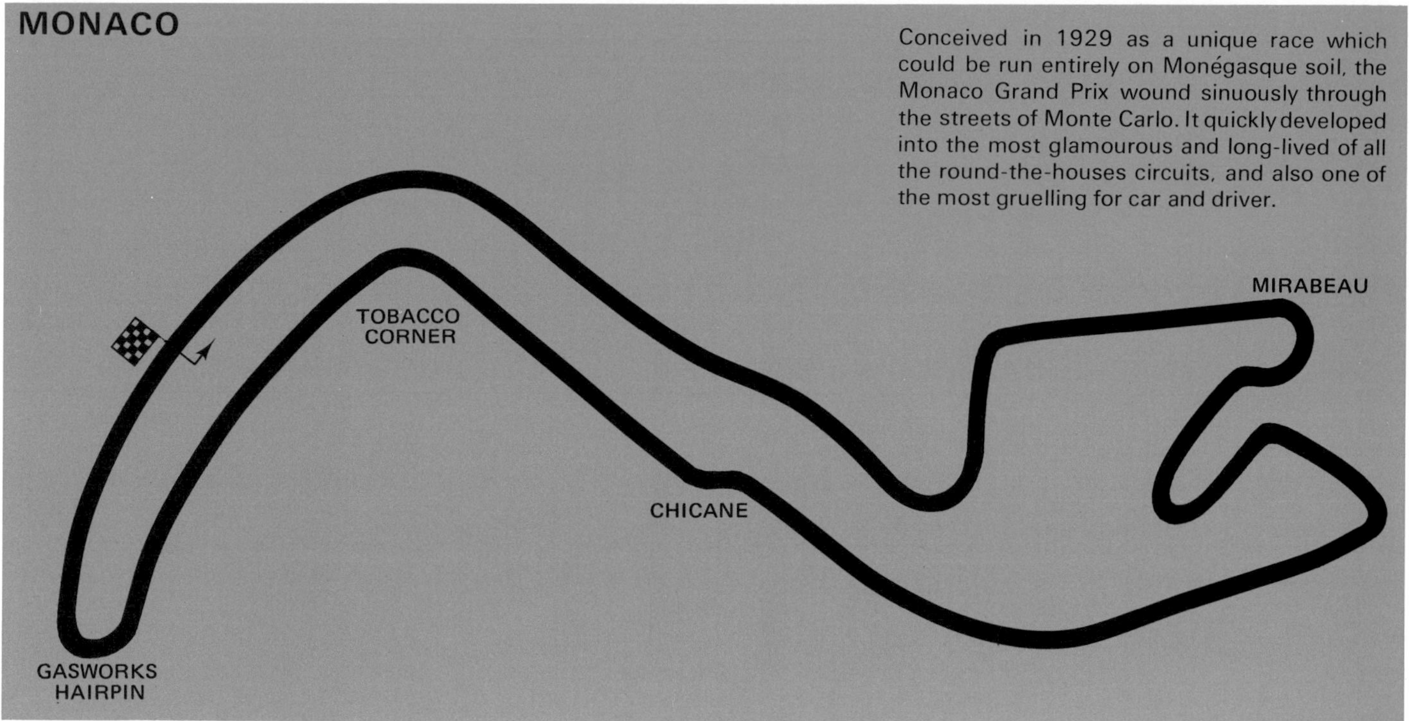

MONTLHERY

Built as a high speed autodrome on the outskirts of Paris in 1924, the banked 1.5 mile (2.5km) track, linked to a road circuit giving a total lap distance of 7.8 miles (12.5km), was the centre of French racing between the wars as well as the site for long duration record attempts. Nowadays it is mainly used for testing.

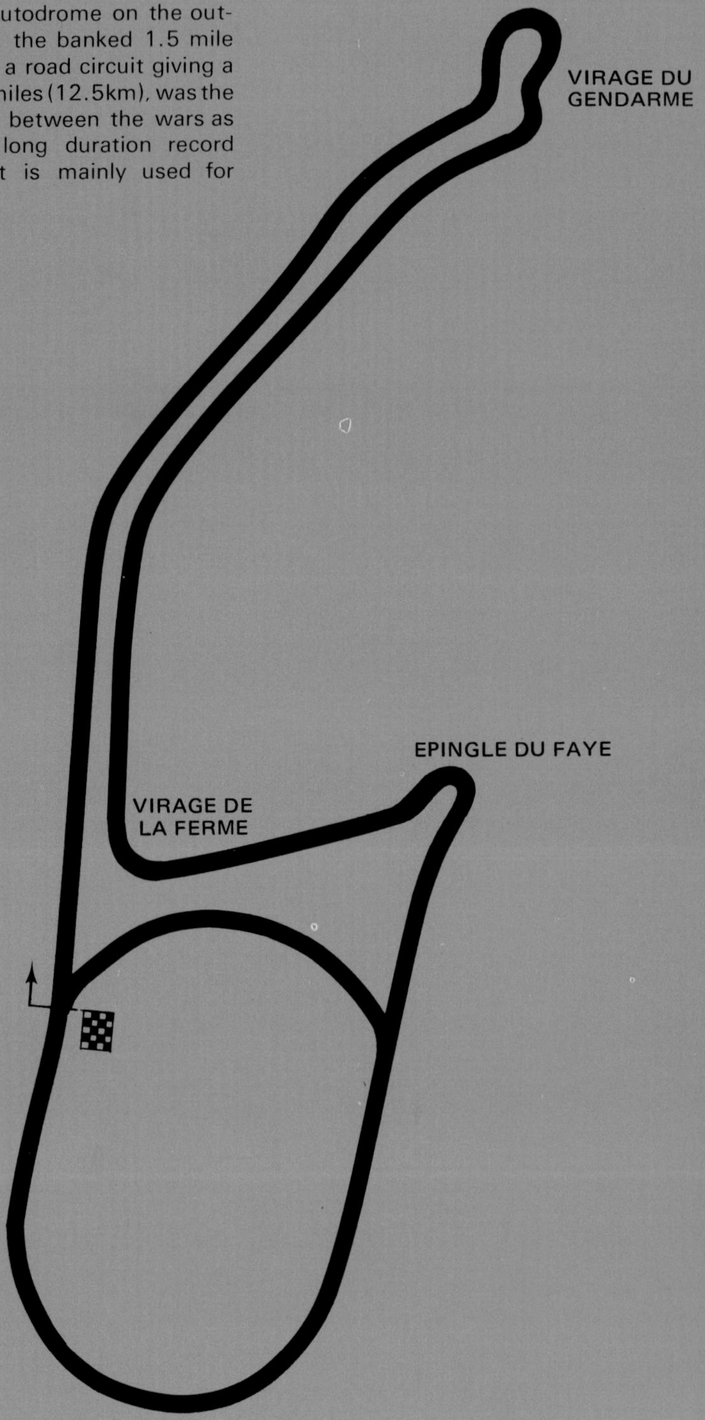

VIRAGE DU GENDARME

EPINGLE DU FAYE

VIRAGE DE LA FERME

Montlhéry, 1936. In 1936 and 1937 the French Grand Prix was a sports car event, being raised to Grand Prix formula status again in 1938. The 1936 race, just about to start in the picture above, was won by Jean-Pierre Wimille and Raymond Sommer, sharing a 3.3 litre streamlined Bugatti, thus achieving the national victory the French so hankered after.

Montlhéry, 1925. The three factory P2 Alfa Romeos move up to the grid, before the start of the French Grand Prix (above). They proved easily the fastest cars, but forfeited the race when their No 1 driver, Antonio Ascari, was killed while in the lead and they withdrew the other cars.

MONZA

Situated in a royal park outside Milan, Monza autodrome, built in 1922, is little short of a shrine to 55 million Italians. Scene of so many historic encounters, and now 3.5 miles (5.7km) in length, the road circuit is one of the fastest in the world.

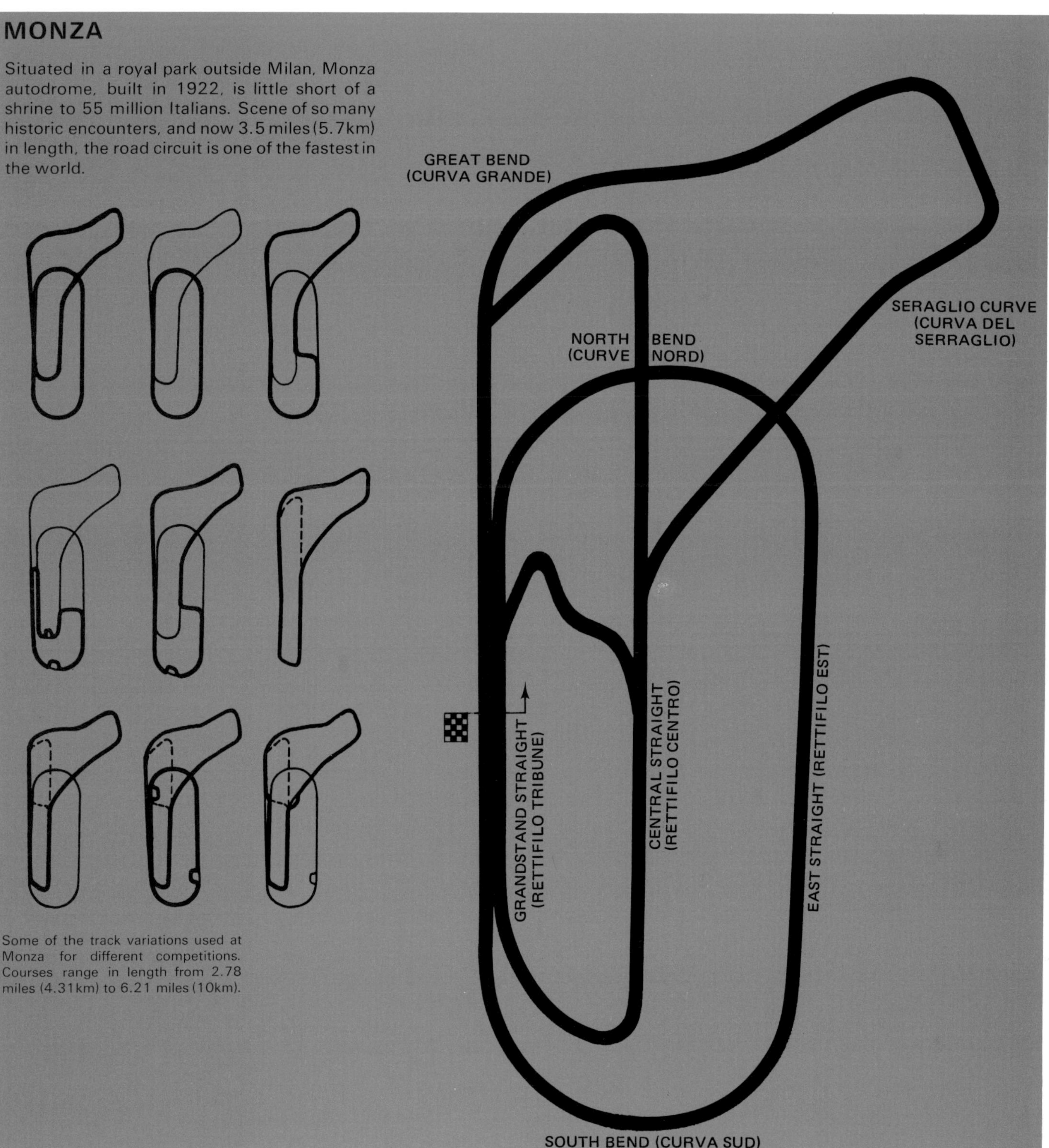

Some of the track variations used at Monza for different competitions. Courses range in length from 2.78 miles (4.31km) to 6.21 miles (10km).

MOSPORT

Stirling Moss won the inaugural race here in 1961 and a corner is named in his honour, though the denomination of this splendid Canadian circuit in the hills of Lake Ontario is actually telegraphese for Motor Sport. Trans-Am, Can-Am and the Canadian Grand Prix are held on the 2.5 mile (4km) long track through the trees.

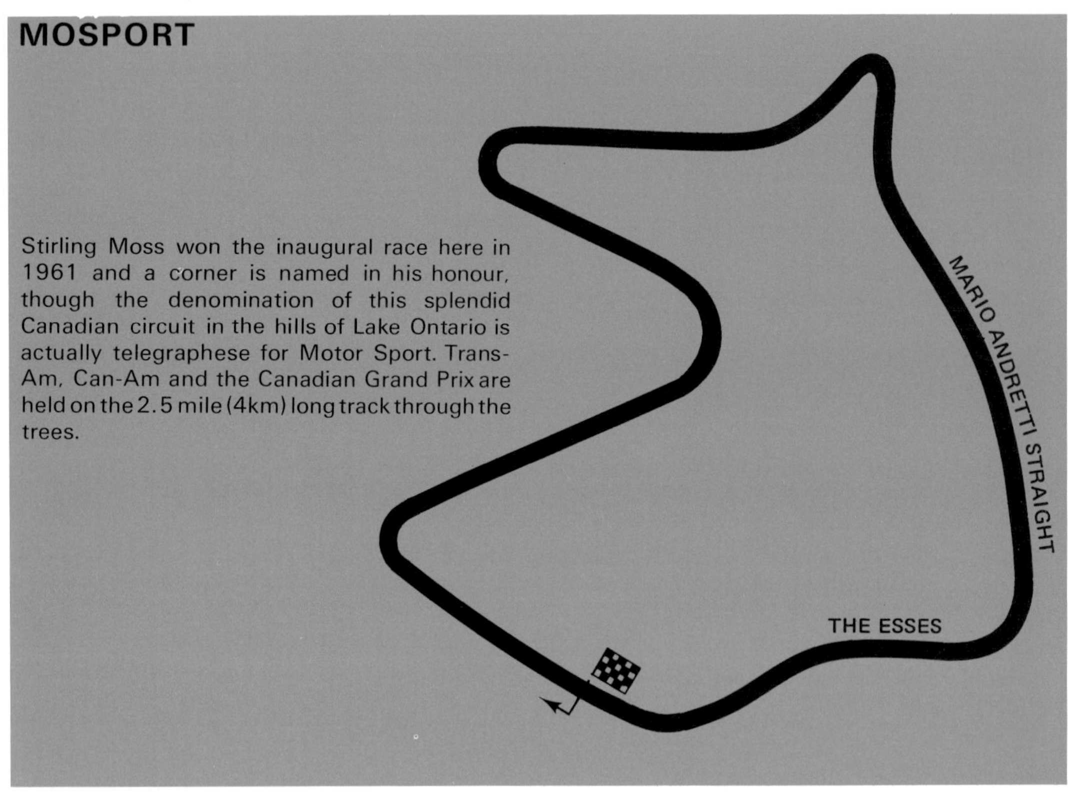

Mosport, 1964. A cool drink for a hot winner! Bruce McLaren (above) cruises round the track for the winner's lap after his victory in both heats of the Players 200 Mile (322km) International Sports Car Race in a Cooper-based Zerex Special.

NÜRBURGRING

Wagnerian in its grandeur up in the Eifel mountains, the 'Ring' was built in 1927 and remains the longest and hairiest of all the great circuits with its 91 left hand bends and 85 right handers.

The combined north and south circuits combine to form a total length of just under 18 miles (29km), but only the 14.19 mile (22.84km) north circuit is used nowadays.

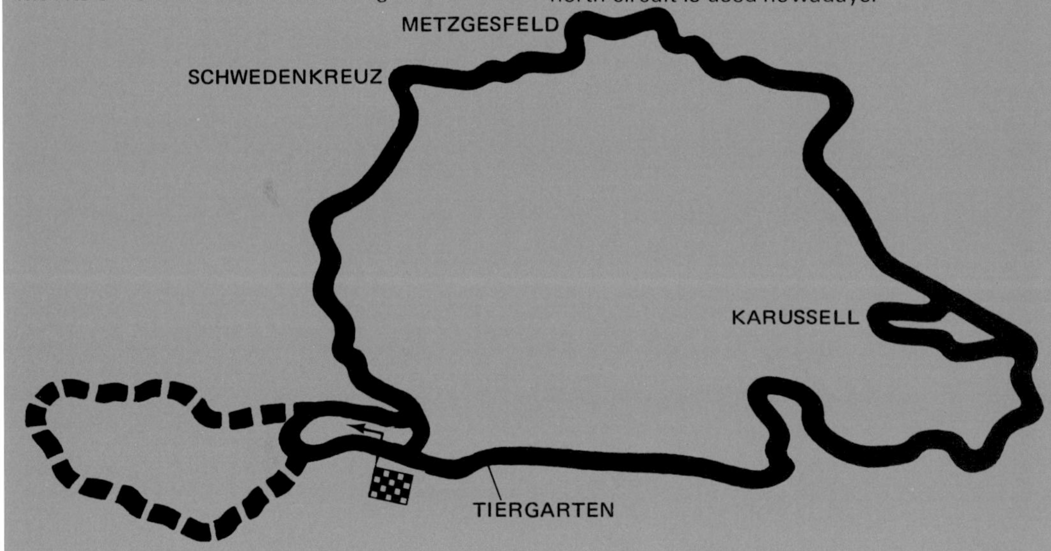

Nürburgring, 1937. The two most famous annual races held on Germany's classic circuit were the German Grand Prix and the Eifelrennen. Here is Bernd Rosemeyer (below) winning the latter event in 1937 with his 6 litre 16 cylinder supercharged rear-engined Auto Union.

Österreichring, 1970. Not so much a race course, more a scenic tour – but at Grand Prix velocity! The Austrian GP at the then newly opened Österreichring in 1970 when the race was won by the Belgian, Jackie Ickx, in a Ferrari.

ÖSTERREICHRING

Austrian races were centered from 1958 on the Zeltweg airfield near Graz until the opening of the splendidly located new international circuit in the hills above. Inaugurated in 1969, the Österreichring has a lap length of 3.17 miles (5.9km).

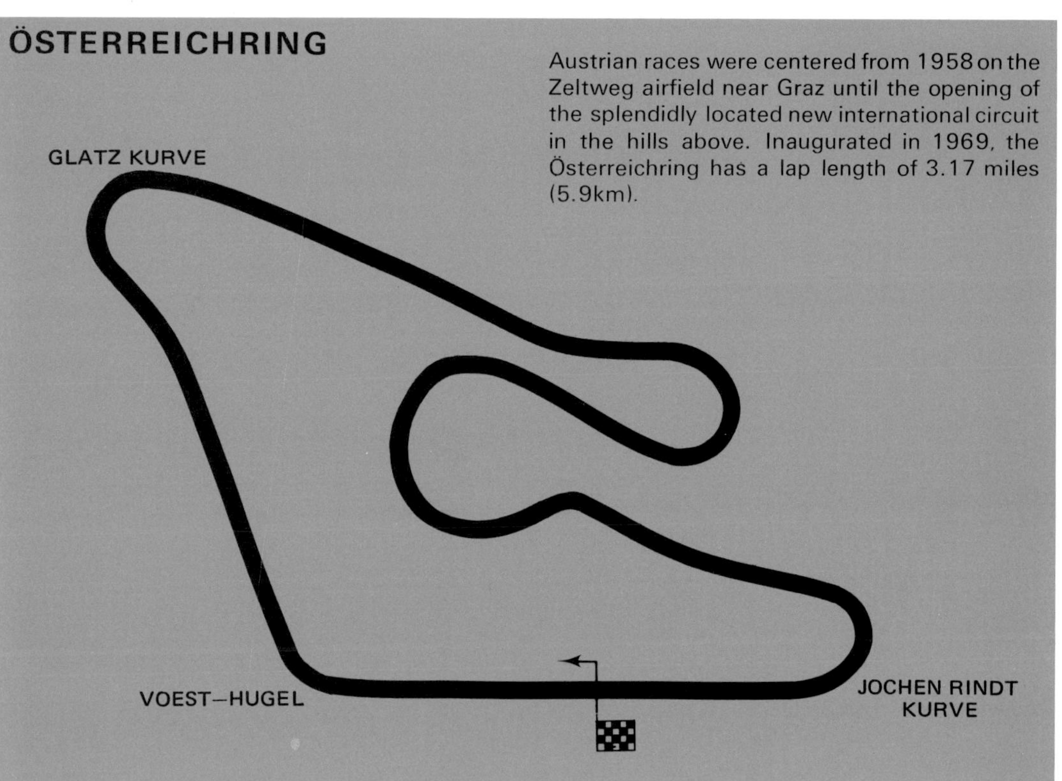

PUKEKOHE

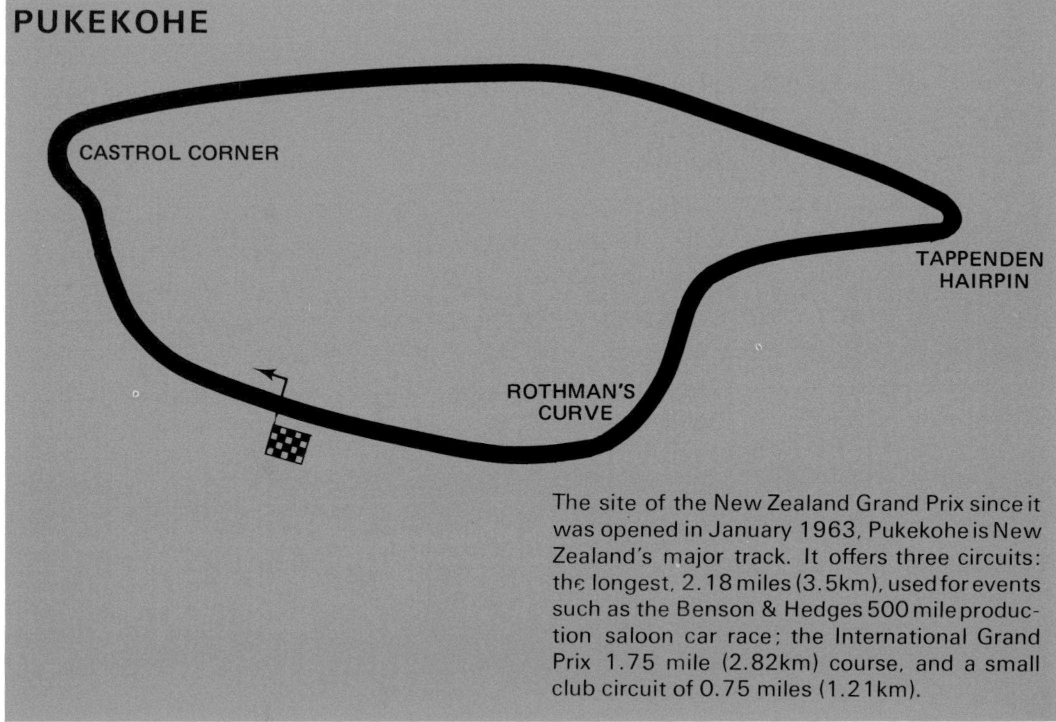

The site of the New Zealand Grand Prix since it was opened in January 1963, Pukekohe is New Zealand's major track. It offers three circuits: the longest, 2.18 miles (3.5km), used for events such as the Benson & Hedges 500 mile production saloon car race; the International Grand Prix 1.75 mile (2.82km) course, and a small club circuit of 0.75 miles (1.21km).

RHEIMS

France's fastest circuit and the venue of the 12 hour race that started at midnight as well as many dramatically fast Grands Prix, the AC de Champagne's *circuit permanent* was run over a 5 mile (8km) triangle of public road just outside the city, the run down the relatively narrow RN31 being known among drivers as 'the best view in Europe'.

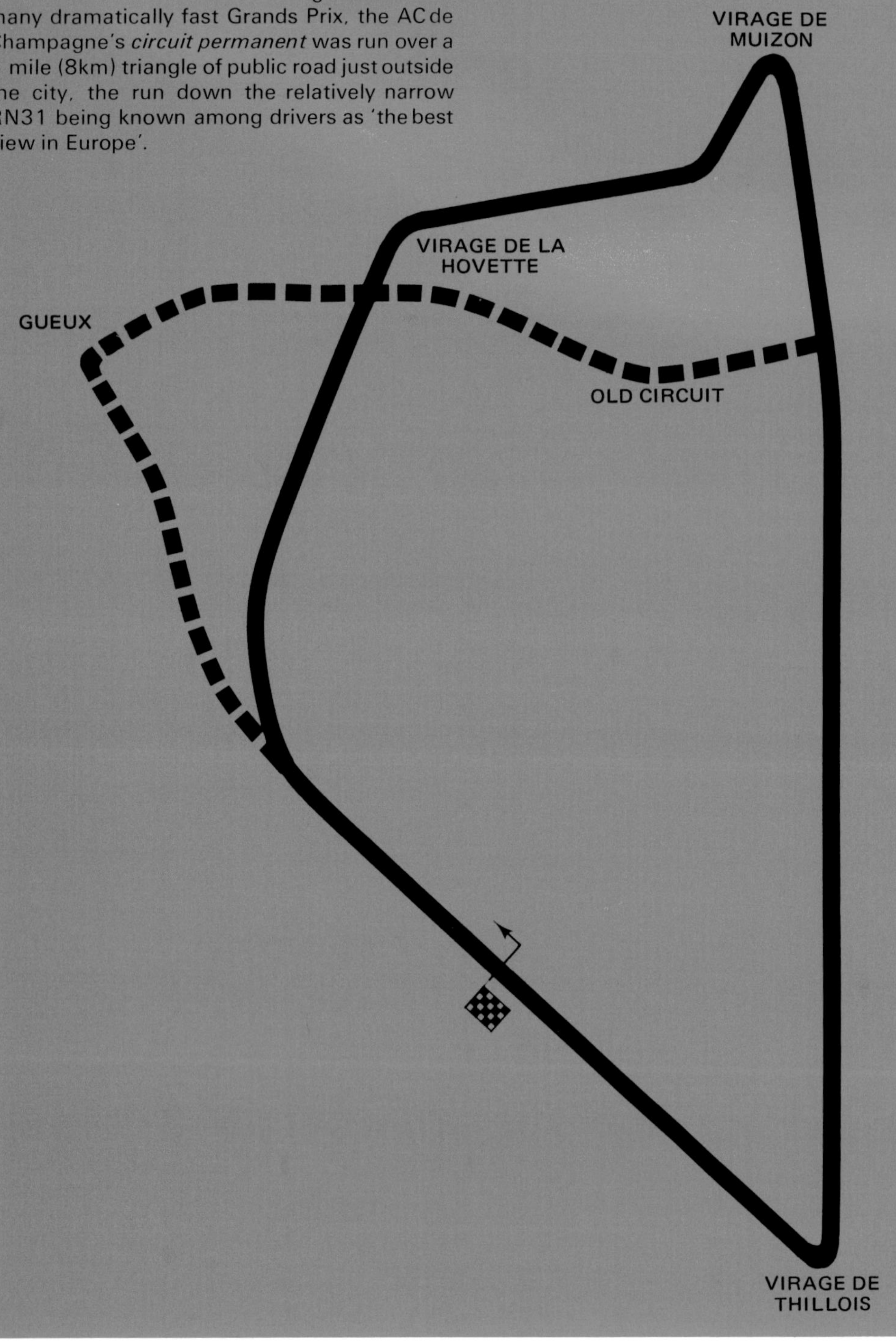

VIRAGE DE MUIZON

VIRAGE DE LA HOVETTE

GUEUX

OLD CIRCUIT

VIRAGE DE THILLOIS

A typical Can-Am McLaren (above) at Riverside. From the traditional autumn sports car races at Riverside and Laguna Seca, sprang the Canadian-American Challenge Cup series, which came into being in 1966, to be largely dominated by McLaren.

Rheims, 1939. The matchless Tazio Nuvolari (above) in a 3 litre Auto Union during the French Grand Prix. Despite beginning car racing in 1922, he was still the maestro throughout the thirties, winning his last major GP at Belgrade, Yugoslavia, in September 1939.

Rheims, 1947. Louis Chiron (above), noted for his artistry at the wheel, seen in a 4.5 litre Talbot, coming into Gueux village during the Marne GP. Subsequently, the village was by-passed when the course was altered in 1952, much to the detriment of the circuit's character, although lap speeds rose correspondingly.

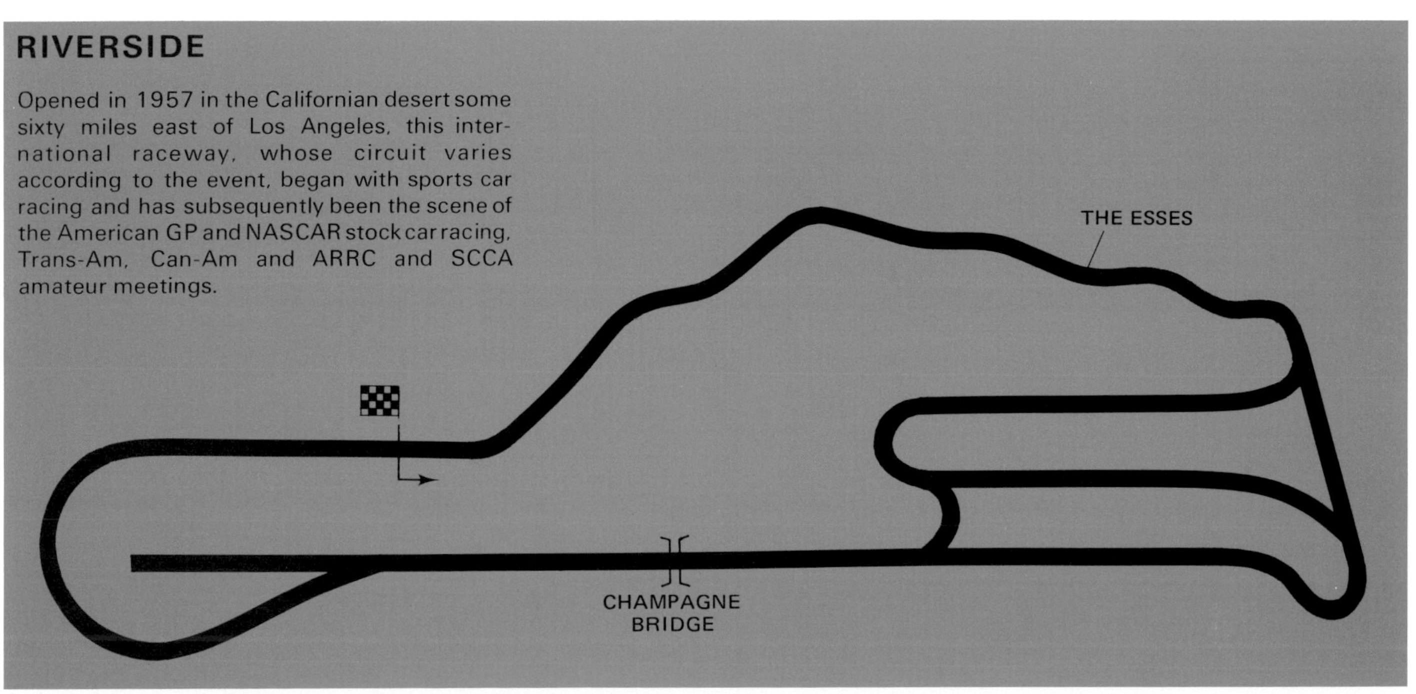

RIVERSIDE

Opened in 1957 in the Californian desert some sixty miles east of Los Angeles, this international raceway, whose circuit varies according to the event, began with sports car racing and has subsequently been the scene of the American GP and NASCAR stock car racing, Trans-Am, Can-Am and ARRC and SCCA amateur meetings.

THE ESSES
CHAMPAGNE BRIDGE

ROAD AMERICA

Built as a result of a Wisconsin state law banning racing on public highways, this 4 mile (6.4km) circuit in the attractive setting of Elkhart Lake began with sports car races in the early fifties and now schedules Trans-Am, Can-Am and Formula A events.

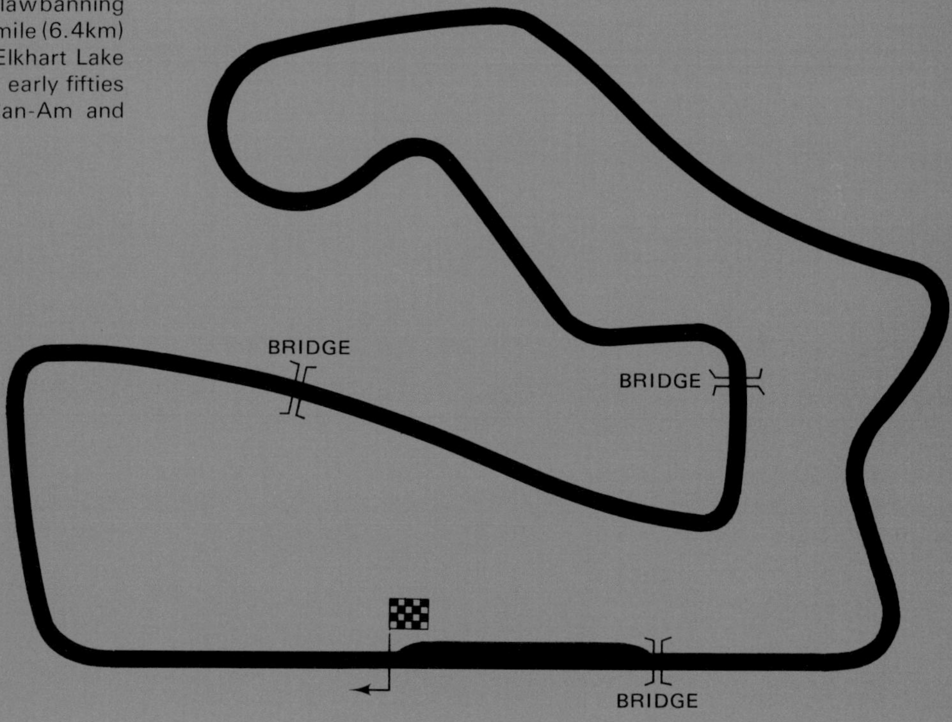

BRIDGE
BRIDGE
BRIDGE

ROUEN

Soon after World War II the compact, twisty circuit just south of Rouen was developed into an impressive, if narrow, 4.1 mile (6.5km) course, which has frequently been the scene of the French Grand Prix as well as the Rouen GP for Formula or sports cars.

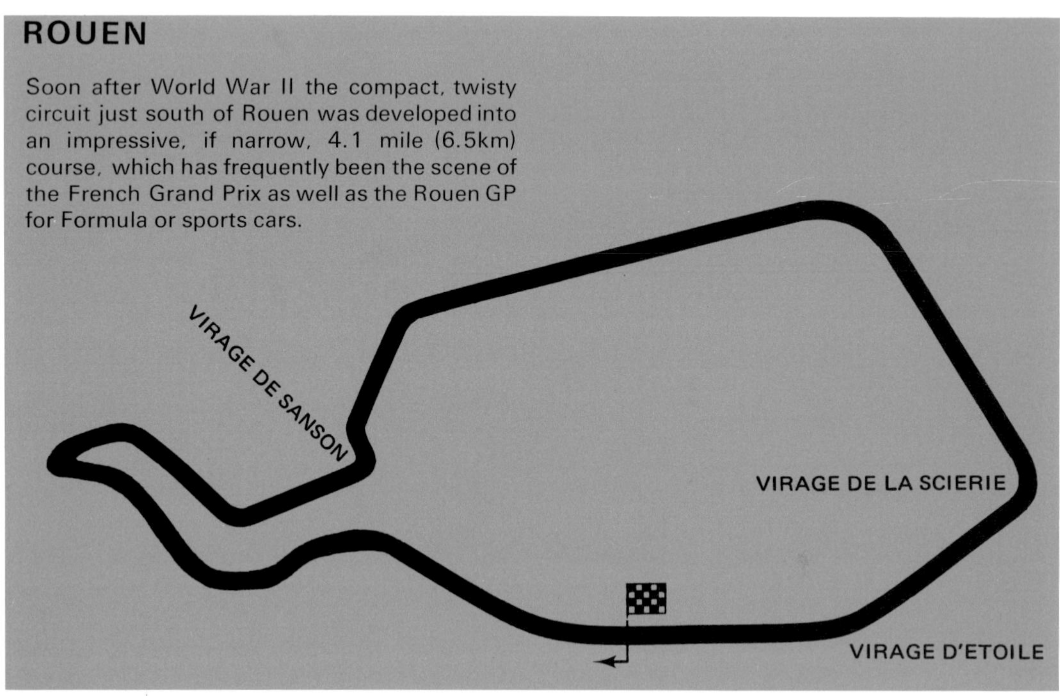

Rouen, 1968. Jo Schlesser, the highly popular French-Madagascan who was killed during the French Grand Prix in 1968. Schlesser was driving the all too new experimental air-cooled Honda seen in the picture. Looking critically on by the off-side rear wheel is the famous motor-racing reporter, Denis Jackson.

SEBRING

Le Mans type sports car racing was inaugurated in the USA by Alex Ulmann on 31 December, 1950, on the abandoned Hendrick B 17 airfield near Sebring in Florida which became the scene of the most famous of American sports car event, the 12 hour 'Noon to Midnight', run over a 5.2 mile (8.4km) combination of runways and connecting roads.

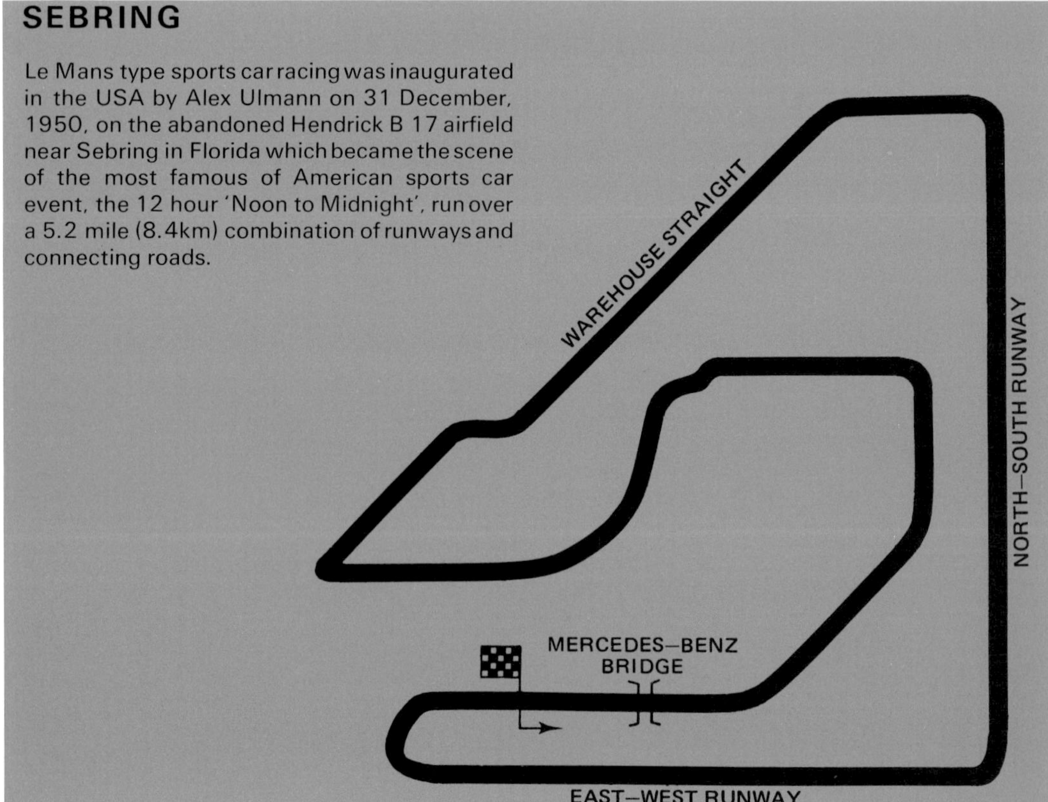

Silverstone, 1956. Stirling Moss (above) in the Maserati 250F during the British Grand Prix. The race was won by Fangio in a Ferrari. Although Moss was coming up to the peak of his performance at this time, Fangio was still the master, Moss being runner-up to the great Argentinian in the world championship for three successive years – 1955, 1956 and again in 1957.

SILVERSTONE

CLUB CORNER

WOODCOTE

STOWE

BECKETTS

Now owned by the British Racing Drivers' Club, this airfield track in Northamptonshire first hit the headlines when the RAC devised a circuit here for the 1948 British Grand Prix, using both runways linked to sections of the perimeter road. In 1952 the circuit was modified to its actual lap of 2.9 miles (4.6km) since when, as the stage for both international and club events, it has become almost synonomous with British racing.

Spa Francorchamps, 1965. Graham Hill (below) in his V8 BRM leading the field during the Belgian Grand Prix, closely followed by Jim Clark, the eventual winner, in a Lotus. Clark went on to win the world championship for the second time, after his victories in the South African, Belgian, British, German and Dutch GPs.

SPA-FRANCORCHAMPS

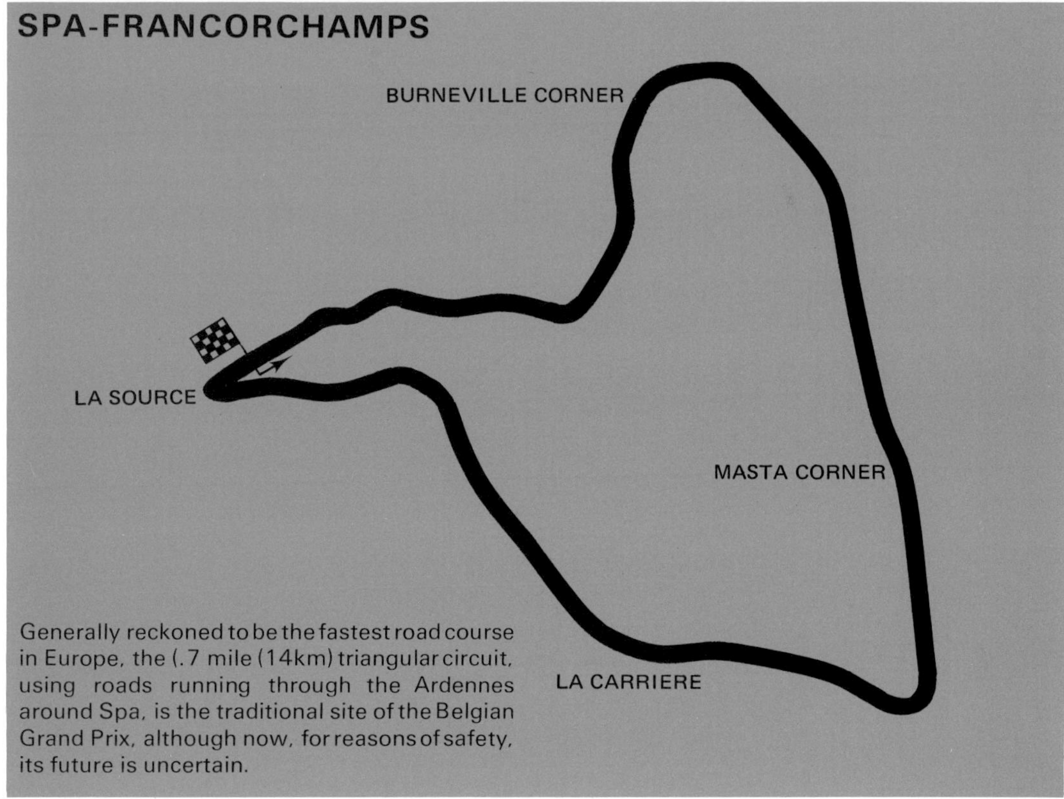

Generally reckoned to be the fastest road course in Europe, the (.7 mile (14km) triangular circuit, using roads running through the Ardennes around Spa, is the traditional site of the Belgian Grand Prix, although now, for reasons of safety, its future is uncertain.

WARWICK FARM

Opened in 1960, about twenty miles outside Sydney, Warwick Farm is Australia's foremost and best designed racing circuit. It is built around a horse racing track, and is owned jointly by the Australian Jockey Club and the Australian Automobile Racing Co Ltd. The full lap is 2.25 miles (3.62km) long, while there is a club circuit of 0.9 miles (1.45km).

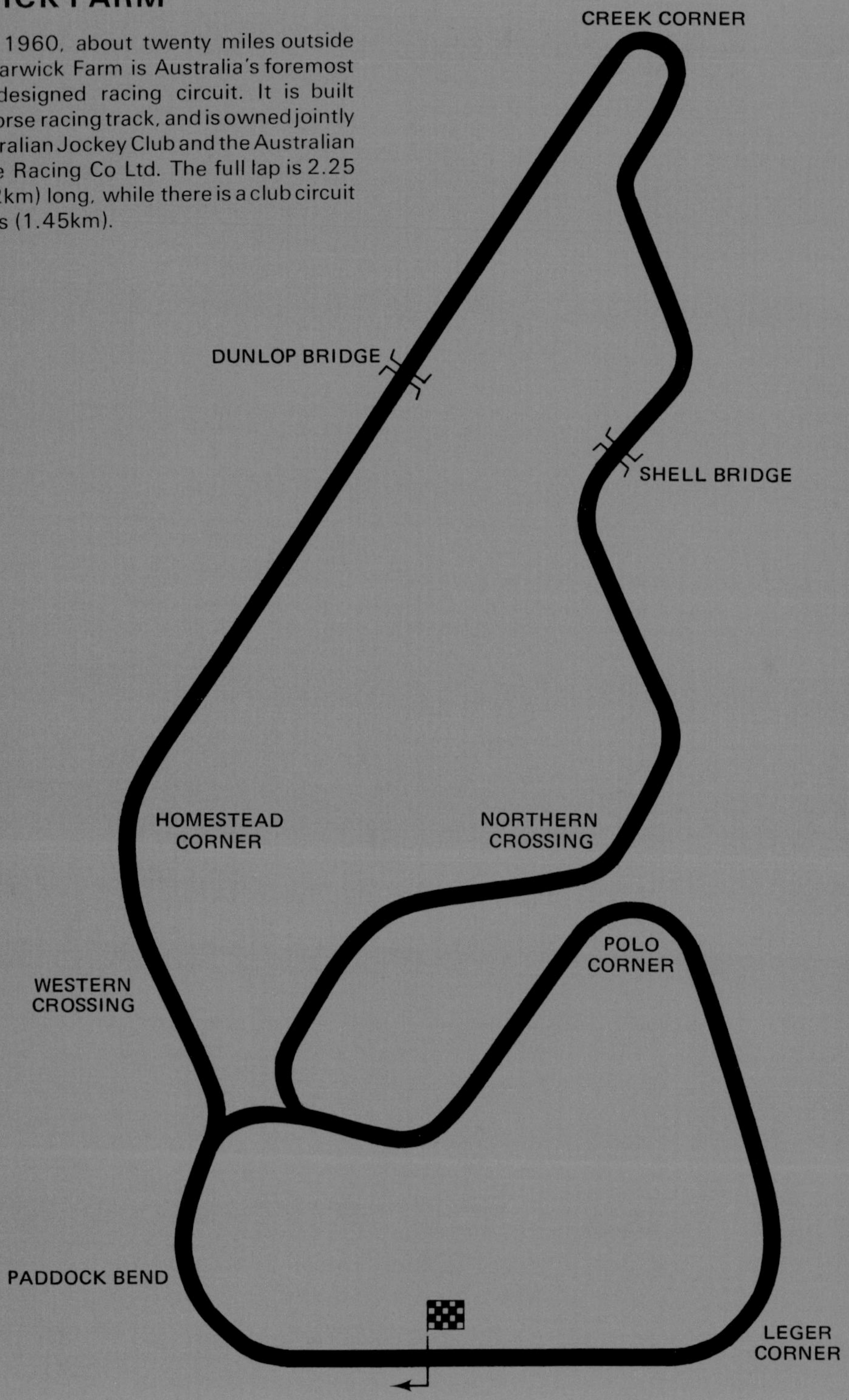

CREEK CORNER
DUNLOP BRIDGE
SHELL BRIDGE
HOMESTEAD CORNER
NORTHERN CROSSING
POLO CORNER
WESTERN CROSSING
PADDOCK BEND
LEGER CORNER

Warwick Farm was chosen as the terminal point for the London to Sydney marathon rally, which ended in December 1968. The rally was sponsored by the English *Daily Express*, who offered a £10,000 ($24,000) prize to the winner. Competitors had to drive overland to Bombay, where they caught a boat to Freemantle, Australia, a total of 10,000 miles (16,000km). The Premier of New South Wales (top picture) symbolically holds the finishing flag over the winning car, the Hillman Hunter GT driven by Andrew Cowan, Brian Coyle and Colin Malkin; and the winning car, No 75 (above), about to head a triumphal procession of all the competitors who finished the course – a total of fifty-six out of ninety-eight starters.

Watkins Glen, 1974. Cars and drivers (above) await the start of the United States Grand Prix. The winner was Emerson Fittipaldi in a McLaren, clinching his second title as World Champion. The circuit embodies the customary modern safety improvements with broad-grid protective guard rail and separate pits road.

WATKINS GLEN

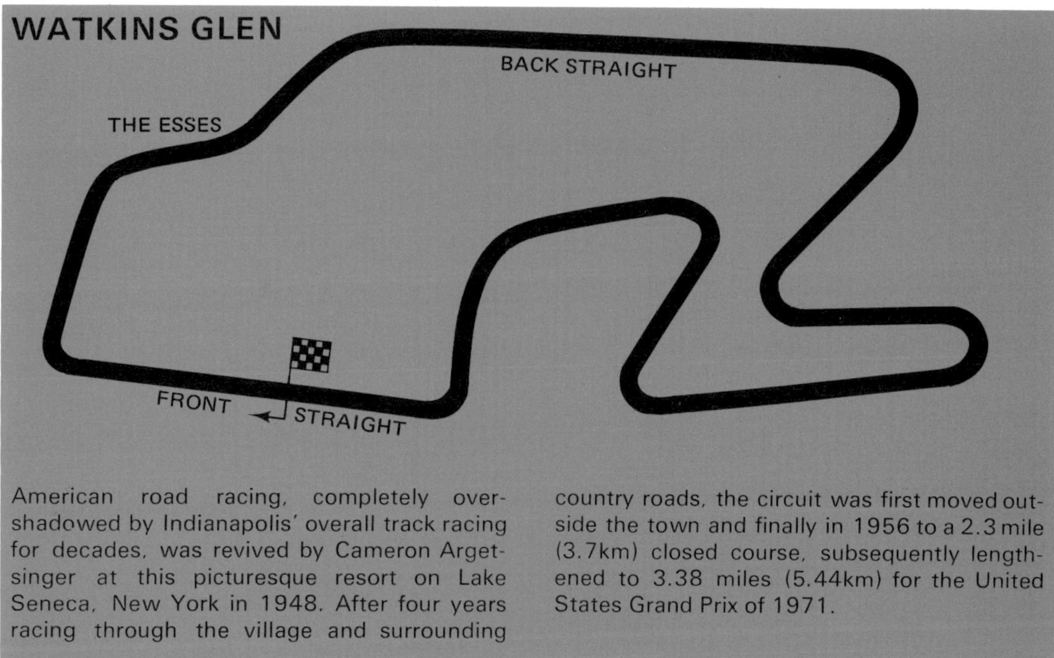

American road racing, completely overshadowed by Indianapolis' overall track racing for decades, was revived by Cameron Argetsinger at this picturesque resort on Lake Seneca, New York in 1948. After four years racing through the village and surrounding country roads, the circuit was first moved outside the town and finally in 1956 to a 2.3 mile (3.7km) closed course, subsequently lengthened to 3.38 miles (5.44km) for the United States Grand Prix of 1971.

ZANDVOORT

Site of the Dutch Grand Prix since 1950, Zandvoort was built soon after the war through the sand dunes along the sea shore. The circuit is 2.63 miles (4.23km) long and the main straight runs parallel to the North Beach. Until recently Zandvoort, in spite of the hazard of sand across the road on windy days, had a good safety record but this has been marred by recent tragedies, costing the lives of Piers Courage and Roger Williamson.

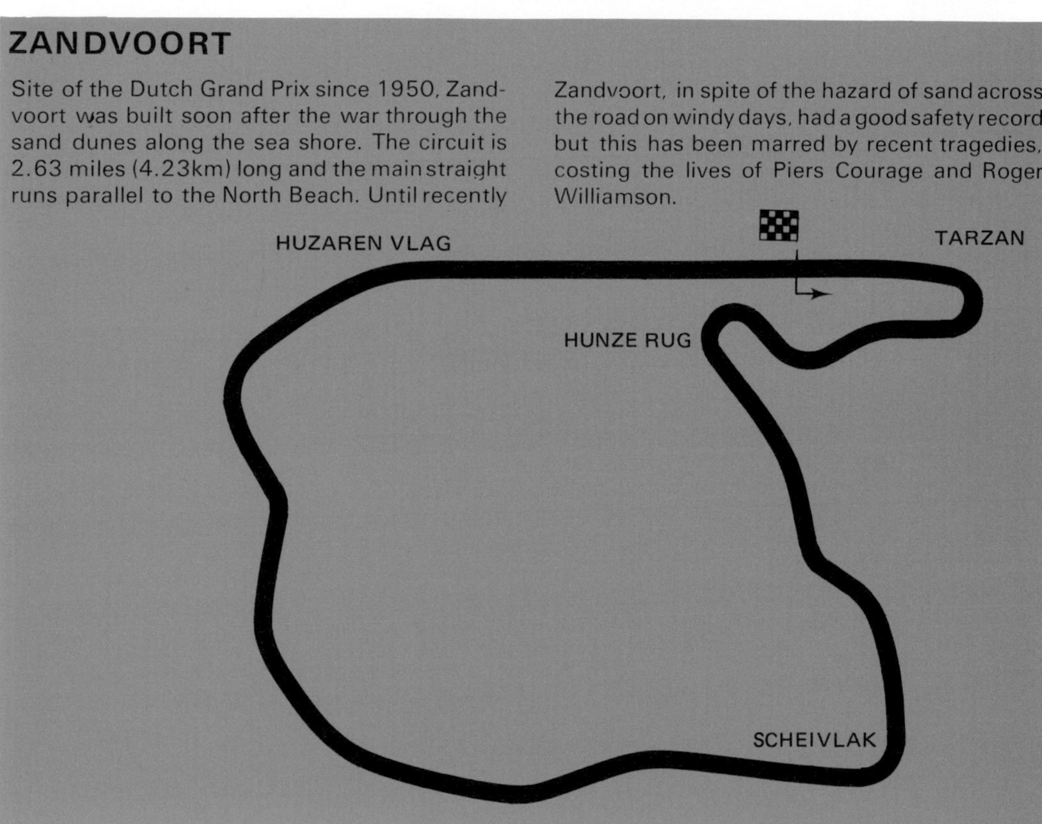

Zandvoort, 1968. First lap scene in the Dutch Grand Prix (below), with cars massed as they take the Hunzerug turn. The race was won by Scotsman Jackie Stewart in a Tyrrell-entered Matra-Ford. This was Stewart's first victory in the Dutch Grand Prix, but not his last, for he was to win again in 1969 and in 1973.

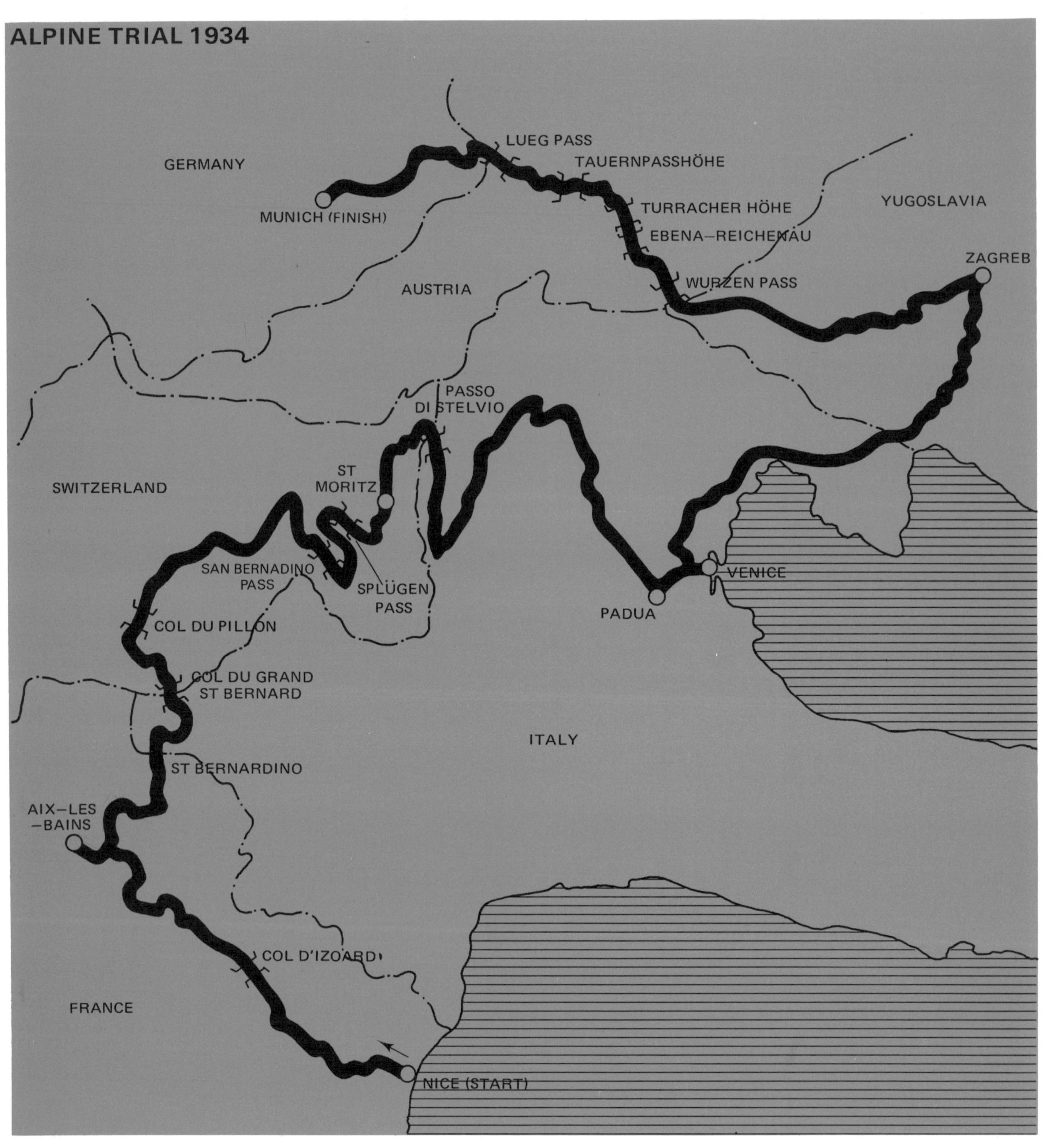
ALPINE TRIAL 1934
GERMANY
LUEG PASS
TAUERNPASSHÖHE
MUNICH (FINISH)
TURRACHER HÖHE
YUGOSLAVIA
EBENA–REICHENAU
ZAGREB
AUSTRIA
WURZEN PASS
PASSO
DI STELVIO
ST
MORITZ
SWITZERLAND
SAN BERNADINO
PASS
SPLÜGEN
PASS
VENICE
PADUA
COL DU PILLON
COL DU GRAND
ST BERNARD
ITALY
ST BERNARDINO
AIX–LES
–BAINS
COL D'IZOARD
FRANCE
NICE (START)

Like most rallies, the Alpine (left) has varied its course (as well as its name – from Austrian Alpine Trial to International Alpine Rally and Coupe des Alpes) over the years. This map of the 1934 route shows a pre-war, pre-Iron Curtain rally passing through France, Switzerland, Austria, Italy, Yugoslavia and Germany. Not until 1956 was the route to pass through Yugoslavia again.

Of recent years the rally, which epitomized the early long-distance endurance tests, has suffered a decline and is frequently not held, or else held just as a French or Austrian event only.

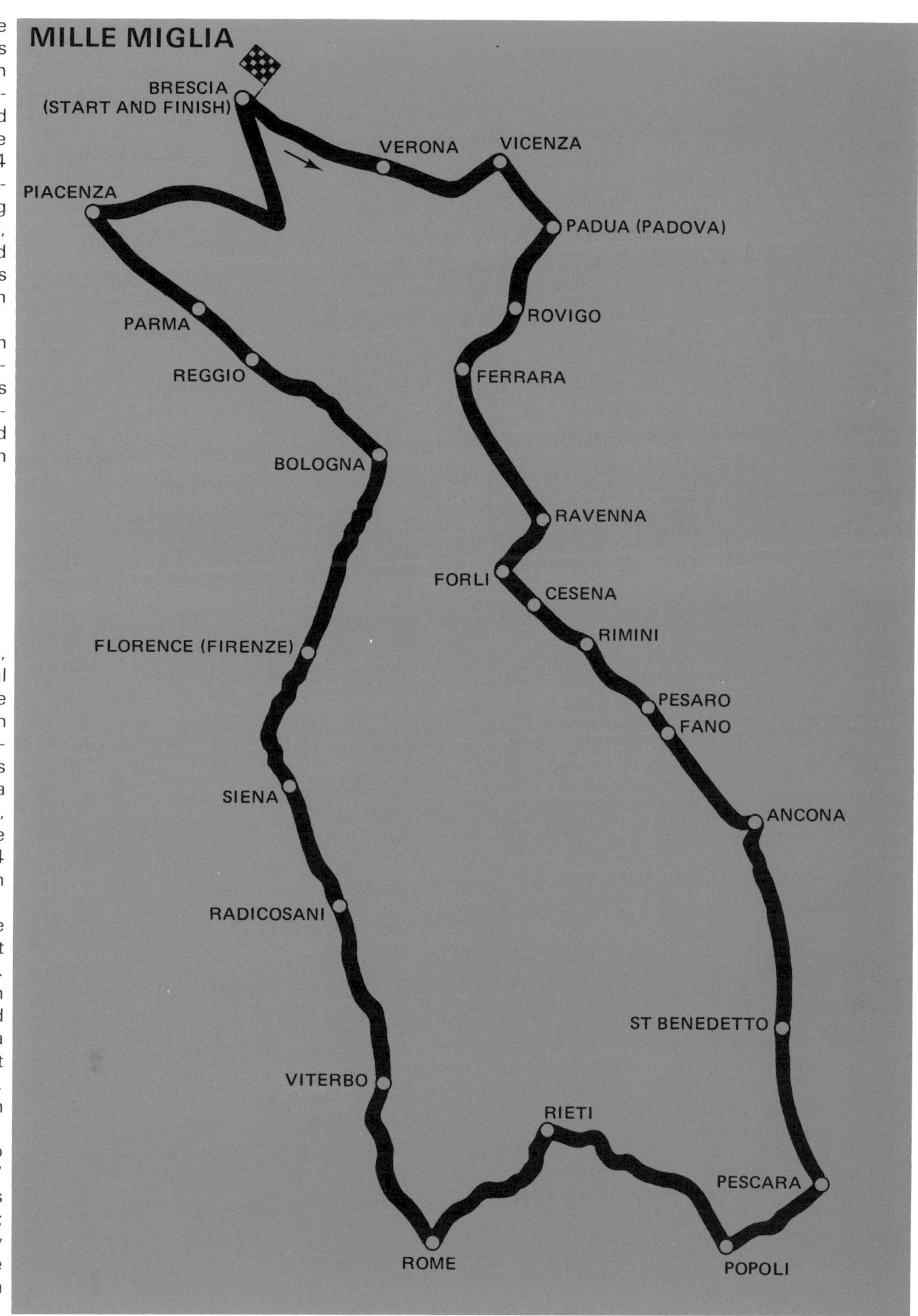

The Mille Miglia (right), now, alas, abandoned after the fatal accident of the Marquis de Portago and Edward Nelson in 1957, in which eleven spectators were also killed, was started in 1927. It was a challenging and difficult race, inspired originally by the success of the Le Mans 24 Hour race, which started in 1923.

Throughout its fifty years the Mille Miglia remained almost exclusively an Italian preserve. The first foreign win came in 1931, when Caracciola and Sebastian came first in a Mercedes-Benz, and the last was another Mercedes-Benz, driven by Moss and Jenkinson in 1955.

There were some attempts to keep the race going after 1957 but Portago's accident was really only the last straw; traffic congestion on the busy Italian roads covered in the rally had made its continuation an impossibility.

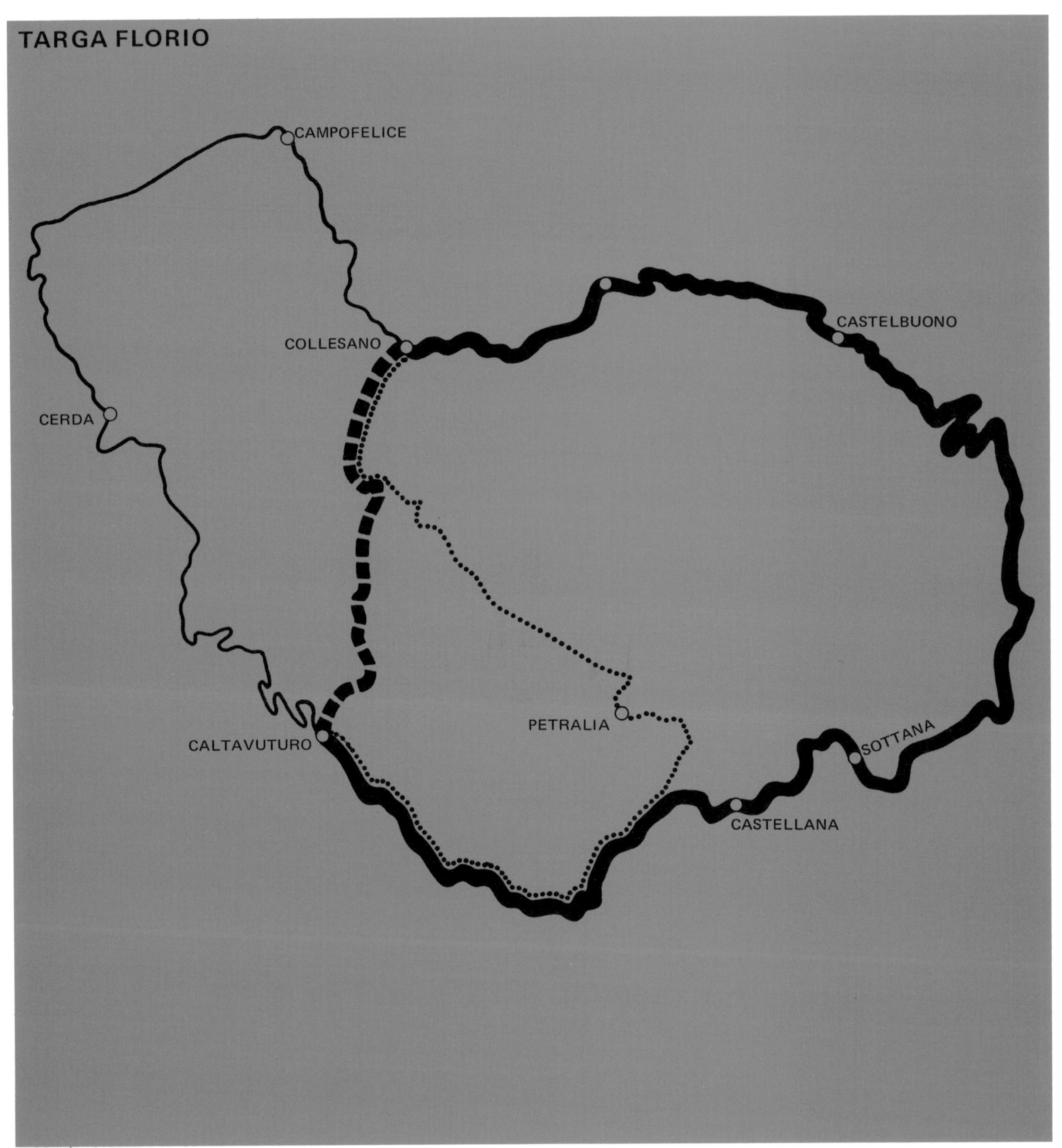
TARGA FLORIO
CAMPOFELICE
COLLESANO
CASTELBUONO
CERDA
PETRALIA
CALTAVUTURO
SOTTANA
CASTELLANA

The Targa Florio (left) was the brain-child of one man, Vincenzo Florio (1883-1958). It was the first held in 1905 and continues to this day, but now in a very much modified form, over a closed track.
The three routes used in its hey-day were the Great Madonie, a lap of 92.48 miles (148.82km), which was used until 1914; the Medium Madonie, a shortened lap of 67.11 miles (108km), used between 1919 and 1930; and the Short Madonie, a 44.74 mile (72km) lap used from 1932 to 1936 and after 1950, up to 1973.

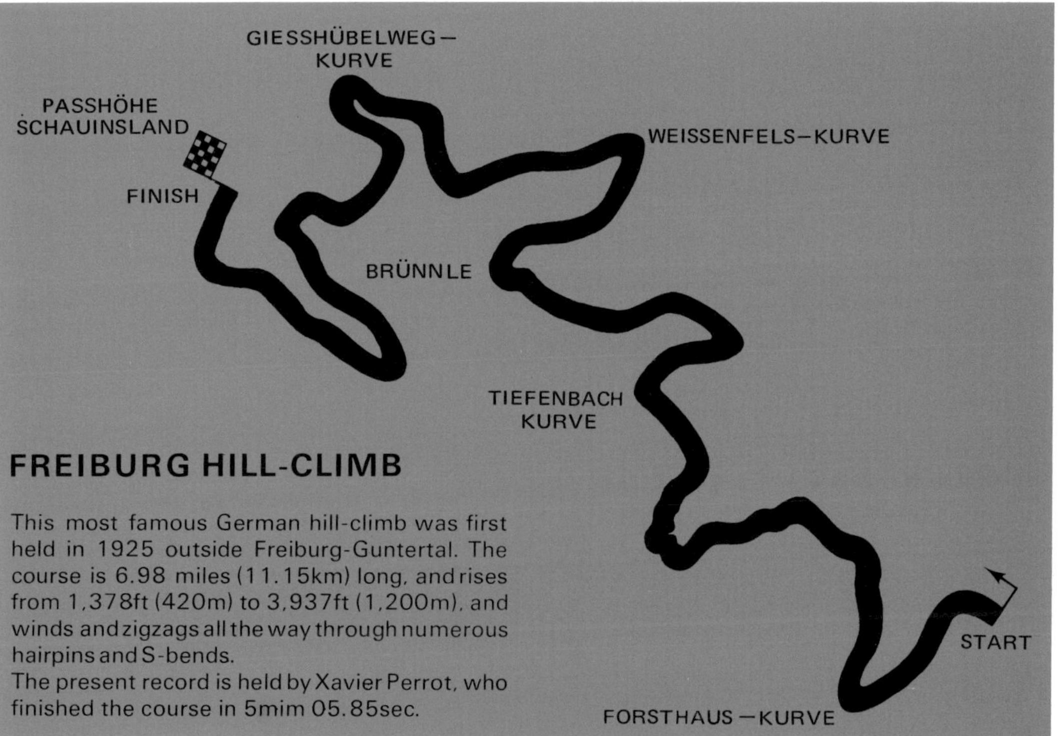

FREIBURG HILL-CLIMB

This most famous German hill-climb was first held in 1925 outside Freiburg-Guntertal. The course is 6.98 miles (11.15km) long, and rises from 1,378ft (420m) to 3,937ft (1,200m), and winds and zigzags all the way through numerous hairpins and S-bends.
The present record is held by Xavier Perrot, who finished the course in 5mim 05.85sec.

MONT VENTOUX

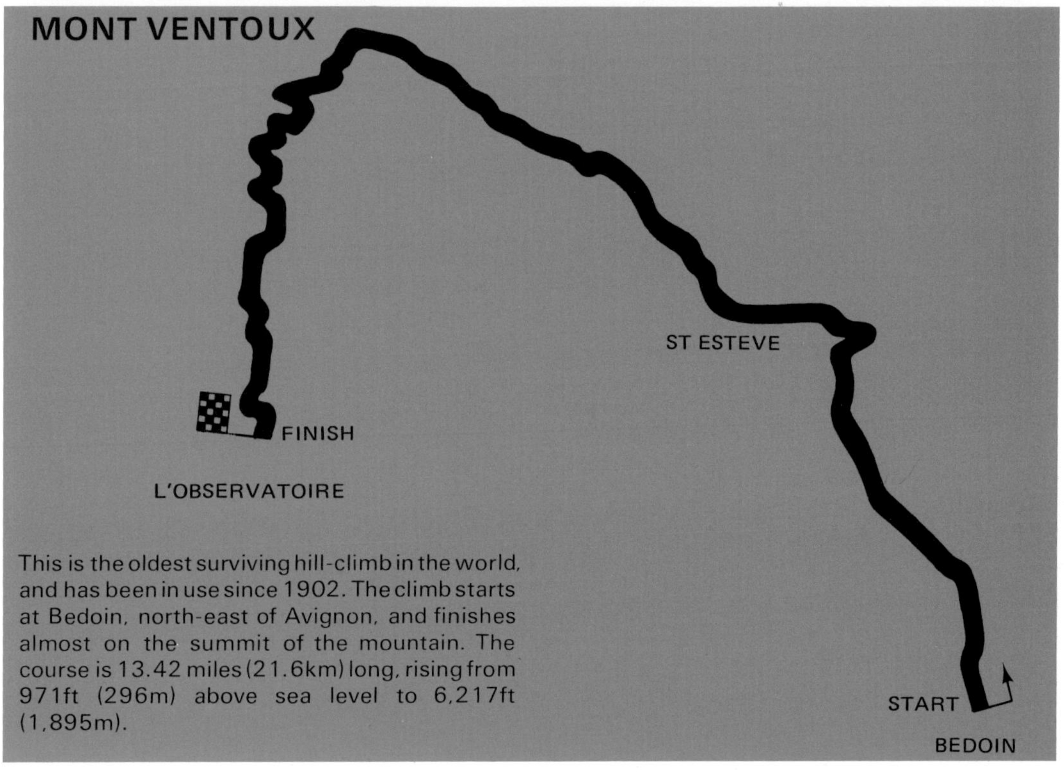

This is the oldest surviving hill-climb in the world, and has been in use since 1902. The climb starts at Bedoin, north-east of Avignon, and finishes almost on the summit of the mountain. The course is 13.42 miles (21.6km) long, rising from 971ft (296m) above sea level to 6,217ft (1,895m).

Index

PICTURE CREDITS

Autocar–39, 43, 45 (top). Auto Múzeum, Budapest–57. Ronald Barker–27, 112, 133 (bottom), 144 (top right), 217 (centre). British Motor Corporation–115, 117 (top). British Museum–10. René Burri–143. Camera Press–170. *The Car*–38. Central Press–216 (top), 230, 232. Colorsport–190-191, 203 (bottom). Daily Telegraph Colour Library–187 (top right), 199, 202. Diffusion Photos de Presse Internationale–178, 179, 182 (top left and right), 183, 186, 187 (left), 194 bottom). Rick Fawcett–194 (top). Jeanne Griffiths–195. *Hot Car*–196, 198 (top and bottom). Indianapolis Motor Speedway–164, 165, 167, 169, 210 (bottom), 221 (centre). Keystone Press–91, 93 (top), 110 (bottom), 125, 131, 137, 141 (top), 145, 155, 156, 157, 159 (top), 160, 163, 181 (bottom), 184 (top), 193, 197, 201, 204, 205, 226 (top), 233. Louis Klemantaski–219 (top), 228 (bottom). E. D. Lacey–181 (top), 216 (bottom). London Editions–36, 37, 228 (top and centre). Mercedes-Benz–22, 23 (top), 24, 29 (top), 46. NASCAR–200 (left), 219 (centre and bottom). National Motor Museum–11, 12, 13, 23 (bottom), 30, 33, 35, 41, 54, 55, 56 (top), 58-59, 60, 61 (bottom), 62, 63, 65, 67 (bottom), 79 (bottom), 80, 81, 82 (top), 85 (top), 86, 87, 89 (bottom), 95, 96, 97, 98, 99, 100, 101, 106 (bottom), 108, 110 (top), 118 (top), 119, 122 (top), 127 (bottom), 130 (top), 133 (top), 135, 139, 141 (bottom left), 147, 151 (bottom), 153, 173, 177 (bottom), 200 (right), 217 (bottom). Peugeot–53 (top), 66, 117 (bottom), 224 (bottom). Radio Times Hulton Picture Library–title page, 21, 25, 31, 47, 48, 50-51, 53 (bottom), 56 (bottom), 61 (top), 68-69, 70, 71, 72, 73, 75, 76, 77 (bottom), 79 (top), 88, 89 (top), 90, 93 (bottom), 94, 103, 118 (bottom), 120, 121, 122 (bottom), 126, 127 (top and centre), 128, 129, 144 (bottom), 149, 151 (top), 220 (top), 231 (top). Peter Roberts–14, 15, 16, 19, 20, 32, 49, 77 (top), 82 (bottom), 83, 85 (bottom), 102, 104-105, 106 (top), 109, 114, 130 (bottom), 141 (bottom right), 144 (top left), 154, 172, 174, 177 (top), 203 (top), 220 (bottom), 222 (centre). Syndication International–45 (bottom), 159 (bottom), 184 (bottom), 185, 222 (top and bottom), 226 (bottom), 227. Roger Viollet–29 (bottom), 40, 74, 123 (bottom), 124, 224 (top). Yardley McLaren–189.